July 23, 1999

for Keith, on the occasion of his birthday and retirement from the "transportation industry" ~

This comes from the library of your old drinking buddy (and a great raconteur). We thought you would like to have it ...

Love,
Kathy and Stan
(and "Ort")

Rails
ACROSS
AMERICA

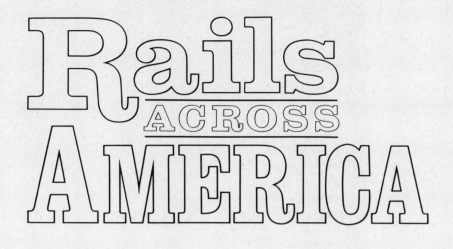

Rails ACROSS AMERICA

A History of Railroads in North America

Consultant Editor: William L. Withuhn

SMITHMARK

A SALAMANDER BOOK

Copyright ©1993 Salamander Books Ltd.

This edition published in 1993 by SMITHMARK Publishers Inc., 16 East 32nd Street, New York, NY 10016.

SMITHMARK books are available for bulk purchase for sales promotion and premium use. For details write or call the manager of special sales, SMITHMARK Publishers Inc., 16 East 32nd Street, New York, NY 10016: (212) 532 6600.

This book was produced by Salamander Books Ltd.,
129-137 York Way
London N7 9LG
England.

Library of Congress Cataloging-in-Publication Data

Rails Across America: A History of Railroads in North America/Consultant Editor William L. Withuhn.
    p.   cm.
Includes bibliographical references and index.
ISBN 0 8317 6482 1 : $24.98
1. Railroad - United States - History. I. Withuhn, William L.
TF23.R325   1993
385'.0973--dc 20   93-24598
                                                                            CIP

Printed in Italy

10 9 8 7 6 5 4 3 2 1

CREDITS
Editor: Will Steeds
Copy editor: Alison Leach
Designer: John Heritage
Artifact photography: Don Eiler, Richmond, VA (©Salamander Books Ltd)
Maps: Janos Marffy (©Salamander Books Ltd)
Index: Edward Leeson
Filmset: The Old Mill, London, England
Color reproduction: Scantrans Pte. Ltd., Singapore

CONSULTANT EDITOR
William L. Withuhn is Curator of Transportation at the National Museum of American History, Smithsonian Institution, Washington, DC. From the very beginning, when he advised on the proposed contents of the title, Bill has played the central role in shaping this book. In addition to writing two chapters, he located authors for other chapters, liaised with railroad museums throughout the United States, recommended sources for photographs, and suggested appropriate subjects for features, sidebars and artifact spreads. Bill has also been closely involved with the production of the book. The publishers express their heartfelt thanks for the very major contribution he has made to the success of this work.

This book is dedicated to David P. Morgan.

ACKNOWLEDGMENTS
John P. Hankey, Senior Curator of the Baltimore & Ohio Railroad Museum, and Walter Gray, Director of the California State Railroad Museum have both, with Bill Withuhn, played crucial roles in shaping this book; they have advised as to the content, suggested subjects for features and artifact spreads, and have written many of those sidebars, features, and artifact spread captions. The publishers would also like to thank Gus Welty of *Railway Age* magazine, and Ron Ziel for the many contributions they have made to the book.

    Grateful thanks are also extended to Robert L. Emerson, Director of the Railroad Museum of Pennsylvania, to Stephen E. Drew, Senior Curator of the California State Railroad Museum, to John Hankey, and to William L. Withuhn for making the outstanding collections held in their respective museums available to Salamander for photography.

    At the California State Railroad Museum, particular thanks go to Stephen E. Drew, Ellen Halteman (Librarian), Blaine P. Lamb (Archivist), and Marilyn Sommerdorf for their help and advice during photography for the artifact spreads, and throughout the entire project. At Baltimore, thanks also to Keith Cranor, and at Strasburg to Ken Riegel.

    In Washington, DC, John Fowler kindly (and patiently) allowed the photography team into his home to photograph his superb collection of railroad artifacts.

    Railroad photography is itself an art form, and some of the top practitioners in the United States have contributed their own work, and also helped us to find historical photographs. Grateful thanks are extended to: Glenn Beier; Ted Benson; Jim Boyd; Shirley Burman; Mike Del Vecchio; Harold Edmondson; Jim Gallagher; Dick Gruber; John Gruber; Joel Jensen; William Kratville; David Plowden; Richard Steinheimer; Wilton S. Tifft; Ron Ziel; Karl Zimmermann.

    For assistance in finding photographs and historical information, particular thanks are extended to: Peter Barton of the Railroaders' Memorial Museum, Altoona, PA; Seth Bramson; Richard Cox; Portia James of the Anacostia Museum, Smithsonian Institution; Joyce Koenemann and staff of the Association of American Railroads; David Letourneau of Burlington Northern; Ken Miller; Jacqueline Pryor of the Railway & Locomotive Historical Society; Bill Schafer; Mark Smith; Don Snoddy and staff of the Union Pacific Museum, Omaha; Gus Welty; Jim Wrinn; and very special thanks to artist Ted Rose.

    In England, the publishers would like to thank Brian Hollingsworth, and Rob Shorland-Ball, Deputy Keeper of the National Railway Museum, York, England, who provided valuable assistance during the very early stages of the project. Finally, thanks to Mark Holt and John Heritage for their inspired laying out of artifacts in Washington, DC, Baltimore, Strasburg, and Sacramento; to Don Eiler for his equally inspired photography; and to Alison Leach for copy editing the manuscripts.

    Full picture credits, and further acknowledgments, are given on page 192.

Editor's note
The final selection and captioning of all illustrations in this book have been the responsibility of Salamander Books Ltd. and not of the individual contributors.

Pages 2-3: The Erie-Lackawanna Railroad's westbound *Phoebe Snow* pauses to take on passengers at Scranton, PA, in 1964. The station is now a hotel, extensively restored to show the grandeur of the building to the best advantage.

Pages 4-5: Freight train of the Quebec Central Railway near Ste. Marie, Quebec.

Pages 6-7: Grain elevators beside the Northern Pacific's tracks at Sykeston, ND.

CONTENTS

ADDITIONAL CONTRIBUTORS:
Stephen E. Drew ('The Gold Coast'); Barry Garland ('Cleaning Up'); Sheila Greene ('Race of the Silk Trains'; reproduced with permission of Burlington Northern Railroad); Blaine P. Lamb ('The Brotherhoods'; 'The Making of the Consumer Society'; 'Railroad Police'; 'Railroad Fairs'); John Lomax (who provided the quote in 'Railroading's Musical Legacy'); David Plowden ('A Ride on the Fast Mail'); Elizabeth Wilde ('Hobo on the CP'; reproduced with permission of Dorrance Publishing); Ron Ziel ('The Gandy Dancers'; 'Keeping Memories Alive').

All other sidebars, features, and artifact spread captions were written by the author of the chapter in which the piece appears, with the following exceptions: John H. Armstrong ('Under the Wires'); Walter P. Gray ('The Brotherhood of Sleeping Car Porters'; 'A Baggage Room of the 1870s'; 'The Telegrapher's Office'; 'Railroads in Popular Culture'); John P. Hankey ('Battling with the Snow'; 'The Art of Railroad Advertising'); William L. Withuhn ('Cry of the Plains'; 'The Engine Crew'; 'Steam Locomotive Builders').

INTRODUCTION

RAILROADING IS ONE OF THE GREAT American adventures, an adventure spanning nearly two hundred years. It is a story of people — of their dreams and achievement, and of their greed and conflict.

During the nineteenth and early part of the twentieth centuries, the United States transformed itself from a vast, thinly populated, agrarian country into a potent industrial nation. A key to that transformation was the railroad. As its tracks spread out across the land, the railroad connected communities and regions together, putting into place the enabling network for a national economy.

There is more to it, however. To begin, one can contrast railroad building on either side of the Atlantic Ocean. Railroads in Europe augmented and improved long-existing pathways of commerce and transport, and distances were relatively short. In America, distances were vastly greater, and — except for concentrated white settlement on the eastern and Gulf seaboards, around the Great Lakes, and along some of the trans-Appalachian and western rivers, together with Hispanic settlement in the upper Rio Grande valley and in California — most of this continental expanse was known only to Native American eyes. In the US in 1830, the center of white population was just 18 miles from Baltimore. Where railroads in Europe connected long-established cities on well-worn routes, in North America they extended rapidly into the hinterlands, laying brand-*new* pathways, and bringing into being brand-new towns and cities, on a continental scale.

Along the way, the railroad put down more than tracks. It laid down cultural patterns and unleashed political forces which became a central part of the American experience. Railroads became — all at the same time — the greatest creators of wealth, the biggest employers, the most energetic sponsors of immigration and nation-building, and the most ruthless displacers of people who could not fit into the new order. The railroad became a social and commercial institution in its own right, and in a way that was unique: it was physically interconnected with every other social and commercial institution. Some important examples, among many:

In our growth as a nation predominantly of immigrants, from a diversity of cultures, most of our ancestors came during a time when railroads were heavily involved in sponsoring 'colonization' and when railroads provided the only feasible means of inland migration. By far the greatest waves of migration to the trans-Mississippi west did not come until after the wagon-train era was over, ended by a rapidly-extending network of transcontinental rail lines.

The railroad permitted a widely dispersed agriculture to feed an entire nation. For the first time, whole regions could now specialize in particular crops, according to which crops were best suited to their soil and climate. The great wheat belt of the upper midwest and northern prairies, for instance, simply would not be economically possible without a rail network to carry the grain to major milling centers and, from there, to distribute the flour to every city and town.

Railroads accelerated the growth of the iron and steel industries, not only by providing cheap transport for the ore, for the coal used in steel-making, and for the finished goods, but by being major consumers themselves of iron and steel.

The relations between big business and working people were fundamentally altered by the ascent of organized labor in the 1880s and 90s. Trade unionism began long before, but the labor strife of the late nineteenth century accelerated unionism, and particularly on railroads. The railroad brotherhoods began as mutual-benefit associations and grew to rank among the country's strongest and most successful craft unions.

The railroad brought widespread use of the telegraph, our first 'real time' communications system. Railroads could not operate without precise coordination.

The railroad permanently altered our sense of personal mobility. In the railroad era, the US became the most mobile nation on earth. Enhanced physical mobility affected our notions of *social* mobility — the ability of people to pull up stakes and to seek fresh opportunity elsewhere.

The railroad reached into every corner of life, affecting every part of society. Many people viewed the railroad's presence as overweening and destructive — which it often was. But the imprint of the railroad on our social fabric is with us still. The railroad has helped shape how we live, where we live, how we communicate, and how we earn our livelihoods. In addition, the railroad has affected our civil rights, our democratic institutions, our business structures, our folk traditions, our music, and even the way we tell time. In none of these things is the railroad the whole story; far from it. We cannot, however, understand the people we are, today, without an appreciation of some of the connected ways we got that way.

Steel rails bound not only the United States together economically and politically, but also Canada. For Canada, what Pierre Berton called 'the national dream' was the epic building of the Canadian Pacific Railway, which ensured that the middle provinces and British Columbia remained part of the Dominion. Despite the implicit rivalry between the US and Canada, their economies became so interlinked that the two countries eventually adopted a truly international rail system — common in gauge, couplings, and clearances — where railcars were entirely interchangeable and, in fact, passed freely and plentifully back and forth across the US/Canadian border. Hence the railroad story of the US is inseparable from that of its northern neighbor.

In the 1990s, railroads have regained a measure of economic health, after a long winter of decline. Today, railroads in the US and Canada are revitalized as providers of the heavy, overland transportation still critical to national economies and to a burgeoning global economy. The resuscitation of railroads, as a new century approaches, is an important part of our story.

Trains are about motion. For people, trains are about their journeys — and all the reasons people have for going and for coming. For goods and cargoes, trains are still about people — and about all their reasons for sending and receiving. To paraphrase Wallace Stegner, trains are 'not about place but about motion, not about fulfillment but about desire.'

This book provides an overview, from the steam railroad's beginnings in the late 1820s, up to and including the high-technology railroading of the 1990s. A team of leading scholars and writers has been put together; each author has taken a chapter covering a time period in which he has recognized competence. Our book is too short to be comprehensive, and our coverage of Canadian rail history is limited, but our hope is that readers will be motivated to learn more. The literature is rich.

Many US and Canadian railroads have had histories written. Maury Klein's two-part work, *Union Pacific* (1987 and 1989), is one of the very best recent such works. Richard Overton's books on the Burlington, James Holton's on the Reading, and Keith Bryant's on the Atchison, Topeka & Santa Fe, are basic for those companies. A case history of a smaller railroad in the American South is Allen Trelease's *North Carolina Railroad* (1991). Authors Dilts, Hofsommer, and Grant have written on the Baltimore & Ohio, the Southern Pacific, and the Erie-Lackawanna, among others. Berton's *The National Dream* (1970) and *The Last Spike* (1971) tell the Canadian Pacific's saga in the nineteenth century.

The listing above is only indicative; dozens of other fine histories are available.

One of the limitations of the present book is that Mexican railroads are not treated. Our working definition of 'North America' is rather archaic now; geographers have always insisted, rightly, on including Mexico, while historians up until recently have tended to think of North America as the territory north of the Rio Grande. Mexico's railroad history began with lines built by private investment — usually with money from Europe and American sources. Today, on the North American continent, the Ferrocarriles Nacionales de Mexico and the Canadian National are the two great nationalized rail systems. By far the best history of Mexican railroads to date is *Los Ferrocarriles de México* (1974; two-vol. paper ed., 1987-88), in Spanish, by Sergio Ortiz Hernán.

The technology of railroads is treated in numerous books. Among the best are John H. White's *The American Railroad Passenger Car* (1978, paper 1985), and his *History of the American Locomotive, 1830-1880* (1968, paper 1979). Modern steam locomotive design is best covered, in short form, in David P. Morgan's *Steam's Finest Hour* (1959); his case study, *Diesels West!* (1963), treats the steam-to-diesel transition on a mid-western line. Basic railroad operations are best covered in John H. Armstrong's *The Railroad: What It Is, What It Does* (3rd ed. 1990).

The cultural and social aspects of railroading have been treated recently in a number of books: James Ward's *Railroads and the Character of America, 1820-1887* (1986), Walter Licht's *Working for the Railroad* (1983), George Douglas's *All Aboard: The Railroad in American Life* (1992), Stuart Leuthner's *The Railroaders* (1983), T.C. McLuhan's *Dream Tracks: The Railroad and the American Indian, 1890-1930* (1985), and Norm Cohen's *Long Steel Rail: The Railroad in American Folksong* (1981) are rewarding. And Botkin and Harlow's *A Treasury of Railroad Folklore* (1953; many times reprinted) is indispensable.

Periodicals that cover both the past and present of North American railroading include *Railway Age* and *Progressive Railroading* (the leading trade journals); *Railroad History* (a scholarly journal); *Trains; Railfan & Railroad; Locomotive & Railway Preservation;* and *Passenger Train Journal.* Indexes to these magazines provide entry into coverage of almost any historical, economic, and technological topic within the railroading arena.

WILLIAM L. WITHUHN,
CURATOR OF TRANSPORTATION,
NATIONAL MUSEUM OF AMERICAN HISTORY,
SMITHSONIAN INSTITUTION.

THE EARLY DAYS

THE STORY OF THE MODERN RAILROAD begins in October 1828 at Rainhill, nine miles east of Liverpool, England, where the Liverpool & Manchester Railway was holding eight days of locomotive trials. Several American railroad promoters and engineers, including E.L. Miller and Horatio Allen of the South Carolina Railroad, and George Brown and Ross Winans of the Baltimore & Ohio Railroad, were among the spectators present.

Allen had already visited England early in 1828 with the purpose of learning about the most recent developments in railroad technology at their source; three engineers from the B&O made a follow-up visit a year later. Both groups toured the Liverpool & Manchester Railway with George Stephenson, its engineer, and observed the deep cuts, huge embankments, and strong stone viaducts that were designed to minimize curves and grades, for Stephenson had laid out the line so it was suitable for locomotives. The visitors discussed these with George Stephenson and his son, Robert, who was also the owner of the engine works that had built the *Locomotion*, the first

steam engine to pull a passenger train on England's Stockton & Darlington Railway in 1825. Prior to Rainhill, the American engineers had reviewed every aspect of railroad operation with their British counterparts, and had heard the arguments then raging in England over the most suitable motive power.

Weary of these disputes and believing that only 'locomotive engines' were capable of continued improvement, the proprietors of the Liverpool & Manchester Railway had offered a cash prize for the best locomotive design. They established rules, selected judges, and set a date. The strange and wonderful machines that ran at Rainhill included a horse treadmill, a small car using Ross Winans's 'friction wheels' that two passengers operated by turning winches, and several 'running coaches.' One of these, the *Rocket*, by George Stephenson, the untutored but brilliant coalfield engineer, and his son Robert, the educated steam engine entrepreneur, won the Rainhill trials. The *Rocket*, which had a horizontal, multi-tubular boiler and steam cylinders directly connected to the driving wheels, also established the prototype

of the modern steam locomotive, and proved once and for all that locomotives were preferable to horses or stationary engines for providing fast, safe, and efficient power for railroads.

The earliest locomotives had gotten up steam in America before the Rainhill trials. The *Stourbridge Lion* was the first commercial, non-experimental locomotive to run. Built by the firm of John U. Rastrick, of Stourbridge, England, the *Lion* was a 'walking beam' engine, similar to the *Locomotion*. Horatio Allen had ordered it for the Delaware & Hudson Canal Company during his 1828 inspection tour of British railways. The company had constructed a 16-mile railroad between Carbondale and Honesdale, Pennsylvania, in an area that was too mountainous for a canal. The trial was not a success. The locomotive weighed seven tons, the line had been built for lighter traffic, and when Allen took the engine down the tracks in August 1829, the timber viaducts sagged so much that the owners, fearing the loss of their investment, placed the *Stourbridge Lion* in storage, and left it there for the duration.

Ross Winans was one of the passengers on

Right: *Peter Cooper's* Tom Thumb *during its race with Stockton & Stokes' horse in 1830. Although built as an experiment, the* Tom Thumb *proved to the B&O that steampower was a viable proposition.*

Below right: *An artist's representation of an early scene at the B&O's Mt. Clare station, Baltimore. The B&O was the most significant of the early railroads in the US.*

Below: *A reenactment of an early B&O scene. The locomotive is a replica of the* Atlantic, *one of the 'Grasshopper' type built in 1832 by Phineas Davis. The cars' design is based on that of a stagecoach.*

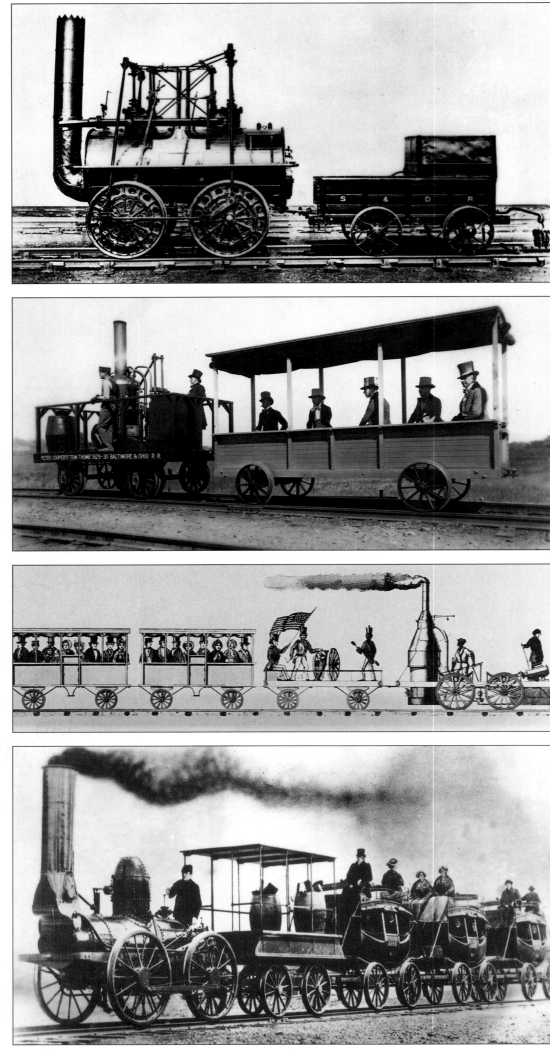

Peter Cooper's *Tom Thumb* when it made a 26-mile round trip on the B&O Railroad in August 1830. Although it later pulled some regularly scheduled passenger trains, Cooper's locomotive was designed as an experiment. Its builder was a prosperous New York businessman and semi-literate mechanic who had based his speculative purchase of several thousand acres in Baltimore on the success of the railroad. Following the Rainhill trials, the B&O had ordered a Stephenson locomotive, but it was evidently involved in an accident while being loaded aboard ship, and never reached the United States. Meanwhile, there was concern among investors that the B&O's sharp curves would prevent the use of steam power.

Cooper set out to prove them wrong. His engine, assembled by a team of Baltimore mechanics, weighed about one ton, and was not much larger than a railroad handcar. The locomotive boasted a vertical, multi-tubular boiler, a single cylinder, drive gears, and rode on the 'friction wheels' designed by Ross Winans, who compared the engine's power favorably to the *Rocket*. With Cooper at the controls, the engine managed to achieve the heady speed of 18mph; some of the passengers pulled out notebooks and wrote down their thoughts to prove that human beings could function normally at such high velocities. About a month later, due to a mechanical failure, Cooper's engine lost its famous race with the 'dappled gray' horse of Stockton and Stokes, the

Left: *The British* Locomotion *(top) was, in 1825, the first steam engine to pull a passenger train.* Tom Thumb *(second from top) pulled the first passenger train in the US in 1829; Horatio Allen's* Best Friend of Charleston *(third from top) was the first locomotive built in the US for general service; and* De Witt Clinton *traveled 17 miles in less than one hour in 1831.*

stage proprietors who had provided the B&O's first motive power, but the *Tom Thumb's* 'triumphant demonstration' removed all doubts about the feasibility of using steam locomotives on the B&O Railroad. *Tom Thumb* also established a tradition of idiosyncratic design that Ross Winans extended during his long career of building engines for the B&O.

In November 1830, the first American-built locomotive for general railroad service, the *Best Friend of Charleston*, made its initial trip on the South Carolina Railroad. Horatio Allen was then the engineer of that line, and E.L. Miller assisted in the design of the engine, which was produced by New York City's West Point Foundry. The *Best Friend* had a vertical boiler, dual-angled cylinders, and direct inside connections to the wheels via axle cranks. Unfortunately, the *Best Friend* exploded five months later when the fireman fastened down the safety valve; the fireman later died. The company's second engine, the *West Point*, bought from the same foundry, had a horizontal, Bury-type boiler. When it began pulling trains, a 'barrier car' stacked with cotton bales protected the passengers in the event of a second mishap.

The significance of Rainhill was not fully realized until long after the event, but the anonymous correspondent for the *Scotsman*, the leading Scottish newspaper of the day, recognized the promise of railroads at the time. After chiding his London colleagues for ignoring the trials in favor of their usual fare of politics and murders, he wrote:

> The experiments at Liverpool have established principles which will give a greater impulse to civilization than it has ever received from any single cause since the Press first opened

the gates of knowledge . . . They may be said to have furnished man with wings, to have supplied him with faculties of locomotion, of which the most sanguine could not have dreamed a few years ago. Even steam navigation gives but a faint idea of the wondrous powers which this new engine has put into our hands. It is no exaggeration to say, that the introduction of steam carriages on railways places us on the verge of a new era, of a social revolution of which imagination cannot picture the ultimate effects.[1]

Nowhere were the railroad's effects to be more dramatic than in the United States. Edward Pease, backer of England's Stockton & Darlington Railway, could have had the United States in mind when he said, 'Let the country but make the railroads, and the railroads will make the country!' Certainly, there was a nation to be made. In 1830, only a few dozen miles of track had been put down, mostly for mine tramways and for the two general-purpose railroads that had made tentative starts from the eastern seaboard. The United States's 13 million population was concentrated in New England and the mid-Atlantic region, and distributed among 24 states, just two of which (Missouri and Louisiana) were west of the Mississippi River. As Frederick Jackson Turner commented in *The Frontier in American History*, 'Prior to the railroad, the Mississippi Valley was potentially the basis for an independent empire.'

No one understood this better than George

Below: *A lithograph of a train at Rainhill on the Liverpool & Manchester Railway in England — scene of the famous locomotive trials attended by Horatio Allen and Ross Winans.*

Washington, the first 'commercial American' who realized the need to bind the disparate sections of the country together with the 'cement of interest,' that is, by ties of trade and commerce. As the result of his personal explorations and military campaigns during the last half of the eighteenth century, Washington anticipated in his diaries and letters the future routes of the Erie Canal, the Pennsylvania Main Line of Internal Improvements, the National Road and, along his beloved Potomac route to the West, the Chesapeake & Ohio Canal. The B&O Railroad also ultimately benefited from Washington's visionary thinking, for it inherited the C&O Canal's western alignments. When the B&O was incorporated in February 1827, western migration had advanced to a point roughly halfway between St. Louis and Kansas City and was moving forward at the rate of about 30 miles per year. But two-thirds of the future United States west of the Mississippi River was still a mostly unexplored region.

Less than a decade before he helped to lay out America's pioneer railroad, the B&O, military engineer Stephen H. Long led the third major US government expedition to the west. Leaving Pittsburgh in 1819 on his custom-designed steamboat, the *Western Engineer*, the soldiers and scientists of the expedition saw emigrant families on the Ohio River aboard 'rude arks . . . floating onward toward that imaginary region of happiness and contentment, which . . . lies always "beyond the place where the sun goes down." '

The following year, from what is now Council Bluffs, Iowa, Long and his group traveled west by horseback along the Platte River, then south at the edge of the Rocky Mountains, and east again to the Arkansas border. The official report

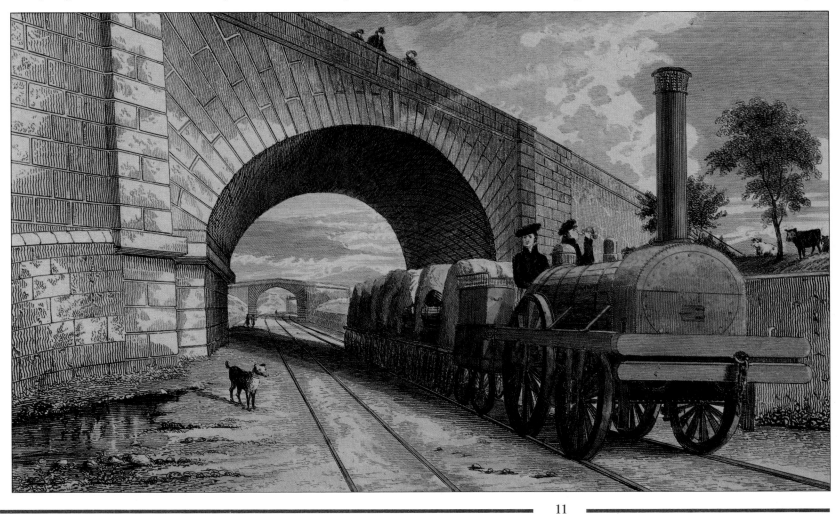

THE FIRST RAILROAD

America began building railroads before anyone fully realized what a railroad could do for a vast country with seemingly inexhaustible resources. The tools of these primitive efforts were the same as those used for surveying roads and digging canals.

The first railroad projects received send-offs worthy of any large public undertaking: parades, oration, solemn ceremonies, and much symbolism. The aprons and ribbons shown here were worn at the impressive ceremony commencing work on the Baltimore & Ohio Railroad on July 4, 1828. Local Grand Masonic Lodges officiated and celebrated the work with rituals which had their antecedents in classical antiquity. The shovel, trowel, and hammer were used in a ceremony that involved placing a symbolic 'First Stone' on the spot where work began.

Two other tasks remained to launch these new enterprises: money had to be raised in unprecedented quantities, and a practical route had to be carved out. The pamphlets, stock certificates, and stock subscriber ledgers shown are early examples of a form of corporate organization which would come to typify American business.

Choosing a route, meanwhile, was often as demanding as raising $10 million in a country where the average laborer's wage was $1 per day. Using a chain — then the basic measuring device — and crude (by today's standards) transits, compasses, painted rods and plumb bobs, the engineers plotted and calculated curves, grades, locations for bridges and tunnels, and made the millions of small decisions required to find the best route.

1 Masonic apron and emblems worn at the B&O's opening ceremonies, 1828.

2, 3, 4 Tools custom-crafted by Baltimore's Association of Black and Whitesmiths, and carried by its officers at the head of the Grand Parade. At the site of the First Stone they were presented to Charles Carroll, who turned the first spadeful of earth.

5 Music written to celebrate the start of construction.

6 A plat book, dating from 1850, showing the surveyor's drawings for the route of the Washington branch of the B&O.

7 B&O stock certificates, 1858-1868.

8 A 'Communication' from the B&O 'to the Mayor and City Council of Baltimore.'

9, 10 Early B&O stockbooks and receipt books.

11 Surveyor's chain and compass, used for the precise measurement of distances and direction when surveying the Washington route.

12 B&O stock certificates, issued in the early 1850s.

13 Glass flask, showing a horse-drawn train on the B&O. 1828.

14 A railroad dinner plate (made in England for the American market in 1828-9), commemorating the founding of the B&O.

15 Surveying transit as used by Jonathan Knight, who became the B&O's Chief Engineer.

16 Masonic sash worn at the B&O's opening ceremonies.

17 C&O Canal scrip.

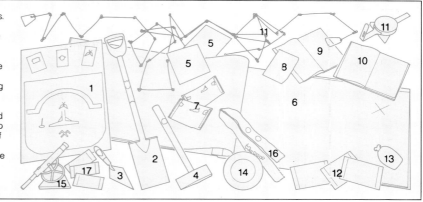

of the expedition contained a map on which Long identified the region he had traversed as 'The Great Desert,' a barren area which, he said, although unsuitable for settlement, would be useful as a frontier to limit expansion and prevent incursions.[2]

For all practical purposes the west in the 1820s was the area between the Appalachian Mountains and the Mississippi, with the river in effect acting as the equivalent of the nation's west coast today. Its towns, as well as those on the Ohio River, were ports of entry for foreign goods. From shipyards as high up river as Pittsburgh, fully-rigged vessels, loaded with western produce, had sailed to Baltimore and on to Europe. Western trade generally followed a counter-clockwise pattern: via raft or steamboat down to New Orleans, then back up on coastal schooners to the eastern seaboard cities; imports and domestic products went west over the mountains mainly by turnpike. This practise lasted well into the 1830s.

But Long had noticed steamboats arriving daily at St. Louis from New Orleans, which meant that foreign and domestic products were finding their way to the interior of the country through the network of western rivers. The Mississippi Valley 'seems destined to become the seat of a powerful, and agricultural, empire,' he proclaimed. The mountains were a barrier to the east, the traditional supply center and market for the western states, Long added, although the Erie Canal, then under construction, and 'the National Road, and the turnpike from Philadelphia to Pittsburgh, will ensure a constant intercourse and some community of interest between the Atlantic states and the countries west of the Alleghenies.'[3]

It was these routes that the settlers (attracted by cheap land: $100 would buy an 80-acre farm) and the entrepreneurs, who traveled in their wake, followed to get to the new west. One of the most popular methods was to travel overland to Pittsburgh, then down the Ohio River. Englishman James Flint did this in 1820, spending ten days on the road in a mail coach and on foot. He passed droves of cattle headed east to market and westbound Conestoga wagons, with babies and the elderly riding inside and the young and strong walking alongside. He met a group of Swiss emigrants, and a man and his wife with their ten children. The oldest carried the youngest on his back while the father pushed a wheelbarrow containing the family's belongings. They were from New Jersey, going to Ohio. 'The Canterbury pilgrims were not so diversified nor so interesting as these,' said Flint. When he got to Pittsburgh, he bought a skiff, some bread, cheese, and beer, and floated off to further adventure in the West.[4] That same year, Long's party had watched a young Philadelphian

Above: *The* Dorchester, *imported from England, hauls the inaugural train on the 14-mile Champlain & St Lawrence Railway. Canada's first railroad, it opened in 1836.*

Below: *The scene at Wheeling in 1872. Before the railroads, freight and passengers moved via river, canal or turnpike — all slow, cumbersome, and expensive, methods.*

disembark from the steamboat below St. Louis with his entire stock of merchandise to set up shop in Kaskaskia, Illinois. 'As the Indians retired the country came into notice as a fine landscape painting is disclosed by the gradual rising of a curtain,' said western editor James Hall, who reminded eastern merchants that they would do well to look over the mountains instead of across the ocean for their commercial fortunes.[5]

Hall's colleague, Timothy Flint, realized at the time what Long did not: that 'The Great Desert' would one day blossom. West of the Mississippi, he wrote in 1826, was a range of territory,

almost beyond the stretch of imagination. For the gentlemen of Long's expedition tell us, that in the political limits of the United States, they found tribes of Indians, whose ears the name of the government that claims their country, had never reached. Nothing can or will limit the immigration westward, but the Western Ocean. Alas! For the moving generation of the day, when the tide of advancing backwoodsmen shall have met the surge of the Pacific. They may then set them down and weep for other worlds.[6]

Back east, the capitalists in the seaboard cities, alarmed by the potential effects on their trade of commercial steamboat traffic on the Mississippi and of the opening of New York's Erie Canal in 1825, made plans to build long-distance internal improvements of their own. Boston chose the railroad, but then did nothing about it for several years. Philadelphia selected a hybrid system consisting primarily of canals, with the Allegheny Portage Railroad over the mountains — the Main Line of Internal Improvements. Baltimore and Charleston picked railroads, and Washington, DC, the Chesapeake & Ohio Canal.

Today, fast, decent, affordable transportation is taken for granted but, in the early nineteenth century, the lack of it had a disabling effect alike on the Philadelphia commission merchant, the farmer in the upper Susquehanna Valley, and the enterprising engineer of western Maryland. The merchant knew that it was cheaper to ship goods from Pittsburgh to Philadelphia via the all-water route down the Ohio and Mississippi rivers and back up the east coast than it was to send them 300 miles overland by turnpike. The farmer was obliged to float his wheat, flour and whiskey down the Susquehanna River and across Chesapeake Bay to Baltimore on keelboats and arks during the spring flood, but because the trade was concentrated in one season, the market soon became glutted; prices thus fell, and the farmer would often have to sell at a loss. And officials of the Georges Creek Coal and Iron Company, a struggling industry in Maryland's bituminous coalfields, were soon made aware of the need for good transportation if their business was to succeed.

In the summer of 1837 the Georges Creek ironworks ordered a steam engine, a blowing engine, and five boilers from the West Point Foundry in New York City (this was the foundry that had built the *Best Friend* for the South Carolina Railroad). The 20 tons of machinery were to be sent by ship to Georgetown, transferred to canal boats and delivered to Williamsport via the Chesapeake & Ohio Canal, and then hauled over the National Road to

Above: *In 1835, traveling by railroad, canal, rail and incline plane, and canal again, it was possible to journey from Philadelphia to Pittsburgh, 'with trifling fatigue,' in six days.*

Lonaconing in Georges Creek. As it turned out, however, only part of this order could be shipped before ice closed the canal to all traffic; the five boilers, each measuring 3ft by 24ft, eventually reached Williamsport late in October. A Lonaconing farmer hired to pick them up from there took a further 11 days to make the 90-mile round trip. Most of the rest of the equipment was sent to Baltimore in late November; three additional months were needed to wagon it to Lonaconing. The final 3 ½ tons of parts reached Baltimore in the August

Below: *This painting by H.D. Stitt captures perfectly the animosity of canal-owners toward the new railroads, which threatened to deprive them of all business.*

of 1838, and were shipped by rail most of the rest of the way.[7]

In the beginning, everything about the railroads was 'new, crude and doubtful,' as one of the directors of the B&O Railroad recalled. Raising money and selecting routes were top priorities. The long-distance roads, canals, and railroads of the United States were built with a combination of public and private funds. The National Road was heavily supported by the federal and state governments, plus private investors. The state of Pennsylvania was an important supporter of the Pittsburgh Pike, and it constructed the Main Line of Internal Improvements. The Erie Canal was built by the state of New York. The major backers of the Chesapeake & Ohio Canal were the federal government, the state of Maryland, and the district cities; together they provided more than four-fifths of its initial capital, with private shareholders contributing the remainder. Later, the state of Maryland was to become virtually the sole financial supporter of the C&O Canal.

The railroads were quite different, however. Although they were regarded originally as public thoroughfares just like the highways and canals (whose users provided their own conveyances and paid tolls), and indeed were treated as such by their neighbors (who drove livestock and private carriages along the rights-of-way to the peril of both themselves and the train travelers), it quickly became apparent that railroads were unique in requiring their operations to be governed by a single entity — a private company. Private investment thus played a much greater role in financing the first railroads than it did in the cases of the turnpikes and canals. Three-fourths of the initial $4 million raised to build the B&O came from individuals and corporations, with the balance being provided by the city of Baltimore and state of Maryland. (In the 1830s, Baltimore and Maryland each issued $3 million worth of bonds to subsidize the B&O's construction.) For the South Carolina Railroad, private shareholders provided about two-thirds, and the city of Charleston one-third, of the start-up funds.

The early internal improvements had been enormous projects for a new nation to undertake. For example, the Erie Canal — 360 miles long from Albany to Buffalo, New York — took eight years to build and cost $7 million. The construction of the Chesapeake & Ohio Canal, 185 miles long from Washington, DC to Cumberland, Maryland, took 22 years, and cost $11 million. In contrast, it required 25 years and $18 million to construct the 380-mile B&O railroad from Baltimore to Wheeling, West Virginia, on the Ohio River.

The federal government gave virtually no direct financial aid to early American railroads, but the favorable legislation and engineering expertise that it did provide were equally valuable. In 1827, in response to a request from the B&O, the Secretary of War assigned about a dozen engineers to conduct surveys. Most of them were graduates of the US Military Academy at West Point, the country's only engineering school. They formulated their theories of location and bridge design on the job. Stephen H. Long, for example, wrote his *Railroad Manual*, a pocket guide for engineers, while on assignment for the B&O. Long later published a book on bridges that explained his truss

Above: *The B&O's Carrollton Viaduct, built 1828 and photographed here in 1872, is the oldest railroad bridge in the US. Some of these early B&O bridges remain in use even today.*

Below: *The bridge carrying the B&O across the Ohio River from Benwood, West Virginia, four miles below Wheeling, to Bellaire, Ohio, was completed in 1871.*

system, which was widely used subsequently in both wooden and iron railroad bridges. This primary cadre of trained military engineers, plus a few self-educated civil engineers who worked with them, formed the basis of the nation's future railroad engineering profession. They showed up on many early rail lines, first as engineers, and then, later, often as company officers on those railroads.

The B&O, in its initial stages, adopted the British form of construction, with substantial embankments and masonry viaducts. (Although the initial cost was high, this proved to be a wise decision, for some of the stone bridges are still in use.) For locomotives, however, the B&O pursued an independent course. The company sponsored domestic mechanics and developed a unique complement of motive power. Its first production model was the 'Grasshopper', whose long connecting rods resembled the back legs of its namesake. The engine tended to jump as well as run down the tracks. Equally odd-looking 'Crabs', 'Muddiggers', and 'Camels' followed, all designed by Ross Winans.

The South Carolina Railroad took an opposite approach after their committee of inquiry reported that there were not many facts to be found about railroads, only theories. Horatio Allen decided against the British system of railroad construction in favor of timber piles, which were cheaper and easier to put up. The piles proved inadequate to support normal railroad operations, however, because they decayed rapidly at ground level and so had to be replaced regularly; they also caught fire easily, thus causing wrecks. Unsurprisingly, the South Carolina Railroad later abandoned the method. In the mid-1830s, the company turned to Great Britain for locomotives, and bought several from Robert Stephenson.

The passenger cars used on the South Carolina and B&O differed widely, too. The first B&O cars resembled stagecoaches with flanged wheels, as did those of a number of other early railroads. But the South Carolina Railroad developed 'barrel cars' for both passengers and freight, complete with iron hoops. One of the

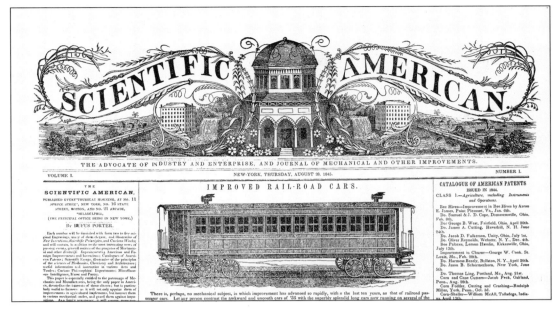

SCIENTIFIC AMERICAN.

THE ADVOCATE OF INDUSTRY AND ENTERPRISE, AND JOURNAL OF MECHANICAL AND OTHER IMPROVEMENTS.

VOLUME I.   NEW-YORK, THURSDAY, AUGUST 28, 1845.   NUMBER I.

IMPROVED RAIL-ROAD CARS.

Above: *Early passenger cars were 'uncouth',* notes this Scientific American *of August, 1845, and bore no resemblance to the 'splendid long cars running on several of the eastern roads.'*

reputed advantages of these 'Hacker's hogs head cars,' as they were known (Hacker was the name of the builder), was that both car and contents would be less subject to damage if thrown off the track. The experience of riding in brakeless, springless cars on narrow iron strips nailed to wooden rails or supported on stone blocks was 'literally, to go thundering along,' said one passenger. Benjamin H. Latrobe, Jr., the future chief engineer of the B&O, recalled a winter trip from Baltimore to the Potomac River and back in early 1834. Halfway there, the train stopped at the top of a ridge for 20 minutes, leaving the passengers shivering while a bitter wind blew through the car. 'Such crazy, uncomfortable carriages never disgraced a public road,' thundered Latrobe; 'I shall represent it to the Prest. of the co. unquestionably.'[8]

The B&O, the South Carolina, the Delaware & Hudson and the other new railroads of the United States all relied at this time on British rails. They deemed the American iron industry to be incapable of producing the necessary wrought-iron flat rails in sufficient quantity and quality, and they considered those made in Britain to be superior, as well as cheaper. This was vigorously disputed by domestic producers of iron, but after a series of political battles between the railroad companies and the ironmakers, Congress exempted imported rails from the tariff (although they remained subject to a small *ad valorem* charge). The B&O saved nearly $ ½ million by importing rails instead of being forced to buy American ones, according to one estimate. There were many problems with the British rails, however, leading to frequent claims against the producers and, in one instance, the appointment of an engineer in Britain to inspect the quality of the iron before it was exported.

The men who laid down the rails at a rate of one mile a day, built up the stone, timber, and iron bridges to support them, set the charges of black powder to blast down the cliffs, tunneled the ridges, filled up the valleys with embankments, and grubbed and smoothed out the rights-of-way, were mainly Irish, driven from home by indigence, famine, and strife. There

were also some Britons, Germans, French, free African-Americans and a few slaves. The European workmen were actively recruited by the turnpike, canal, and railroad companies whose agents made promises, offered free passage, and signed up thousands of indentured laborers. After they arrived — if they stayed on the job, which many failed to do — they first had to work off their passage and then toil for from 50 cents to $1 per day. Sometimes free board and a few ounces of whiskey were provided as well. The workers lived in shanties thrown up near the right-of-way, or in 'house cars,' which were mobile dormitories stationed at the end of the tracks. Considering the numbing and dangerous labor that the workmen performed for ten and more hours a day, it is remarkable that they had the strength left to engage in pitched battles and riots, which were usually over wages. As one writer put it, 'An Irish war followed the canal and railroad lines.' The Irish were truly ferocious builders.

By 1840, the few dozen miles of railroad in operation ten years earlier had become 3000, and substantial improvements had been made in the level of comfort offered to passengers. The first eight-wheeled coaches — the prototype of the American railroad passenger car — appeared on the B&O's Washington Branch in 1835. Designed by Ross Winans, they rode on four-wheeled trucks (bogies), featured steel leaf springs, and were equipped with mechanical brakes. The interiors were more comfortable, with center aisles, upholstered seats, and windows that opened. Locomotive design was also evolving. The 4-2-0 engine, with a four-wheel leading truck, two driving wheels, angled cylinders, direct connections, and a horizontal, Bury-style boiler, became popular duing the 1830s; William Norris and Thomas Rogers built many of them. Passenger stations, though, remained basic. The rural depots of the period consisted of rough stone or timber buildings — essentially, they were freight sheds. The passengers might gather in an adjoining room, or more likely at a nearby tavern or inn. In the cities, special provision was sometimes made for them; this could be a roofed, fenced-in area, but the tired traveler's strongest impression was likely to be of a howling mob of 'runners' for the various hotels and connecting stage, steamboat, and other railroad

lines that greeted him on arrival. Much shouting, shoving and (occasionally) violence were involved in deciding who went where and with whom. It was, said a British tourist, 'pandemonium let loose.'

The safe arrival of a train at a station, meanwhile, was guaranteed (if that is the correct word) by the watches and rule books of the conductors — a method that created great problems for operators and passengers alike, as will be seen in Chapter 3.

Signaling, in the form of daytime flags and nighttime lanterns, had been introduced on the B&O as early as 1829, but it only really came into its own during the 1830s on the nearby Newcastle & Frenchtown Railroad. This line employed a system of 30ft poles, spaced about 3 miles apart along the track, on which white and black balls were raised and lowered to give different commands: a white ball at the top of the pole, for example, was the signal to proceed. On a clear day, the train's progress could be tracked from station to station by watching the movement of the balls. (A century later, a similar system of ball signals was still in use on some lines of the Boston & Maine Railroad.)

By 1850, there were 7500 miles of railroad in the United States and, during the previous decade, substantial improvements had been made to the permanent way. In 1844, the first heavy rails to be made in the United States were rolled at Mount Savage, Maryland. The company used them to lay a track to link its ironworks with the B&O at Cumberland. The next year, the Mount Savage ironworks rolled its first wrought-iron 'T'-rail, and obtained a blast furnace blowing engine from the same West Point Foundry that had sent the earlier one to Lonaconing. How the new engine got to Mount

Above: *The first railroad public relations campaign? In 1858, the B&O invited prominent artists, photographers and journalists on an excursion between Baltimore and Wheeling.*

Below: *Few railroad stations as such existed before the Civil War: passengers usually had to wait in an inn. On arrival they were likely to be mobbed by 'runners' paid by local hotels.*

Savage is not known, but by then it could have traveled almost the entire distance by rail.

The 4-4-0-engine made its appearance in the 1840s, in a clunky version that by the end of the decade had nearly completed its evolution. The first dining, or refectory cars, as they were called, also came into use. Passenger coaches had armchairs and berths, and there were special cars for women, furnished with sofas, mirrors, carpets, venetian blinds, and washstands; enough to encourage them to think, a reporter noted, that they were 'in their own neat apartments.' Stations were still at a primary stage of development, but the American railroad itself was at the threshold of achieving real maturity and economic power.

During the decade prior to the Civil War, the number of railroads mushroomed, forming a 30,000-mile system: a map of the United States east of the Mississippi resembled a glazed surface struck by a hammer. Iron arteries spread west from Boston, north from New Orleans, and up and down the east coast from Maine to Georgia, while capillaries extended out into the Great Plains. The central part of the South, however, was still mostly bereft of railroads.

The four great eastern trunk lines also finally reached the 'western waters' in this period. The New York & Erie Railroad was the first to open officially, on May 17, 1851. A 6ft, broad-gauge line, it extended from Piermont on the Hudson, 25 miles above New York City, to Dunkirk on Lake Erie. The Pennsylvania Railroad (which replaced the former canal-railroad system), was completed from Philadelphia to Pittsburgh on November 29, 1852. The B&O arrived at Wheeling, the next big city below Pittsburgh on the Ohio River, on New Year's Day, 1853. The New York Central, a chain of smaller railroads,

was born on July 6, 1853, and Cornelius Vanderbilt later merged it with other lines to link New York City with Buffalo by rail.

The extension of the trunk lines to Cleveland, Detroit, Chicago, and St. Louis established the geographical territories of operation of the main railroads. The north was dominated by the New York Central and the Erie, with lines via Buffalo, Cleveland, and Chicago; the lower route to the midwest marked the fiefdom of the B&O, with its line going via Cincinnati and St. Louis. In between lay Pennsylvania Railroad territory, with its route through Philadelphia and Pittsburgh to Chicago.

In 1830, when two of the B&O's original engineers drew an early map of it, Chicago had been little more than a mudflat with a population of 100. But the city was to grow prodigiously over the next two decades as migrants flowed westward over the Erie Canal. With the coming of the railroads, Chicago became the central point of connection between the Atlantic Ocean, the Great Lakes, and the Mississippi Valley (see Chapter 5 for the story of Chicago's subsequent development, and its emergence as the 'second city').

Travel times and rates fell precipitously over the same period. In 1832, it took three days for passengers and mail, and 15 days for freight, to reach Wheeling from Baltimore on the National Road. Twenty years later, it took one-and-one-half days and three days, respectively, on the B&O. Fares declined from $18.75 for stagecoach passengers to $5 for rail passengers; freight rates

fell from $45 a ton to $25 a ton for railroad express goods. It became possible to travel great distances between cities entirely by rail, although long waits were still necessary at junctions between lines or for ferries across unbridged rivers. But journeys that had required several days of travel, riding first in a railroad coach, then in a stagecoach, and finally on a steamboat, were mostly a thing of the past.

The railroads' influence could be seen everywhere — even in buildings. In the mid-1850s, for example, wrought-iron beams virtually identical to railroad 'T'-rails were used in the structure of the Cooper Union building in New York. The railroads also changed the daily lives of the people who occupied the new buildings. Foundries closely affiliated with the railroads, for example, not only offered cast-iron stoves for delivery by rail, but also the coal to burn in them. Before long these foundries were producing — and the railroads were delivering — hundreds of tons of bridge, viaduct, and assorted building components for their own construction programs, and even entire cast-iron fronts for buildings (an innovation that was to change the aspect of downtown areas throughout the United States).

At this time the 30-ton, 4-4-0, 'American'-type engine with its bright livery, bonnet stack, and proud individual name — *Arrow* or *Saturn* — was becoming a classic. The B&O's *William Mason* was a prime exponent of the type. Passenger cars also increased in size and comfort as journeys of hundreds of miles, as well as overnight travel, became common on railroads. Weighing between ten and 12 tons, the 40-ft-long passenger coaches of the 1850s seated 56 people, had increased headroom with their clerestory or monitor roofs, and featured

Below: *John A. Roebling's span linking Canada and the US was erected at Niagara Falls by the Great Western Railway. Opened in 1855, it was an engineering marvel of the times.*

TRAVEL IN THE EARLY DAYS

The 'tools of the trade' for train travel in the nineteenth century took different forms, but their functions survive to this day on every passenger railroad in North America.

Richard Imlay built a full-size version of the model in the late 1830s. It was one of the earliest American 'first class' cars, with a rest room, a counter and lockers for buffet food service, and interior seating. The form of the car — resembling a stretched stage coach — shows the experimental nature of many early cars. But it did not take passenger car builders long to figure out the basic rectangular box design of the American car.

Before the water cooler became common on coaches after the Civil War, water-sellers made a living by supplying passengers with cool water at a few pennies a glass. Our notions of hygiene were somewhat less advanced then, and all passengers shared the glasses. The successor of the water-seller was the 'news butcher,' selling candy, tobacco, magazines and newspapers, and sometimes advice to travelers as well.

The water-seller — and anyone else moving about aboard the train — had to be somewhat agile to remain standing; for the crude system of coupling cars with links and pins left a certain amount of space between each car, known as 'slack.' As the locomotive accelerated and decelerated, the slack ran in and ran out, producing a series of shocks and lurches sufficient to knock the legs out from under even the most surefooted train crew. Links or pins sometimes failed under the strain, calling for quick work by the crew to prevent a crash or runaway.

1 A model of the passenger car 'Victory', by Richard Imlay, 1835. Imlay built the B&O's first cars; this is a representation of a later Imlay design built for the Philadelphia, Norristown & Germantown Railway. The model was used as a sales piece, to illustrate the novel features of the design to the railroad's officers; it is to a scale of 1½in. to the foot.

2 An original link-and-pin coupler, of the type fitted to the Imlay coach.

3, 4 Conductors' badges dating from the 1860s.

5 Trainman's whale-oil lantern, probably dating from the 1860s.

6, 7 Baggage checks as used in the 1860s.

8 Early ticket punch, as used by conductors.

9 An advertisement of the 1860s. From an unknown source.

10 B&O tickets, dating from the 1850s, validated for travel on the newly extended line from Baltimore to Wheeling.

11 A B&O conductor's ticket, 1860. This type of ticket was issued on the train itself.

12 A B&O 'Time Book' for 1857, showing the running times of the trains on the Baltimore to Wheeling section of the line. The book was issued to engineers, conductors, trainmen and other employees who were involved with operating trains.

13, 14 Water kettle and glasses, dating from 1841, used by W.P. Horton to sell water to passengers on B&O trains.

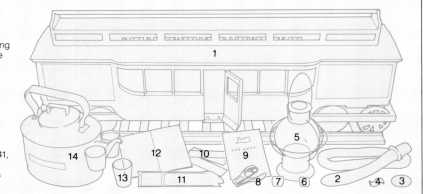

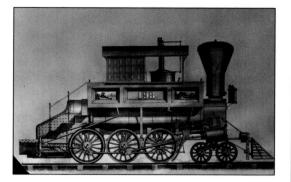

Above: *A 'Hayes Ten-Wheeler'. Named for Samuel Hayes, the B&O's 'Master of Machinery' who devised them, the engine was a development of Ross Winans's 0-8-0 'Camel' design.*

reclining seats, heating, lighting, and some ventilation. Despite these new amenities, the trip was not always tranquil.

None of these innovations was to have as great an impact on the railroads as the events of September 22, 1851, however. For it was on that day that Charles Minot, superintendent on a New York & Erie westbound train that had been stopped at a station to await an eastbound express, telegraphed the operator at Goshen, NY, with the message: 'Hold eastbound train till further orders.' Having issued this first telegraphed train order, Minot then assumed control of the westbound train, as the engineman had refused to run it on other than 'time-card rules.' Minot ran the train to Goshen. On arrival there, the eastbound express had still failed to appear, so Minot repeated the orders and ran the train on to Port Jervis, NY, saving two hours on the schedule overall. The system of dispatching trains by telegraph was subsequently adopted on the NY&E, albeit with strong resistance at first from conductors and enginemen; the idea soon spread quickly to other lines. The first practical demonstration of the telegraph had taken place over the B&O's Washington Branch right-of-way on May 24, 1844, when Samuel F.B. Morse wired the famous 'What hath God wrought?' message from the Supreme Court chamber in the Capitol in Washington, DC to the B&O's downtown depot on Charles Street in Baltimore. But the railroads were rather slow to adopt the invention that would become as important as the conductor's watch and timetable in governing train movements.

Of all the celebrations that attended the completion of the eastern trunk lines to the western rivers in the 1850s, probably none equalled, at least in duration, the B&O's opening of the line from Baltimore to St. Louis in 1857. Aboard the excursion trains that left Camden Station in June of that year were Secretary of State Lewis Cass, Henry Ward Beecher, George Bancroft, Charles A. Dana, Abram S. Hewitt and Commodore Perry, among other notables. Many ceremonial dinners, toasts, and speeches later they arrived at their destination, and in mid-July, they did it all again on the way back, culminating in more parades, banquets and entertainments in Baltimore. Much after-dinner rhetoric was expended on the subject of 'The Union', such as New Yorker James Brooks' comment, after they had reached St. Louis, that 'Hence whatever disunionists or sectionalists may do or say, the more they try to tear us apart, the more the iron

The railroad revolutionized the gathering of news and its dissemination. So did the telegraph, although the press was quicker to utilize the device that was to have such a great impact on railroad operations.

The Baltimore *Sun* in 1837, its first year, cut the time for publishing the President's annual message from two days to one by having it sent 30 miles by rail via the Washington Branch of the Baltimore & Ohio Railroad, which had opened two years earlier. 'The President's message, which will be found entire in this day's paper, was received at our office at 2 o'clock precisely — the transmission from Washington to Baltimore occupying less than two hours,' the newspaper proudly reported.[1]

The *Sun* bettered its own record at the end of the year by printing an extra with another of President Van Buren's addresses the same day it was given — December 6, 1837. This time a courier aboard the train took only one hour and 17 minutes to reach Baltimore. He

was met at the depot by the *Sun*'s messenger, who raced on a pony to the office where 49 compositors stood ready to set the message in type. The newspaper hit the street at 5p.m.; 15,000 copies were distributed.

On March 4, 1841, by means of a similar arrangement involving other railroads and newspapers, the text of President Harrison's inaugural address was rushed from Washington, DC to New York: 'By agreement with the Post Office Department, the Baltimore & Ohio and Philadelphia, Wilmington & Baltimore Railroad Companies ran expresses from Washington to Philadephia,' the *Sun* said.[2] The train from Washington, DC reached Baltimore's outer depot in one hour and 15 minutes. A man on horseback carried the dispatches across town to the PW&B's depot (locomotive use was restricted on city streets at that time), and from there the dispatches were rushed by train to Philadelphia and New York.

The *Sun*'s alliance with New York newspapers also resulted in the 'horse

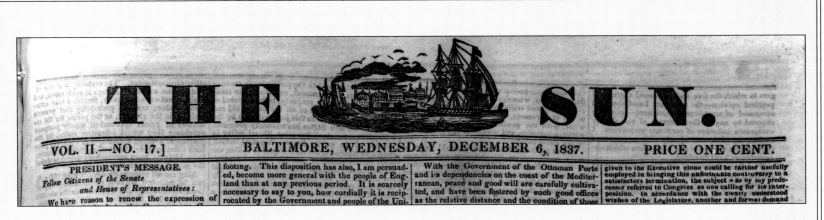

THE SUN.

VOL. II.—NO. 17.]   BALTIMORE, WEDNESDAY, DECEMBER 6, 1837.   PRICE ONE CENT.

Above: *The December, 1837, edition of the Baltimore* Sun *— the day the newspaper broke all records by printing President Van Buren's address the same day it was given.*

Left: *By enabling rapid delivery of mail and newspapers, the railroads freed communities from isolation, bringing in accurate news about national and international events.*

express' across Nova Scotia in 1845. Halifax, Nova Scotia, the first port of call for mail steamers from Europe, had no rail connections. The *Sun* and its allies therefore established relays of horses and riders to carry the urgent news dispatches 150 miles across the peninsula, where they were again put aboard steamers for Portland, Maine, which was connected by rail to Boston, New York,

Below: *Washington DC's B&O station in 1872, with the Capitol's dome to the right. With the advent of railroads, governments could be more effective.*

Philadelphia, and Baltimore. The 1000-mile total distance was covered in 50 hours.

In 1844, the *Sun* backed the bitterly contested Congressional appropriation of $30,000 for a practical demonstration of Samuel F.B. Morse's telegraph along the B&O's Washington Branch right-of-way, but buried the two-sentence story of the transmission of the first 'What has God wrought?' message in its *Local Matters* column on May 27. A Baltimore competitor had already printed the first telegraphed news dispatch, but the *Sun* quickly adopted the new system. President James K. Polk's 1845 swearing-in was reported by wire to Baltimore, with Morse himself at the key, and on May 11, 1846, the *Sun* obtained Polk's Mexican war message to Congress in its entirety by telegraph.

The *Sun*'s new headquarters in Baltimore, the five-story, structurally unique Sun Iron Building, designed by James Bogardus and built in 1851, was typical of the newspaper that had pioneered the collection of news by railroad, telegraph, and pony express. On the

second floor, one floor below the composing room and editorial offices, were three telegraph companies — the Magnetic, the Western, and the Southern. The telegraph wires strung from the building, which were necessary for the companies' operation, blackened the sky for many years on Baltimore Street. It was the country's first integrated telegraph-news operation. When, in January, 1853, the B&O Railroad officially opened its new line, the correspondent for the Baltimore *Sun*, who was aboard the first train, filed his definitive account by telegraph from Harpers Ferry and Wheeling.

To cities across America, the telegraph spread. In smaller towns, the railroad telegrapher dispatched both trains and news.

Notes

[1]Baltimore *Sun*, Sept. 6, 1837, quoted in Gerald W. Johnson, Frank R. Kent, H.L. Mencken, Hamilton Owens, *The Sunpapers of Baltimore*, (New York: Knopf, 1936), p. 55.
[2]Ibid., p. 64.

The pioneer locomotives, such as the Stourbridge Lion, *were built in Great Britain (see artworks), but domestic builders designed engines more suited to America's rough track. The better-tracking 4-2-0 evolved into the classic 4-4-0, which became the 'standard' North American type into the 20th.C. Freight engines, though, needed more driving wheels for better pull.*

roads and lightning wire must bind us together.'[9] Despite such rhetoric, the iron road was in fact to enable the Unionists and 'disunionists' to tear each other apart far more effectively. For the Civil War was to be the first railroad war.

There was no experience in the use of railroads in warfare prior to the Civil War; after it, a great deal had been learned about their strategic importance, and also about how to disable a railroad and make it useless to the enemy. At the beginning of the war, the North possessed two-thirds of the national railroad mileage; the South's one-third, furthermore, was poorly laid out and connected. And between them, the four major northern trunk lines

owned as much motive power and rolling stock as did all the Southern rail lines put together.

Of all the railroads, north and south, the one that occupied the most crucial position relative to the conflict, and suffered some of the gravest damage, was the B&O. The B&O was the only line into the nation's capital from the north, and its western extension was also of critical importance in delivering the materials of war — coal, iron, and provisions — to the east. The B&O even shaped the eastern panhandle of West Virginia, a state that came into existence during the Civil War. John W. Garrett, the B&O's president, was the most important wartime railroad official, and because of its unique location, the line was the scene of some of the war's most dramatic episodes.

John Brown's shocking night raid on Harpers Ferry helped to precipitate the conflict. With a band of followers, who had been staying at a farm in the nearby hills, he captured the US arsenal, stopped an eastbound B&O express, and shot the African-American station porter, Hayward Sheppard (or Sheppard Hayward, as

in some accounts), who later died. Toward morning, the train pulled out from the small town where the Shenandoah and Potomac rivers joined and together poured through a ragged gap in the Blue Ridge Mountains. The subsequent exchange of telegrams between the conductor and his supervisor has lost none of its drama or immediacy:

Monocacy, 7.05a.m., Oct. 17, 1859
W.P. Smith, Baltimore

"Express train bound east under my charge was stopped this morning at Harpers Ferry by armed Abolitionists. They have possession of the bridge and of the arms and armory of the United States . . . They are headed by a man who calls himself Anderson and number about 150 strong. They say they have come to free the slaves, and intend to do it at all hazards . . . It has been suggested that you had better notify the Secretary of War at once. The telegraph wires are cut east and west of Harpers Ferry and this is the first station that I could send a despatch from." A.J.Phelps

Norris-built 4-2-0, 1837, with four-wheel leading truck (or bogie) for better tracking.

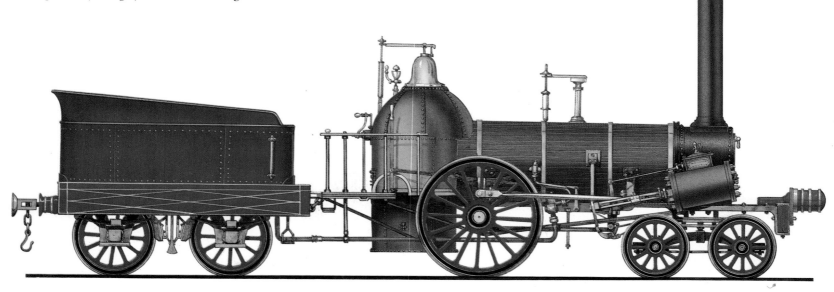

A typical 4-4-0 'American' type, circa 1857, built for passenger service.

Col. Robert E. Lee arrived at Harpers Ferry instead, by train, with a company of US Marines and Baltimore militia. In the ensuing battle at the armory's engine house, which Brown had used as a fort, ten of his 21 followers were killed and Brown was taken prisoner. He was later hanged.

In February, 1861, Abraham Lincoln traveled by rail to his first inaugural, with stops at major cities to give addresses. As the party approached Baltimore, General Winfield Scott and detective Allan Pinkerton, in charge of Lincoln's safety, countered rumors of a plot to sabotage the train and assassinate the President-elect by secretly re-routing him via the Pennsylvania Railroad to Philadelphia, the PW&B Railroad to Baltimore, and the B&O to Washington, DC. The transfer between the PW&B's President Street Station in Baltimore and the B&O's Camden Station several blocks away was then made by horsepower. On the night of February 22, Lincoln rode through the city in a closed coach and reached Washington, DC safely.

On April 19, 1861, a week after the firing on Fort Sumter which marked the official beginning of the war, the Sixth Massachusetts Regiment, on its way to Washington by rail, attempted to march through an angry crowd over the same route between the two Baltimore train stations. The result was a riot, during which shots were fired; four soldiers and 12 citizens were killed, and many more were wounded. After that, Union troops were diverted around Baltimore, and its rail lines and the city itself were put under military rule.

The B&O's situation was summarized a week later by a Wheeling editor: 'The terminus at one hand is among the mobocracy; at the other end, here in Wheeling, among good, order-loving Union men. At Harpers Ferry it is completely under military despotism, and every train has to run the gauntlet of cannon and armed espionage.'[11] This was Stonewall Jackson's main theater of operations: the great Valley of Virginia beyond Harpers Ferry, which the B&O line crossed to Martinsburg. Garrett managed to keep the B&O in Union hands and operating for most of the war, but Jackson was one of his prime antagonists. The South lacked motive power and rolling stock and in the summer of 1861, Jackson bottled up 56 B&O locomotives and over 300 cars in the Valley of Virginia, hauled some of the equipment overland to a connection with the Confederate railroad system and burned the rest, destroyed bridges and track, and closed the line to through traffic for ten months. One of the Union soldiers who helped to repair the 1861 damage at Harpers Ferry by building suspension bridges was Washington Roebling, later of Brooklyn Bridge renown, and son of John Roebling.

Herman Haupt also worked on repairing the bridges at Harpers Ferry. He had already established his reputation as a bridge and railroad man before the Civil War, but gained even more respect for his activities during the conflict. Although he was a West Point graduate, Haupt served as the civilian director of the United States Military Railroads established by federal statute in May, 1862. In fact, it was largely due to Haupt that the military railroads, although under the central control of the Quartermaster General of the Army, were independently operated by their civilian personnel rather than the military officers who tried continually to commandeer them. Haupt, a field manager himself, wrested control of the railroads from the generals and got the men and supplies to the front at

A 'Consolidation' 2-8-0, 1866, an early locomotive for heavy freight.

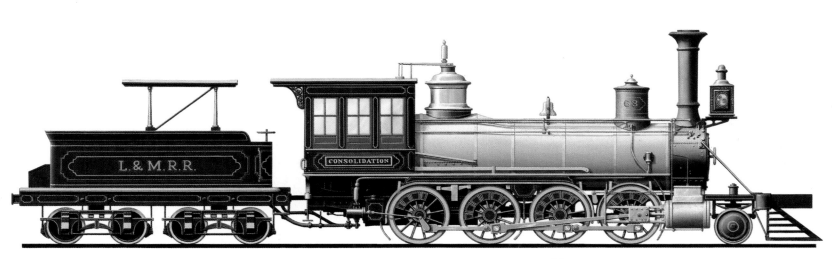

Fredericksburg, Chancellorsville, and Gettysburg. Haupt formed a Construction Corps, made up primarily of fugitive slaves, who could lay a mile of track or put up a timber replacement bridge in a day using prefabricated, interchangeable parts. He improvised a system of runners and men on horseback to communicate between trains when the telegraph was out of order, and sent such timely and accurate dispatches to Washington, DC that the War Department often had a much superior grasp of the military situation than the generals in the field.

Haupt left the service in September, 1863 and missed the great troop movement that began at the end of that month, when more than 20,000 soldiers of the Army of the Potomac were transported 1200 miles in 11½ days from northern Virginia to reinforce Rosecrans at Chattanooga, Tennessee. This successful Union troop movement, which changed the fortunes of the war in the west, proceeded initially in 30 trains of 20 cars each over the B&O to the Ohio River, then by Ohio and Indiana rail lines to Louisville, Kentucky. From there the convoy traveled on the Louisville & Nashville Railroad to Nashville, and finally via the Nashville & Chattanooga to Bridgeport, Tennessee.

Sherman employed all of these methods in his famous march to the sea from Chattanooga, Tennessee to Atlanta, Georgia in the spring of 1864, a march which has been called 'a classic in efficient military railroading.' From Atlanta, Sherman continued his march to Savannah, Georgia, which he reached at the end of the year, and then on into South Carolina, rebuilding the railroad ahead of him and destroying the line and everything else in his wake.

The war ended with Lee's surrender at Appomattox, Virginia, on April 9, 1865. Lincoln was assassinated on April 14 and, on April 21, his body was loaded onto a special train to begin the long journey that reversed the route of his 1861 inaugural trip to Washington, DC. The greatest and most solemn funeral procession in American history marked a transition for both the nation and the railroads. In the new era, the railroads dominated the transformation of the United States that was to occur over the next 50 years, fulfilling Edward Pease's comment that 'the railroads will make the country'.

Even more so was this true of Canada, where the 1867 federation of the provinces was based largely upon the need for a central authority to plan railroad construction. British Columbia joined Confederation in 1871 on being promised a railroad linking it to the eastern provinces, and when in 1885 the Canadian Pacific Railway was completed to Vancouver, Canada was at last one nation. Before that, the country lagged substantially behind the United States, with good reason. Its population was relatively 'scanty and scattered' (in 1830, Canada had about one million people), there was little investment capital, industrial development was

Right: *The station at Richmond, VA, (top) in 1865 following a Unionist attack. In 1862, US Military Railroad officials recover an engine derailed by Confederate raiders (center) during an attack on General John Pope's lines. A bridge (bottom) built by soldiers, a USMRR train and guards. Both sides became adept at making quick repairs to track and bridges.*

slow, and the physical obstacles were daunting.

'Here we have comparatively few or no good roads, we have often to wade through mud and swamps for many miles together, and except in the sleighing season, find it almost impossible to go any distance,' wrote a resident of what is now western Ontario arguing for railroads in 1836.[12] In that year, with a locomotive imported from England, Canada opened its first railroad, the 14-mile Champlain and St. Lawrence south of Montreal that improved trade between that city and New York. A few years later, the earliest locomotives were employed in the Maritime Provinces on short coal lines in Nova Scotia. But by 1850, only 60 miles of railroad were in operation in all of Canada, and the author of a pamphlet on railroads lamented: 'Far away to the South is heard the daily scream of the steam whistle — but from Canada there is no escape: blockaded and imprisoned by Ice and Apathy, we have at least ample time for reflection.'[13]

During the next decade, however, railroad construction in Canada surged ahead. In 1853, the St. Lawrence and Atlantic Railway, an important line between Montreal and Portland, Maine, was completed, and in 1855, the Great Western linking Buffalo and Detroit across Ontario opened for business. A year later, the Grand Trunk Railway, which had acquired the St. Lawrence and Atlantic, finished its Montreal to Toronto line, which was later extended westward to Sarnia near Lake Huron and eastward to Riviere du Loup high up on the St. Lawrence River.

Altogether, 2000 miles of railroad were constructed in Canada between 1850 and 1860. The St. Lawrence and Atlantic, the Great Western, and the Grand Trunk were broad gauge lines, however, while many of the smaller companies were narrow gauge. Rail travel was further hampered by snow. Even in good weather, a British officer reported in 1857, the average train speed was 10mph on the Grand

Above: *A giant 13-in. mortar — named 'The Dictator' — used by the Unionists to bombard the Confederate lines around Petersburg. The mortar fired a mammoth 200-pound shell.*

Trunk. The line was then deeply in debt, soon went bankrupt, and was rescued during the next decade only by a government reorganization.

Canada invested much more heavily in its rail network than did the United States: in 1867, the year of union, there were 2459 miles of railroad, built at a total cost of $155 million, to which the provincial government contributed $33 million. Although the early Canadian railroads had failed in their original intention of turning American

Below: *The locomotive that hauled President Lincoln's funeral train from Washington, DC to Springfield, IL. Lincoln's coffin was carried in his hitherto unused private car.*

trade into the St. Lawrence Valley, they had succeeded in opening wide the curtain of Canada's isolation from itself and the United States, and had established the pattern for the nation-building that would follow.

Notes

[1] Undated news clipping, ca. Oct.-Nov., 1829, (B&O Rr. Pamphlets, B&O Railroad Museum, Baltimore).

[2] Edwin James, *Account of an Expedition from Pittsburgh to the Rocky Mountains* . . . 2 vols. (Philadelphia: Carey & Lea, 1823; Readex Microprint,1966), 1: 16-17, 110; 2: 9-10.

[3] Ibid., 2: 440-41

[4] James Flint, *Letters from America* . . . London: 1822, in Reuben Gold Thwaites, *Early Western Travels, 1748-1846*, (Cleveland: Clark, 1907), 31 vols. 9: 72.

[5] James Hall, *Notes on the Western States* . . . Philadelphia: 1838, p. 214; same author, *Letters from the West* . . . 1828; (Gainesville, Fla.: Scholars' Facsimiles, 1967), p. 77.

[6] Timothy Flint, *Recollections of the Last Ten Years* . . . (Boston, 1826), p. 203.

[7] Katherine A. Harvey, "Building a Frontier Ironworks: Problems of Transport and Supply, 1837-1840," *(Maryland Historical Magazine*, Summer, 1975), pp. 156-57.

[8] Benjamin H. Latrobe, Jr., *Journal*, Jan. 26, Feb. 1, 1834, (Mrs. Gamble Latrobe Collection, MS 1638, Maryland Historical Society).

[9] William Prescott Smith, *The Book of the Great Railway Celebrations of 1857*, (New York: Appleton, 1858), p. 258.

[10] Edward Hungerford, *The Story of the Baltimore & Ohio Railroad, 1827-1927*, 2 vols. (New York: Putnam's, 1928), 1: 336-37.

[11] Wheeling *Intelligencer*, Apr. 27, 1861, quoted in Elizabeth Cometti and Festus P. Summers, eds., *The Thirty-Fifth State; a Documentary History of West Virginia*, (Morgantown, W. Va.: West Virginia University Library, 1966), p. 299.

[12] G.P. de T. Glazebrook, *A History of Transportation in Canada*, (Toronto: Ryerson press, 1938), p. 147.

[13] Ibid., p. 161.

RAILS WEST!

THE PIONEERS OF THE American state of California were not men who had to learn that upon facilities of rapid transit and transportation depended the development of resources, material, political, and social. They brought that knowledge with them.'[1]

Thus did the dean of California's nineteenth-century historians, Hubert Howe Bancroft, characterize the raw, undeveloped land that would become California, and in the same words outline the attitude of the entire nation during the period of western expansion. What America came to know as the West, the gigantic spaces beyond the Mississippi River, was considered perfect save for the fact that no white people lived there. The development of these open lands was seen as a national entitlement. The doctrine of Manifest Destiny — that it was

fundamentally inevitable that the United States should in time come to own and develop the entire continent from the Atlantic to the Pacific — was an article of unshakable faith. Towns, cities, farms, and manufactories were destined to fill this new territory, but they depended on transportation — the railroad — to make this march of progress possible.

Russia, Great Britain, France and the United States all had designs on the Pacific coast, and the idea that it was Americans who should ultimately take over the west was encouraged in the popular mind by accounts like Richard Henry Dana's *Two Years Before the Mast:* 'In the hands of an enterprising people, what a country this might be!'

The nationalistic catchphrase of the nineteenth century, Manifest Destiny, was coined in

1845 and came to symbolize the idea that 'American' culture and values were ordained to prevail over the entire continent from the Atlantic to the Pacific. The railroad was heralded as the most sublime of mankind's mechanical creations, and was accorded the popular stature of 'Agent of Civilization'. It was the force which would permanently alter the face of the land, for it had a transforming power capable of building cities, moving the products of mine, mill and factory, and capturing the maximum potential of agriculture. The west would become irrevocably American only after the railroad came.

Asa Whitney, a New Yorker made wealthy in the China trade, talked about a railroad from the Great Lakes to the Pacific in 1845: 'It will bring the world together as one nation; allow us to

and for the next two generations every self-respecting railroad company with transcontinental aspirations made sure it had 'Pacific' in its name.

Despite the lack of transportation, the lure of the west appealed to the adventurous and those looking for new opportunity. Groups of settlers traveled overland via a number of routes, braving the hardships of a three- or four-month walk from the midwest for the promise of good farming land and fair weather. Immigration to California was steady but extremely slow. By 1845 the annual total of immigrants from 'the States' was 250, doubling the next year.

Manifest Destiny motivated national action, and prompted the United States to take what had been the Spanish southwest. The United States declared war on Mexico in May, 1846 and triumphed over its adversary in a series of short, sharp military actions. The Treaty of Guadalupe Hidalgo was concluded in February, 1848, ceding to the United States a vast tract of land from Texas to Oregon.

Unknown to the treaty negotiators, gold had been discovered along the American River in the central Sierra Nevada foothills on January 24, nine days before California was officially given up by Mexico. The results were stunning and unanticipated. The largest voluntary worldwide mass migration, the California Gold Rush, transformed the new territory into a state almost instantly. California became the thirty-first state

A.J. Russell took this photograph (below) seconds before the final spike was driven to complete the first transcontinental railroad on May 10, 1869. In his painting of the scene (above) Thomas Hill romanticized the event, and included several dignitaries who were not present.

traverse the globe in thirty days, civilize and christianize mankind, and place us in the center of the world, compelling Europe on one side and Asia and Africa on the other to pass through us.'[2] The concept was vivid and appealing. The proposed line was called the 'Pacific Railroad,'

under the Compromise of 1850, being admitted to the Union on September 9, 1850. The census of 1852 counted 223,856 Californians, up from only 15,000 in 1848. Nearly all had trudged across the continent or braved the voyage in sailing ships around the tip of South America. The new state wanted to be connected with the rest of the Union by a railroad.

But where would a railroad to the Pacific begin? Where would it end? Anti-slavery interests in Congress feared that a railroad which began in a slave state would result in this 'peculiar institution' being carried into the new states which would inevitably arise along the route. Similarly, those who favored slavery were worried that free states would develop along a railroad which commenced in a free state. Either way, the delicate balance of power between free and slave states in Congress would be upset, and most people believed that the enormous costs of building such a railroad made government involvement essential. The issue was thoroughly discussed, the railroad was favored by many, but North-South conflict deadlocked Congress and any possibility of action on a Pacific Railroad.

While Congress debated, the new citizens of California were making their own destiny. In 1854 a small group of Sacramento businessmen proposed a railroad from the capital city east into the foothills. A New York firm was hired to plan and construct the new line, and a young civil engineer, Theodore D. Judah, came west to superintend the project.

Judah was a brilliant, energetic, capable and difficult man. The Sacramento Valley Railroad, the first railroad west of the Mississippi, was completed to the new town of Folsom on February 22, 1856, and Judah turned his attention to the fabulous idea that a railroad could be built from near sea-level in Sacramento over the 7000ft summit of the Sierra Nevada only 100 miles away, and then across Nevada and Utah Territories to a connection with the railroads of the east. Practical minds had declared the idea foolish and impossibly expensive, and Judah found no encouragement in San Francisco's business community. But Theodore Judah was not about to have his idea rejected, and he became a forceful and single-minded advocate for a railroad over the mountains to the east. He pursued the matter with a disturbing intensity in the face of much scorn and derision, earning the name 'Crazy Judah' for the strength of his beliefs. He made trips to Washington, DC to lobby for a Pacific Railroad, and spent nearly every waking hour planning ways to convince people to support his efforts.

The issues of slavery and states' rights were straining the very fabric of the nation when Judah made a presentation to a group of Sacramento businessmen in November, 1860. The most prominent of these — Leland Stanford, Collis Huntington, Mark Hopkins and Charles Crocker — were members of the new Republican Party and saw possibilities in Judah's ideas. They all supported the candidacy of Abraham Lincoln, who had been elected the sixteenth President on November 6, and they combined patriotism with an equally strong sense of enlightened self-interest. A railroad along the central route east from California would bind the state to the Union in the event of civil war — and war looked like a certainty

Left: Officers of the UP and CP, (clockwise, from top): Oliver Ames; Charles Crocker (CP construction supervisor); Oakes Ames; Sidney Dillon; D. H. Moffat; Leland Stanford (CP President); C. P. Huntington (CP Vice-President). Mark Hopkins, CP Treasurer, is not shown.

— and a line into Nevada would capture lucrative traffic to the Comstock mines of western Nevada.

Lincoln's election triggered the secession of eleven southern states, with the final rending of the national tapestry taking place early on the morning of April 12, 1861, as Confederate guns fired on Union Fort Sumter in Charleston Harbor, South Carolina, commencing formal hostilities between North and South. Back in California, the time to carry out Judah's plan had arrived. An organizational meeting for a new company, the Central Pacific Rail Road of California, was held on April 30, with the

company being incorporated on June 28. Stanford became president of the company, with Huntington vice president, Hopkins treasurer, and Judah as chief engineer.

There could not have been a more favorable moment to launch the enterprise. The Union Congress no longer had reason to debate the route of a railroad to the Pacific: the line would clearly be in northern territory. Construction of the road was now a matter of national urgency. But the Government of the United States, fully engaged in a war for its very survival, was in no position to build such a railroad. Said Lincoln, 'Private enterprise must build the Pacific Railroad. All the government can do is aid, even admitting its construction is a political as well as a military necessity.'

Judah and his associates spent the summer of 1861 surveying the projected route over the mountains — and with a growing sense of confidence that the railroad would actually be built. A Sacramento newspaper crowed that 'when the Pacific Railroad next comes up in Congress, Californians will be able to say to members: We are now prepared to lay before you a perfectly reliable report of a competent engineer. The problem as to crossing the Sierra Nevada has been solved.' That summer Stanford campaigned for the governorship of the state, winning election in September to a two-year term.

Judah was sent east in October '. . . as the

Below: The Gov. Stanford, Central Pacific locomotive No. 1, was built on the east coast in 1862 and delivered to California by ship — an arduous and lengthy 15,000-mile voyage.

MISTON & LEONARD RAILROAD POSTERS, CHICAGO.

Left: A UP poster announcing the beginning of through train services to San Francisco. As the poster proclaimed, the new route cut the journey time to the west coast to 'less than four days'.

ment was given a first mortgage on the entire undertaking. The railroads were required to be completed within a period of 12 years.

The idea of land grants dated from 1850, when the Illinois Central and Mobile & Ohio Railroads received support for their route from the Great Lakes to the Gulf coast. Land grants were eventually made available to about 80 railroads, and four of the first five transcontinental lines received federal lands. The government considered most of the lands in the west to be essentially valueless unless they were made accessible by a reliable transportation system, so exchanging unclaimed land — about 130 million acres in total — for the benefits of railroad development seemed to be good federal policy.

Groundbreaking for the new railroad occurred on January 8, 1863, at the foot of 'K' Street in Sacramento. It was a drizzly, muddy day; bundles of straw had to be spread around to provide dry footing for the participants. The Sacramento *Union* decried the 'disagreeable necessity' for female onlookers to wear pantaloons in consideration of the weather. A speaker's stand decorated with bunting and flags furnished the backdrop for '. . . a ceremony of vast significance in Sacramento, California and the Union. With rites appropriate to the occasion, and in the presence of the dignitaries of the State . . . ground was formally broken at noon for the commencement of the Central Pacific Railroad — the California link of the continental chain that is to unite American communities now divided by thousands of miles of trackless wilderness . . .' The real work of railroad construction could now begin.

With materials beginning to arrive from the east, grading and track construction progressed in a northeasterly direction into the foothills. The work was much slower and more costly than anticipated, and the government bond subsidy would not be available until the first 40 miles had been completed. By early summer things were not going well. The railroad was running out of cash, and a widening rift had developed between Judah and Stanford, Huntington, Crocker and Hopkins — who were now becoming known as the 'Big Four.' Judah disliked the fact that Charles Crocker was given the contract to build a section of line, and wanted to use the completed part of the railroad as collateral for loans to stay afloat until the government bonds became available. The Big Four instead favored going deeper into personal debt to support the railroad rather than lower the line's credit rating by borrowing against it. There were other disagreements, and Judah was excluded from many important decisions. Matters came to a head in September when both camps adopted a put-up-or-shut-up compromise. The Big Four agreed to buy out Judah's interest in the railroad for $100,000, and in turn offered to let him buy them out on the same terms if he could raise the money. If Judah wanted to run the railroad here was his opportunity, otherwise he could take the money and leave. He boarded ship for New York giving the impression that he was about to secure

accredited agent of the Central Pacific Company of California, for the purpose of procuring appropriations of land and US bonds from the government, to aid in the construction of this road.' This was his fourth attempt to induce Congress to support such a railroad, and he was better prepared than ever with surveys, the support of a company actually ready to build the line, and the pressure of a national emergency to lend urgency to the matter. A cautious Congress, its attention focused on the war, debated a railroad bill through the winter and spring of 1862, and it finally passed the House on May 6. The Senate approved the matter on June 20, with President Lincoln signing the Pacific Railroad Act on July 1, 1862.

The act empowered the CP to build from California toward the east, and chartered a new company, the patriotically named Union Pacific Railroad, to build west from Nebraska Territory into Nevada. The railroads were granted right of way over federal lands, and ceded alternate sections — 6400 acres — of public lands for each mile of track completed. The lines would also receive a construction subsidy in the form of United States bonds in varying amounts for each mile of track. This was actually a loan, as the bonds were to be repaid with interest at 6 percent within 30 years, and the federal govern-

CRY OF THE PLAINS

Moment of Excitement, 1879, *by Howard Fogg, depicts a clash on the Plains.*

For Native Americans, the coming of the railroad was a disaster, not an opportunity. In the early wars to defend their ancestral lands against white settlers, Indians could steal guns and outmaneuver the invaders. Against the railroad in the end, however, they could do nothing: for the railroads brought settlers in such huge numbers that resistance became futile.

For Plains Indians, white buffalo hunters were the first serious encroachers. At the beginning of the century, North American bison — the vital mainstay of all Plains Indian culture and economics — were so numerous that single herds numbered in the hundreds of thousands; it could take such a herd several days to migrate past one spot. White buffalo-hunters first came for skins to ship back east. Between 1872 and 1874, 1.5 million hides were carried by the Kansas Pacific Railroad alone. Later the buffalo-hunters were employed by the railroads who were building west across the prairies. Shooting enough bison to feed the track gangs was only one of their tasks; the main purpose was to eradicate the bison altogether so that train movements would not be hindered.

William F. Cody — 'Buffalo Bill' — gained fame working for the Kansas Pacific Railroad; by his own count, he killed over 4000 bison in less than 18 months — more than even the ravenous track workers could eat. (Using a heavy Sharps .45 caliber sporting rifle, a hunter could kill scores of animals without moving from one spot.) Bison carcasses littered the land. The great chief of the Hunkpapa Lakota, Sitting Bull, bitterly commented on such hunters: 'What is this? Is it robbery? You call us savages. What are *they*?' Later, in 1883, Cody parleyed his notoriety into a wild west show that toured the US and Europe for many years. The Indian horsemen who were part of Cody's act must have had mixed emotions about taking part. For it was Buffalo Bill and the other hunters, working on behalf of the railroads, who had destroyed the Native Americans' very means of existence.

For many Americans, the train whistle was to become a haunting, romantic call, as has been celebrated in countless folk songs. There are other perspectives. 'When older people heard that whistle out on the prairie,' commented Lakota Sioux historian Albert White Hat, Sr., 'they would cry.'

THEODORE JUDAH: MAN OF VISION

Planning the Pacific railroad required vision and audacity, qualities possessed in ample measure by Theodore Dehone Judah (below, right), first Chief Engineer of the Central Pacific Railroad.

Like the 'Big Four' who would become his partners in the enterprise, Judah was a Yankee. Born in Connecticut on March 4, 1826, he was raised in upstate New York, where he studied engineering at Troy's Rensselaer Polytechnic Institute. By his early 20s he had developed a reputation as a sometimes temperamental genius, and garnered a degree of fame for his work on the Niagara Gorge Railroad.

An older brother had been in California and it is possibly he who enthralled Theodore and his wife Anna with stories of the Pacific Coast, inspiring Judah's dream of building a railroad to the west. He told Anna that a Pacific railroad '. . . will be built, and I'm going to have something to do with it.' Thus it seemed providential when the promoters of the Sacramento Valley Rail Road hired an upstate New York contracting firm — and Theodore Judah — to build the first railroad in California.

The Sacramento Valley line was completed in early 1856 and Judah began to devote considerable energy to his idea of a railroad over the mountains. Few other thoughts occupied his mind. He went to Washington DC in 1856 and 1857, impressing supporters and adversaries alike with his dedication, zeal, and energy.

By 1860 Judah had performed a reconnaissance for a line over the Sierra

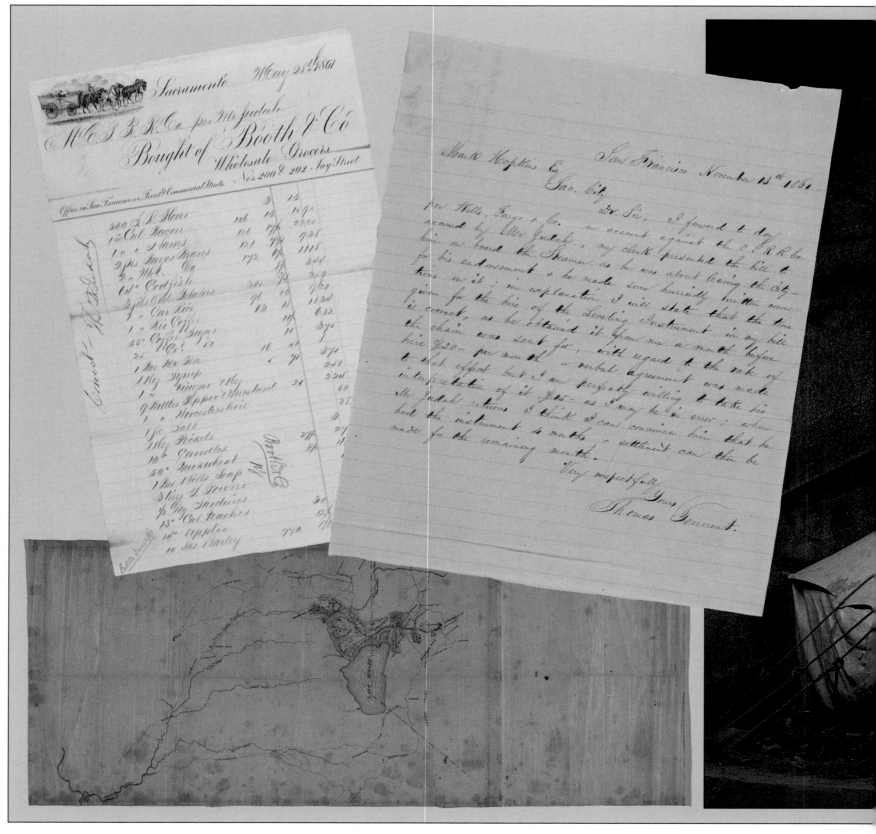

Nevada but was unable to secure financial support for further surveys. In the fall of 1860 the Sacramento merchants Huntington, Hopkins, Stanford and Crocker became involved with the project, and they would ultimately carry it to completion. Judah, sometimes accompanied by Anna, who prepared his maps, continued his surveys and spent weeks in the mountains during late 1860 and 1861 refining the proposed route. This work ultimately resulted in Congressional approval of the railroad project.

Judah's relationship with the Big Four

cooled during 1863 and was finished by the fall of that year. He died in New York on November 2. Anna returned to the east, and promoted the idea that her late husband had been exploited and cast aside by the Big Four. In fact, Judah had an almost constitutional inability to work with other people.

Nevertheless, Theodore Judah was one of the pivotal personalities in building the first transcontinental railroad, and is memorialized in the collections and exhibits of the California State Railroad Museum in Sacramento. Located just a few feet from

where the Central Pacific Railroad broke ground in January 1863, a typical surveyor's tent (below) is the centerpiece of exhibits about Judah and the planning of the railroad. As well as the recreation of Judah's tent, this feature shows a bill for provisions supplied to Judah for his May 1861 surveying expedition (left); a letter from Thomas Tennent to CP Treasurer Mark Hopkins regarding payment for a surveying instrument supplied to Judah (right); and an ink-on-linen map, attributed to Judah, showing the location in red of the line of the CP from Sacramento to Nevada.

Above: *Jack Casement, with some of the work crew building the UP under his direction, poses by a work train during the building of the UP in Wyoming in 1869.*

financial backing sufficient to buy out his partners and take over the enterprise. Whatever his plan, Theodore Judah did not live to carry it out. While crossing the Isthmus of Panama he contracted yellow fever, and died in New York City on November 2, 1863.

The Big Four now had complete control of the CP. In one of those ironies of history, the railroad's first locomotive, the *Gov. Stanford*, arrived by schooner from San Francisco on October 6, four days before Judah departed on his final, fatal trip east. It was difficult and costly to secure equipment for the railroad. All the rails, locomotives, and other supplies — literally everything except timber and the few iron castings which could be made locally — had to be sent on an 18,000 mile, five-to-eight-month

voyage by sailing ship around Cape Horn from Atlantic coast ports. With the nation embroiled in the Civil War, the Union had first call on railroad equipment, and scarcity drove up prices. Only small, obsolete locomotives were available; larger, more modern engines went to

Below: *Racing to lay track — and to keep the flow of government money up — the UP and CP often built temporary wooden bridges such as this trestle over the Green River, Wyoming.*

the war effort. Confederate privateers preyed on the shiploads of valuable supplies, and while few shipments were lost the cost of insurance became astronomical.

Construction was slow, but things began to look up in 1864. Additional locomotives arrived, and the road began hauling paying passengers in March. Another cash crisis occurred in the spring, and Congress was induced to pass an amended Pacific Railroad Act in July which increased the amount of land available and let the railroad borrow more money. The financial situation was stabilized by January of the next year, when construction really took off. Gangs of surveyors and location engineers ranged far out ahead of the end of the track, refining Judah's survey and establishing the final location for the course of the line. Graders followed, making cuts and fills and preparing the roadbed. Giant timber trestles were constructed, and stations, water tanks, engine servicing facilities, and yards built.

The line moved east. Tracks were completed to Colfax, 54 miles from Sacramento, on September 1, 1865. The long, difficult, dangerous task of blasting a ledge for the roadbed a thousand feet above the American River at Cape Horn was not completed until May of the following year.

The line reached Alta, 69 miles from the start, in July. Alta remained the railhead through the fall and winter of that year as enormous cuts and the railroad's many tunnels were prepared ahead. The work was grueling and endless, and was all done by hand.

In the fall of 1866 the CP reported that 'The construction work is also progressing at several of the most difficult points on the line; among which are included a tunnel at the summit of the Sierra Nevada mountains 1600ft in length, and one 800ft, seven miles east of the summit, on which laborers are working night and day.'

Below: *A CP diamond-stack in Bloomer Cut, in the Sierra. The Cut — 85ft deep and 800ft long — was one of the most challenging construction jobs on the entire CP line. It was excavated by Chinese using primitive tools and black powder.*

Tunneling was the most arduous and dangerous part of the work.

In the vicinity of Cisco, the rock was so hard that it seemed impossible to drill into it a sufficient depth for blasting purposes. Shot after shot would blow out as if fired from a cannon. A nitroglycerine factory was established near the summit tunnel. Some of the nitroglycerine was used on the summit tunnel and the two tunnels to the eastward. Its use was abandoned after a disastrous explosion, and Charles Crocker ordered them to 'bury that stuff.' Dynamite was invented in 1866, but was never used on the Central Pacific.[5]

The majority of the CP's workforce was Chinese, who with pick, shovel, wheelbarrow and one-horse dump cart literally moved mountains. The railroad was built without the use of mechanized equipment. There were no steam shovels to excavate the cuts, and no power drills to bore holes in the granite rocks for blasting. Everything was accomplished by hand, making the CP the last, and largest, of the nation's great civil engineering achievements of the pre-mechanized era.

The winter of 1866-67 was one of the harshest on record, and caught the crews of the railroad in the midst of drilling eleven tunnels at the highest elevations. Work was rushed in the fall to ensure that each of the tunnels had a good start. The tunnels were worked from both ends, and an intermediate shaft was placed in the middle of the summit tunnel to give four working faces. A civil engineer later recalled that 'By the time winter had fairly set in, the headings were all underground. The work was then independent of the weather, except as storms would block the tunnel entrances, or avalanches sweep over the shanties of the laborers.'

There were no less than 44 storms that winter, some depositing as many as six feet of snow, with drifts of 40ft and more. The workers lived a curious mole-like existence in tunnels under the snow, where debris from blasting could be deposited.

The problem of snow would plague the CP for years. There was no way that men with shovels or the simple snowplows of the time could be relied upon to keep the railroad open in the winter. Judah had assumed that the line would stay clear by the simple expedient of running plow-equipped locomotives back and forth during storms, but he never actually experienced how harsh the winters could be in the Sierra. Leland Stanford is reported to have conceived the idea of building wooden sheds over the track. Some experimental snowsheds were built in the summer of 1867 and tested the following winter. The initial designs were not satisfactory, and were modified for the first permanent snowsheds, built in 1868. Eventually 34 miles of tunnels and snowsheds protected the Sierra crossing from the effects of winter, giving the CP the reputation of being a 'railroad in a barn.' Such sheds, modernized and improved, continue to be used to this day.

While work progressed at the summit, a crew of about 3000 graders had pushed ahead toward the state line. All the tunnels were passable by August, 1867, and even before track had been installed in them three locomotives, 17 cars and 20 miles of rail were hauled on sledges to the

east side of the mountains so work could continue almost uninterrupted through the winter; by the spring grading crews were nearly 300 miles ahead of the end of the track.

The crews of the CP were not building blindly east in a vacuum. The Union Pacific was moving just as inexorably toward the west at the same time. The UP was formally organized in October, 1863 to build from the Missouri River west across the Great Plains and Rockies until it met the CP coming the other way.

The UP was to receive the same land grants and government bond loans as the CP, but the railroad got off to a much slower start than the CP because of the Civil War raging literally in its backyard. Lincoln had decided that the UP line would begin at Omaha, Nebraska Territory, on the Missouri River: 100 miles from the nearest railroad connection. Ground was broken on a bitterly cold December 2, 1863, amid high hopes, but it was to be one-and-a-half years before any track was built.

Even though it was half a continent farther away, the CP's oceanic supply routes were easier than the UP's. Everything the UP needed, even timber for ties, had to be secured in the east at war economy prices, transported by rail to St. Joseph, Missouri, and then steamboated north to Omaha. The Missouri River, described as too thick to swim in but too thin to walk on, was fickle, treacherous and only navigable for a few months of the year. The war meant that there was a severe labor shortage — most young men were either in the military, or working hard to avoid being in the military — and the UP couldn't easily tap immigrant groups such as the Chinese. The UP's executives, initially General John A. Dix as president and Thomas C. Durant as vice president, were not as clever as the Big Four in raising funds.

The situation was dramatically improved by the ending of the Civil War in April, 1865. Hordes of able young men were released from the armies of both North and South. Used to life outdoors and somewhat tamed by military discipline, they swarmed west looking for adventure. Many were recent immigrants from Ireland, northern Europe and Great Britain. In addition to manpower, new sources of investment capital opened up and supplies became more readily available. The Union Pacific's progress increased dramatically.

Like the Big Four, who made a deal with one of their own, Charles Crocker, to build much of the line, the UP's promoters created a complex financial and contracting apparatus, the Credit Mobilier of America, to build most of the UP. The railroad company's officers and directors were secretly owners of the Credit Mobilier, and essentially paid themselves at inflated rates to build their own railroad. Durant, the shovel-making brothers Oakes and Oliver Ames, George Train and Sidney Dillon all invested in this company. Oakes Ames, an influential member of Congress, sold Credit Mobilier stock at a discount to fellow legislators and even Vice President Schuyler Colfax in order to secure favorable political treatment. The scheme unraveled in 1872 when Colfax and other prominent federal officials were accused of accepting bribes from the UP's promoters. The scandal widened, and Oakes Ames and fellow Congressman James Brooks were censured early the next year. Discredited and

THE CHINESE: BUILDERS OF THE CENTRAL PACIFIC.

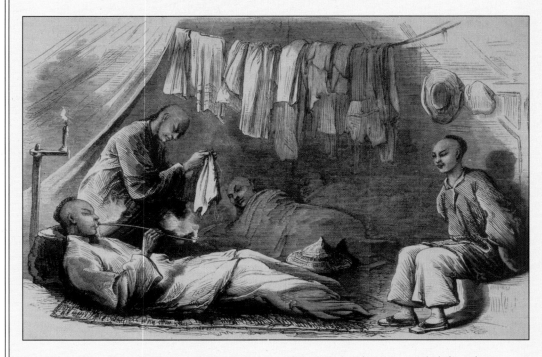

The Central Pacific Railroad was built entirely without the use of mechanized equipment. The incredible feat of constructing the railroad was accomplished by Chinese workers.

The CP Railroad was in desperate need of a reliable labor force as the tracks approached Auburn in the spring of 1865. Seven hundred men had been employed to build the railroad, but most Caucasian laborers disliked the arduous work of grading and track construction and, as construction superintendent James H. Strobridge would later testify, '. . . [They] were unsteady men, unreliable. Some would not go to work at all . . . some would stay until pay day, get a little money, get drunk and clear out.' Work was slow and inefficient; drastic steps were urgently required.

The San Francisco & San Jose Railroad had put a few Chinese laborers to work, and the idea of doing the same was suggested to Strobridge by CP contractor Charles Crocker. Nearly 20,000 Chinese lived in California in 1864, most drawn by the lure of the Gold Rush but driven out of the mines by racial prejudice. Crocker overcame his admitted bias enough to try a small number of Chinese in the summer of 1865. In Strobridge's words, '. . . the experiment has proved eminently successful.'[1] Strobridge hired more and yet more, eventually employing over 10,000 at one time.[2]

Workers were initially recruited from the mining areas of Central California until the available population of Chinese in the state was exhausted. The railroad later contracted with labor agents in southern China to furnish workers by the boatload. By 1869 between 7000 and 12,000 Chinese men had been imported specifically for railroad work. Most came with the intent of eventually returning to China with sufficient money to marry and live honorably, but relatively few were actually able to make the journey home.

Limited at first to the simplest tasks because

of disdain for their size and ability, the Chinese soon proved to be capable of any job given them. Construction foremen found them willing to do any of the dirty, dangerous, backbreaking work which the whites rejected, in any weather. They felled trees, cleared the earth, moved mountains of dirt by wheelbarrow or one-horse dump cart, drilled and blasted 13 tunnels, cut ties, shoveled snow, and built trestles. Literally every aspect of the railroad's construction involved the adaptable Chinese.

Organized into gangs of about 30 men each, Chinese laborers worked six days a week with Sundays off. In tunnel construction the shift was eight hours around the clock; for other work the day was usually 12 hours long. They received between $30.00 and $35.00 per month, in gold, somewhat higher than the prevailing wage but less than that paid white workers, who also received room and board.

The Chinese supplied their own food and accommodations, each gang having a cook who prepared traditional Chinese foods. The Chinese had a better diet than the other workers, and tended to avoid diseases which beset the white labor force by boiling their water for tea instead of drinking it unboiled. Also unlike the majority of whites, they bathed and changed their clothes regularly.

Usually depicted as a docile group, the Chinese asserted themselves several times to secure better working conditions. Small strikes were common during tunnel construction in the Sierra, and in the summer of 1867 several thousand walked off the job for higher wages and a shorter day. Crocker cut off food supplies and threatened to fine anyone who stayed away from work, ending the strike without any apparent gain. A short time before the strike, however, the CP had increased wages by four dollars a month, perhaps hoping to avert the walkout.

The work of the Chinese has become part of the heroic legend of building the first

Left: *A lithograph, published in* Frank Leslie's Illustrated Newspaper *in 1870, shows four Chinese construction workers relaxing in their lodgings after a hard day's work.*

Right: *Official CP 'China Pay Roll' No. 217 for June, 1865. The roll not only recorded the days worked and deductions for food, but also misdemeanors — such as lateness.*

transcontinental railroad, and has spawned doubtful tales of laborers precariously hanging in baskets from Cape Horn and hundreds killed by premature blasts and avalanches. Nevertheless, the CP wouldn't have reached Promontory if not for the skill and tenacity of the Chinese workers. But only Charles Crocker's brother Edwin, a man of authentic liberal spirit, took pause to recognize their accomplishment on May 10, 1869. Concluding a speech before the State Assembly in Sacramento, he offered a toast to the railroad, adding: 'I wish to call to your minds that the early completion of this railroad we have built has been in large measure due to the poor, despised class of laborers called the Chinese — to the fidelity and industry they have shown.'

The ceremonies at Promontory meant the end of a job for thousands of Chinese laborers who went on to become a mobile,

Below: *Building the Secrettown trestle, 1867. The photograph clearly shows the crudity of the tools the Chinese were given.*

bachelor work force available to undertake any enterprise requiring pick-and-shovel labor. Many found their way back to California, aggravating an already high unemployment situation. Others continued to build railroads in the west. Chinese workers graded the Tehachapi Loop, bored the 6975ft San Fernando Tunnel, and pushed tracks across the blistering Mojave Desert and the windblown wilds of Montana. More still found work building irrigation and

reclamation projects, roads, levees, and on farms. The west is still dotted with the remnants of small Chinese settlements which are quiet reminders of the distant time when the railroads were new, and the men who built them were from Canton.

Notes
[1]Report of the Chief Engineer, 1865.
[2]Hubert Howe Bancroft, *History of California*, VII (San Francisco: The History Company, 1890), p.567.

broken, both men died soon after. A later president of the UP, describing the machinations, characterized the Credit Mobilier as 'another name for the Pacific Railroad ring. The members of it are in Congress; they are trustees for the bondholders; they are directors; they are stockholders; they are contractors; in Washington they vote the subsidies, in New York they receive them, upon the plains they expend them . . . they receive money into one hand and pay it into another . . .'[4]

Financial shenanigans notwithstanding, the UP marched across the plains. General Grenville Dodge, late of the Union Army, became superintendent of the work on May 1, 1866, and built 293 miles of track by the end of the year. The effort had the logistical precision of a military operation. Gangs built two or three miles of track a day in a carefully organized campaign involving graders, tracklayers and lining gangs.

The ever-advancing end of track was followed by a sort of portable town whose primary residents were saloonkeepers, gamblers, prostitutes, toughs and sharks of every stripe. Any vice could be fulfilled, and whiskey, gambling and the gratifications of the flesh became payday staples for the legion of trackworkers who flocked to the tents and shacks of this temporary city. It was rough beyond belief, and the traveling Gomorrah was given the apt moniker 'Hell on Wheels.' Most of these temporary settlements vanished without leaving even memories, but a few survived the experience to become respectable, upright communities. Cheyenne, Wyoming, began as just such a Sodom-at-the-end-of-the-line, prompting this description of its early days:

When it was known that this was to be the winter terminus of the road, there was a grand hegira of roughs, gamblers and prostitutes from Julesburg and other places down the road to this point, and in the fall of that year [1867] and the winter of '68, Cheyenne contained 6000 inhabitants. Habitations sprang up like mushrooms. They were of every conceivable character, and some were simply holes in the ground . . . Every nation on the globe, nearly, was represented here. The principal pastimes were gambling, drinking villainous rot-gut whiskey, and shooting. Shooting scrapes were an everyday occurrence. Stealing anything from anybody was the natural habit of the thieving roughs. Knock-downs and robberies were daily and nightly amusements. But these things had to come to an end, and their perpetrators, some of them, to a rope's end.[5]

Obviously not every worker succumbed to the leisure opportunities on offer — if they had, the general level of dissipation would have been so great as completely to paralyze the railroad's progress. For progress did continue across Wyoming and into the mountains of eastern Utah. Meanwhile, the CP railhead moved rapidly through the Nevada deserts.

Both railroads crossed lands that had been occupied for thousands of years by Indians. In California, a century of Spanish, Mexican and American occupation had decimated their numbers and relegated the few survivors to the status of ranch hands and fugitives. The Washoes

Above: *A railroad supply camp at Victory, near Promontory. On April 28, 1869, a CP crew laid ten miles of track in one day — at a speed of one mile per hour.*

Below: *Bear River City, one of the notorious 'Hell-on-Wheels' construction towns, boasted some 200 inhabitants in 1868. Note the high number of saloons lining the main street.*

and Piutes of Nevada had been considerably reduced in number by intermittent warfare with settlers earlier in the 1860s. Minor conflicts attended the passage of the CP through their lands — mostly grading crews shooting at the Indians — and the company was careful to distribute food, liquor, free passes, small amounts of money and a few jobs among tribal leaders to ensure their tractability. Tradition holds that the CP allowed Indians to ride freight trains at no cost for years after the line was completed as a sort of reward for leaving the railroad to its own affairs. The CP considered the Indians a picturesque nuisance.

Matters were different on the UP. The tribes of the Great Plains, the Northern Cheyenne and the Sioux, were well organized, mobile, and able to resist the encroachment of the railroad onto their land. These groups had been engaged in almost constant conflict with overland emigrants and settlers since the start of the California Gold Rush, and the Army frequently found itself in the position of trying to stop the

Americans from exterminating the original inhabitants of the land.

Indian anger was strong, and the coming of the railroad made matters much worse, but actual attacks against railroad construction workers or trainmen were not common. The few real instances were wildly magnified in the eastern press and have become the stuff of legend. The most celebrated incident — told and re-told as a key part of UP's mythology — was on August 6, 1867 when a party of Cheyenne derailed a freight train between Plum Creek and Willow Island, Nebraska. Although scalped, a telegraph repair worker named William Thompson survived the attack and walked four miles back to Plum Creek, scalp held carefully in hand, to report the incident. A surgeon tried to reattach Thompson's scalp after it had been rejuvenated in a bucket of brine, but without success. Several railroaders were killed in the attack, and Thompson's sensational story elevated it from a tragic but limited skirmish to a major atrocity perpetrated by ruthless savages. This prompted the customary equally ruthless retaliations against the Cheyenne by the Army and its Pawnee scouts.

In April, September and October of 1868 other successful attacks against trains occurred, culminating in the Army's summer 1869 campaign against the Sioux and Cheyenne and the killing of more than 200 Indians. In the end, the destruction of the buffalo — 12 million killed during the 1860s and 1870s — and the increasing number of permanent American settlements on the upper Plains doomed the Indians. Deprived of their means of livelihood, decimated by disease and warfare, their land occupied, and with no political support, the Indians ultimately were powerless to prevent their forced (although incomplete) assimilation into the culture which sought to eliminate them, all in the name of progress.

The CP's Chinese track gangs crossed the California state line in May, 1868, and spiked down 305 additional miles of track by the end of the year. Work progressed at the rate of three miles a day, and the two roads suddenly found themselves in competition with each other to be the first to reach the Salt Lake Valley.

By the spring of 1869 competing grading crews had passed each other by 100 miles. The two companies were paid by the mile, and it seemed absurdly possible that they might keep building parallel lines forever unless they were forced to connect. Under considerable pressure from the public and Congress, a deputation led by General Dodge met with C.P. Huntington in Washington, DC on April 9 to agree where the railroads should be joined. It was decided that Promontory Summit, north of the Great Salt Lake, would be the final meeting place. The next day, a joint resolution of Congress ratified that this would be the spot '. . . at which the rails

shall meet and connect and form one continuous line.'

The CP had one final burst of flamboyance on April 28 when a crew of Irish and Chinese tracklayers built ten miles and 56ft of track in one day. The effort was in response to a wager of $10,000 between Crocker and Durant, which Crocker had no intention of losing. The CP men put down ties and rails at the pace of a walk. Six miles went down before lunch, with the rest completed by 7p.m., setting a record which has never been bettered. It was perhaps not an accident that the UP's end of track was less than eight miles from Promontory.

The CP reached Promontory Summit two days later and waited for the UP to arrive. Plans were made for a ceremony on May 8 — a Saturday — and the telegraph wires which followed each railroad carried the news back to the respective coasts. A trainload of CP dignitaries appeared on schedule, only to learn that a washout and a labor dispute (the UP owed money to some of its workers, who delayed Durant's train until they were paid) would keep the UP contingent away until Monday, May 10.

On May 10, 1869, on the top of the world in the desolate Utah uplands, at about 12.45p.m., the dream of Manifest Destiny was symbolically achieved and the continent girdled at last by iron rails. One thousand onlookers, mostly soon-to-be-unemployed laborers, gathered to commemorate the completion of the Pacific railroad. The day was breezy and cool, with a threat of rain: most days of significance to the history of the enterprise had been cold, or wet.

Below: *A UP pay car and a few of the 10,000 workers — mostly Irish — employed to build the UP at Blue Creek, Wyoming, in 1868. The men were paid in cash — paper or coin.*

Hubert Howe Bancroft described the setting:

The spot where the joining of the Atlantic to the Pacific took place was a grassy plain sunken between green hills. The horizon was bound on the east by the silver-rimmed summits of the Wasatch, whose rosy-violet atmosphere was in harmony with the iridescent hues of the Great Salt Lake on which they looked. In the immediate vicinity were a few canvas tents. Moving about the ground, mingling in a picturesque confusion, were people from the Occident and the Orient — Mongolian, Celt, full-blooded aborigine, and half-caste Mexican, garbed in national costumes, or innocent of any, mixing freely with American citizens and soldiers, each regarding only the significant preparations. At 11 o'clock a train from the west drawn by a decorated engine approached the gap left between the rails. Soon another train from the east, with no less elegant appointments, drew up on that side of the breach, each debouching some principal actors on the scene.

The 'Last Tie,' of California laurel, handsomely finished, and having a silver plate, bearing the names of the officers of both companies, was placed beneath the connecting ends of the rails, and a spike of gold placed in a cavity made to receive it, was driven home by a silver hammer in the hands of President Stanford of the Central Pacific. Other significant and precious articles were displayed, the gifts of neighboring territories. There followed addresses of which everyone will be able to conjecture the import. Congratulatory telegrams were read from cities east and west. Cheers, music, and banqueting followed, and the royal marriage was consummated.

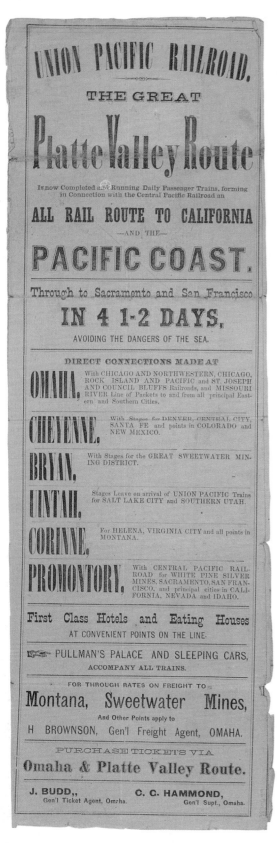

Obscured by Bancroft's flowery eloquence is the fact that numerous special spikes — silver, iron-silver-gold, and other gold spikes in addition to the well-known one — were driven, or more likely ceremonially tapped, into the last tie. The real last spike appears to have been a regular iron spike, the driving of which was transmitted by telegraph in the first coast-to-coast broadcast of an electronic media event. The signal 'Done' flashed from Staten Island to the Golden Gate, igniting a national celebration of unprecedented magnitude and emotion. Speeches, parades and congratulatory banquets were held in every city. A long-sought national goal had been at last, heroically, achieved.

The new railroad generated paeans of rapturous praise from nearly every section of American society. As Charles Nordhoff succinctly summarized, 'On the plains and in the mountains the railroad is the one great fact.'[6] The wounds of the Civil War were symbolically healed by this great national feat. The dream of Manifest Destiny had been achieved, and every detail of the accomplishment was described with the loving enthusiasm of a proud parent. Guidebook authors wrote with the boundless opulence of language only known to shameless boosters and copywriters:

> The grandest of American scenery borders the magnificent route of the Pacific Railroads. Since their completion, the glorious views of mountain grandeur in The Yosemite, The Yellowstone, have become known. The sublimities of Colorado, the Rocky Mountains, canyons of Utah, and the Sierra Nevadas, have become famous. The attractions of the Far West for mining, stock raising and agriculture have added millions of wealth and population.[7]

In October 1869, just a few months after the Gold Spike was driven, 23-year-old Cornelia E. Comstock and a friend made the journey from upstate New York to a small town north of San Francisco, where she had a teaching job. Securing a section in a Pullman sleeping car at Omaha, 'not to make another change until Promontory should be reached in three days and two nights distant,' she recorded her trip across the continent. Her account captured the popular enthusiasm most Americans felt for the Pacific railroad, and the wonderful freedom to travel conferred by railroad technology:

> We are not near so tired now as when we first started. We are used to the motion of the train, and rather enjoy the prospect of a long ride in this most elegant, comfortable car. Every convenience is at hand, and a pillow ready for us when we feel like lounging. We are crossing the great Platte Valley of Nebraska — one unending, dead level without a tree or even a fence to break the monotonous stretch of plain, only once in a while a poor thatched cottage, a hut more like.

Above: *An Andrew J. Russell photograph of locomotive No. 23 at Wyoming station, 15 miles west of Laramie, in 1868. No. 23 was built by the Schenectady Locomotive Works.*

Left: *A poster advertising services on the newly opened transcontinental makes much of the fact that 'Pullman's Palace and Sleeping Cars' are part of consists.*

Cornelia and her friend shared an upper berth — two to a bed was standard on the railroads — in which they slept that first night comfortably 'notwithstanding the storm of cinders that fell upon our faces all night, one of the ventilators having been left slightly open.'

Arising the next morning the two women waited their turn to freshen up in the ladies' dressing room as their train moved across the plains at a steady 25mph. They ate breakfast during the meal stop in Cheyenne, much subdued from its notoriously unruly 'Hell on Wheels' days.

> We reached Sherman, the highest point of mountains which we would cross, at about noon — a strange looking place, as all these mountain villages are. The people live mostly in tents. Soldiers are stationed all along the route. It seems natural to see so many blue uniforms. We felt sorry for them, away out in these lonesome places. Thought we would show our sympathy by singing *John Brown* and waving our handkerchiefs. Our kindness met with no response except a prolonged stare from every one of them. We decided that they had been out here so long they had forgotten the usage of civilized society. We saved our voices after this and used our handkerchiefs for more legitimate purposes.
>
> Salt Lake smiles upon us suddenly. I am sorry that my ideas of paradise will borrow coloring from the view, which we enjoy for two hours. Utah Mountains in the distance. Great Salt Lake, an arm of which we cross, lying at the foot, not a ripple visible on its clear surface — the loveliest, softest shade of blue, Heaven's ever-blue, the mountains borrowing (it would seem) the same hue only tinged more with the purple indistinctness which distance gives. I thought, 'Can anything be more lovely?'

And so we reach Promontory at about six o'clock. We took supper here. Had a great time before going to eat, disposing of our baggage. Engaged a stateroom on one of the Silver Palace sleeping cars. Had to get our baggage checked — our satchels, I mean; they are not allowed in the cars.

Next day the ladies learned that their conductor, Charles Kimball ('a fine-looking young man'), was from their town in New York, and arranged that he be introduced to them.

He was very entertaining, tried to make a pleasant day of journeying for us. Told us that his engineer, Charles Arnold, was also from Owego and would be glad to see us. Invited us to ride on the engine. We were pleased with the idea of traveling in that way away out in Nevada, so when we reached the next station Mr. Kimball took us off and helped us on. We liked Mr. Arnold very well. We rode 24 miles with him along the foot of the Humboldt Mts., by the side of the Humboldt River, and through Humboldt Canyon. We made short runs and rode by deep ravines. We could see all the seeming danger from our position in the engine, which seemed to be possessed with life and judgement — it bore us so safely and steadily onward.

The last day of Cornelia's trip began as the train struggled arduously up the mountain grades, gradually surmounting the steep eastern approach to the Sierra Nevada.

We went out on the platform when it commenced getting light. Saw objects distinctly but missed Donner Lake, much to our regret. We came to the snowsheds before daylight. They were tedious enough — 50

Above: *A rather lonely-looking passenger on a car of the 1870s; note the bed already made up for use (in the background), and the truly plentiful supply of spittoons.*

miles of snowsheds! I had no idea what it meant until I passed through. Only once in a while an opening. We were glad when we left them and were once more out in the pure mountain air. And then the view, once seen, can never be forgotten. We realized what was meant by 'high rocks on one side, nothing on the other.' We stood on the platform . . . for a hundred miles at least.

Below: *Columbus, Nebraska in 1878 — by now a firmly established and prosperous township. The special railroad photography car near the depot was used by the UP photographer.*

This side around Cape Horn is wonderful. We are descending a steep grade one minute, in three minutes afterward are ascending one in an exactly opposite direction. We can see the engine and the last coach of our train at once. O, the scenery! There can be nothing to compare with it, I am certain.

Our descent was rapid. We saw a good deal of hydraulic mining on our way, and learned how it was carried on. We reached Auburn at about half past nine. We are getting down into the Sacramento Valley. Everything in Nature has changed from the wild mountain scenery to wide fields and dusty roads, to live oaks instead of the mountain spruce and laurel. We began to breathe more naturally, and find when Sacramento is reached that we are extremely tired.

We change cars at Sacramento. We have a tiresome ride before us on account of the heat and dust. We reached Alameda at about six or half past — I could not tell accurately. I looked at my watch every time and guessed. There was three hours and 17 minutes difference when I reached San Francisco between mine and R.R. time. We rode on trestlework down to the Bay, even to the ferry boat. The ferry boat is very fine and very large, much like a steamboat, with upper and lower decks. The Bay is five and a half or six miles wide at this place. We crossed in about half an hour. We . . . reached the Exchange at about nine o'clock. Could get no supper here and were obliged to go to a restaurant. Retired at once on our return to the Hotel, glad to have a room and a genuine bed.[8]

Thousands of others made the passage west under more challenging circumstances, riding the emigrant trains which transported would-be Americans to new homes and the promise

of opportunity in the territories. The Scottish writer Robert Louis Stevenson crossed the United States by train in 1879, experiencing a hard side of railroad travel that was familiar to many but never mentioned in guidebook descriptions of luxurious Pullman accommodations. Stevenson appreciated the scenery along the route, but focused his descriptive powers on the social component of the trip. Five days after commencing his journey at Jersey City, New Jersey, on the Pennsylvania Railroad, he continued his narrative at Council Bluffs, Iowa, preparing to board a Union Pacific emigrant train:

It was about two in the afternoon of Friday that I found myself in front of the Emigrant House, with more than a hundred others, to be sorted and boxed for the journey. A white-haired official, with a stick under one arm, and a list in the other hand, stood apart in front of us, and called name after name in the tone of a command. At each name you would see a family gather up its brats and bundles and run for the hindmost of the three cars that stood awaiting us, and soon I concluded that this was to be set apart for the women and children. The second or central car, it turned out, was devoted to men travelling alone, and third to the Chinese. The official was easily

Above: *A newly built CP emigrant car outside the Jackson & Sharp car works in Delaware in the 1870s. The interiors of such cars were austere and very uncomfortable.*

Below: *The last emigrant wagon train heading west meets the first locomotive heading east, as they pass at the north shore of the Great Salt Lake on May 8, 1869.*

Above: *A Chicago, Rock Island & Pacific RR emigrant ticket. Traveling on an emigrant train, Robert Louis Stevenson commented that 'Civility is the main comfort that you miss . . .'*

moved to anger at the least delay; but the emigrants were both quick at answering their names, and speedy in getting themselves and their effects on board.

I suppose the reader has some notion of an American railroad-car, that long, narrow wooden box, like a flat-roofed Noah's Ark, with a stove and a convenience, one at either end, a passage down the middle, and transverse benches upon either hand. Those destined for emigrants on the Union Pacific are only remarkable for their extreme plainness . . . and for the usual inefficacy of the lamps, which often went out and shed but a dying glimmer when lit. The benches are too short for anything but a young child. Where there is scarce elbow-room for two to sit, there will be not space enough for one to lie.

It was a troubled, uncomfortable evening in the cars. There was thunder in the air, which helped to keep us restless. The day faded; the lamps were lit; a party of wild young men, who got off next evening at North Platte, stood together on the stern platform, singing 'The Sweet By-and-By' with very tuneful voices . . . and it seemed as if the business of the day were at an end. But it was not so; for, the train stopping at some station, the cars were instantly thronged with the natives, wives and fathers, young men and maidens, some of them in little more than nightgear, some with stable-lanterns, and all offering beds for sale. Their charge began with twenty-five cents a cushion, but fell before the train went on again, to fifteen, with the bed-board gratis . . .

A great personage on an American train is the newsboy. He sells books (such books!), papers, fruit, lollipops, and cigars; and on emigrant journeys, soap, towels, tin washing-dishes, tin coffee pitchers, coffee, tea, sugar, and tinned eatables, mostly hash or beans and bacon. Early next morning the newsboy went around the cars . . . [and Stevenson with two new-found comrades bought] . . . coffee, sugar, and the necessary vessels, and their operations are a type of what went on all through the cars. Before the sun was up the stove would be brightly burning; at the first station the natives would come on board with milk and eggs and coffee cakes; and soon from end to end the car would be filled with little parties breakfasting upon the bed-boards. It was the pleasantest hour of the day.

Above: *A lithograph, probably from* Frank Leslie's Illustrated, *titled 'Waiting at a station on the plains.' Thousands of emigrants made the dismal trip in the hope of a new life.*

. . . [A] great deal of your comfort depends on the character of the newsboy. He has it in his power indefinitely to better and brighten the emigrant's lot. The newsboy with whom we started from the Transfer was a dark, bullying, contemptuous, insolent scoundrel, who treated us like dogs. Indeed, in his case, matters came nearly to a fight . . . On the other hand, the lad who rode with us in this capacity from Ogden to Sacramento made himself the friend of all, and helped us with information, attention, assistance, and a kind countenance. He told us where and when we should have our meals, and how long the train would stop; kept seats at table for those who were delayed, and watched that we should neither be left behind nor yet unnecessarily hurried. You, who live at home at ease, can hardly realise the greatness of this service, even had it stood alone. When I think of that lad coming and going, train after train, with his bright face and civil words, I see how easily a good many may become the benefactor of his kind.

At Ogden we changed cars from the Union Pacific to the Central Pacific line of railroad. The change was doubly welcome; for, first we had better cars on the new line; and, second, those in which we had been cooped for more than ninety hours had begun to stink abominably. Several yards away, as we returned, let us say from dinner, our nostrils were assailed by air. I have stood on a platform while the whole train was shunting; and as the dwelling-cars drew near, there would come a whiff of pure menagerie, only a little sourer, as from men instead of monkeys. I think we are human only in virtue of open windows. I do my best to keep my head the other way, and look for the human rather than the bestial in the Yahoo-like business of the emigrant train. But one thing I must say: the car of the Chinese was notably the least offensive, and

that of the women and children by a good way the worst. A stroke of nature's satire.

The cars of the Central Pacific were nearly twice as high, and so proportionally airier; they were freshly varnished, which gave us all a sense of cleanliness as though we had bathed; the seats drew out and joined in the center, so that there was no more need for bed-boards; and there was an upper tier of berths which could be closed by day and opened at night. Thus in every way the accommodation was more cheerful and comfortable, and every one might have a bed to lie on if he pleased. It was the first sign I could observe of any kindly purpose toward the emigrant.

Stevenson completed his journey to San Francisco, enduring more days of tedium crossing Utah and Nevada, and recording for us all the commonplace experiences of the lowly emigrant.[9]

The completion of the Central Pacific-Union Pacific was not an unalloyed benefit for the states of the far west. The sudden influx of manufactured goods into California by rail plunged the state's economy into a recession, from which it did not fully recover for five years. The state was also filled with people who had come west during and after the Gold Rush, and who wanted to return 'back east' but were unwilling to face the rigors of Panama or Cape Horn. The CP made trips home easy and safe, triggering an out-migration of people heading east to take care of long-neglected personal matters, see family and friends, or re-settle after their sojourn on the Pacific coast. As many as 35,000 more people left California each year during the 1870s than entered.

One of the promises of the west was mineral wealth, and railroads figured prominently in the mining industry. Those who would exploit these underground resources were convinced that nature existed for the convenience of man, and that railroads were merely tools to achieve their ends. Ore could be transported to concentrators or smelters, often a considerable distance from the mines, much more cheaply by rail than by freight wagon. Dozens of shortline railroads, often of 3ft gauge, branched off the main trunk lines to serve mining regions, carrying ore as well as construction materials, mining machinery, food, and the miners themselves.

Luxurious or plain, passenger or freight, the trains served all segments of society, and the railroad network expanded to connect nearly every part of the nation. Total United States railroad mileage at the end of the Civil War was just over 35,000. This had doubled by 1873, and more than doubled again, to 156,082, by 1888. In one single year alone, 1882, more miles of track were built than in the first 20 years of the railroad in America.[10]

Numerous other 'Pacific' railroads were built toward the west. The Kansas Pacific was completed to Denver in 1870, the Texas & Pacific to El Paso in 1882. 1883 saw completion of several important lines. Henry Villard's Northern Pacific — the next true transcontinental after 1869 — had been chartered in 1864, although construction only began in 1870. Progress was difficult and slow, and the line's fortunes figured prominently in the collapse of Jay Gould & Company in 1873, which event triggered a national depression. Only in 1880 did things

THE RAILROADS AND IMMIGRATION

Once railroad lines reached beyond the established cities of the eastern seaboard they began to serve as a conduit for settlers into new, open lands. Extension of the railroad network past the Appalachian barrier coincided with the start of an explosion in immigration to the United States. Two and a half million immigrants — nearly one million from Ireland alone — journeyed to the US during the 1850s: more than had come in the previous 40 years. Similar numbers made the trip in each of the next two decades, with the total doubling, to 5.2 million, between 1881 and 1890.

The railroads conveyed this influx of humanity to the Missouri River frontier and beyond after the Civil War, with the 1880s transcontinental routes bringing huge numbers of northern and eastern European immigrants to the states and territories of the upper Great Plains.

The railroads actively sought the business of immigrant groups, often working in concert with steamship companies, and it was sometimes possible to book passage directly from Liverpool, Hamburg, or even Odessa straight through to Minnesota or Nevada.

Another important business involved encouraging rural residents of the states of trans-Appalachia and the Old northwest — Ohio, West Virginia, Kentucky, Indiana and Illinois — to resettle farther west and perhaps adopt new forms of agriculture. There were opportunities for ranching and wheat farming in the intermountain states, and the climate of the Pacific coast permitted fruit growing in California, Oregon and Washington.

1 Broadside, in Greek, promoting settlement in California. Published by Western Pacific.
2 Northern Pacific 'Section Land Map' for immigrants, showing parcels of land still available alongside the NP's route in eastern Washington State and Idaho. Late 1880s.
3 Southern Pacific land grant register, recording which parcels of land had been allocated.
4 SP ledger, detailing the land sold each day, and the price paid. 1884.
5 Ink-on-linen drawing of an AT&SF emigrant car, 1889.
6 *Crofutt's . . . Guide*, 1872.
7 California Western Railway and Navigation Company advertisement for the 'Noyo River Apple Land'.
8 Scrapbook showing advertisements for land for settlement.
9 Broadside advertising colonist fares to California. Chicago & Alton, 1912.
10-29 A selection of brochures, booklets and magazines promoting different areas and often aimed at settlers with

specific skills (for example, the Union Pacific's 'Dairying in Nebraska' brochure from the early 1900s (14). Many railroads also published magazines for new settlers, for example AT&SF's *The Earth* (24). The items range from a 1901 issue of *Sunset* magazine (28), to the *Vegetable Guide* (UP, 1957) (11).
30, 31 UP timetable of 1893 advertising connections with the Midland Railway in Great Britain, and (31) UP rate schedule, 1902.

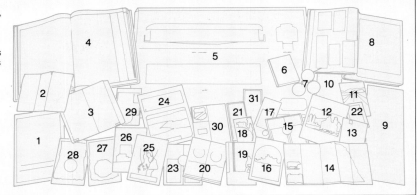

Above: Across the Continent: Westward the Course of Empire Takes its Way. *Fanny Palmer's painting, published by Currier & Ives in 1868, celebrates the fulfilment of the dream of Manifest Destiny.*

Below: *Triple-decked dormitory cars for the construction crews of the St. P, M & M Railroad in the 1880s. This line was to become part of Jim Hill's Great Northern in 1890.*

start moving again, and Villard took over the railroad and pushed it to a triumphal completion in 1883. Also finished in the same year were the Denver & Rio Grande's Denver-Salt Lake City route, the Southern Pacific's line to New Orleans and the Santa Fe's competing route across the southwest via the Atlantic & Pacific. James J. Hill's Great Northern was finished to Great Falls, Montana, in 1887, and pushed to the Washington coast in 1893.

The 30 years after Promontory saw the entire west divided, tamed, and placed under some form of governmental organization. This transformation was largely the result of the proliferation of railroad lines, which gave a durability to the occupation of the land and were a conduit for American civilization in all its forms to reach into what had heretofore been considered wilderness. Only Arizona, New Mexico and Oklahoma remained as territories. The proud and once independent native peoples were subjugated as wards of the United States, pushed off their lands by settlers and squatters, by the floods of miners entering their territories, and by the army sent to protect them.

Perhaps the deepest and longest-lasting consequence of connecting the east and west by rail was the creation of the concept we call today 'The West'. The Oregon Boundary treaty of 1846, the Treaty of Guadalupe Hidalgo in 1848 and the Gadsden Purchase of 1853 established in final form the United States' continental dimensions, but the railroads transformed the notion of vast unknown lands into the psychological image of the West, a wonderful place which ordinary people could visit, understand, desire, and romanticize. The railroads made travel to the west possible for nearly everybody, encouraged the creation of National Parks, and popularized a conception of the west as the land of the cowboy, the cavalryman, the yeoman farmer, and the stoic Indian. The reality was far more complex, of course, but the simplest symbols have proved the most durable.

Railroads were very costly to construct, and their capital-intensive nature made the railroad industry by far the largest outlet for investment capital in the country. By 1860 the total amount invested in American railroads was just over one billion dollars.[11] The great railroad trunk lines built during this period — the Erie, the Pennsylvania, the Baltimore & Ohio, the New York Central, the Union Pacific, the Michigan Central and the Illinois Central — were capitalized at between ten and 35 million dollars each. Hardly any railroad project could be undertaken for less than two million dollars.[12] By 1888 more than nine billion dollars had been spent to develop the national railroad network, at an average of more than 400 million dollars per year since 1876.[13]

This tremendous volume of capital was almost entirely derived from private investors, often in Europe. The United States literally did not possess the surplus funds necessary to build so many expensive railroads at the same time. Economic markets became centralized, with New York City the center for railroad financing. A number of firms began to specialize in railroad securities to meet the demands of American railroads seeking funds and European investors looking for opportunities in the United States. The instruments of investment, stocks and bonds, came into being as known today, as did new techniques of speculative buying and selling of these securities. In the 1850s and 1860s — as in the 1980s — skilful and clever securities manipulators became national celebrities. Daniel Drew, Jim Fisk and Jay Gould all achieved their dubious reputations by sharp dealing in railroad securities, often at the expense of unsuspecting smaller investors.

This was an era of pure, absolute, devil-take-the-hindmost competition, almost unfettered by regulation or even common ethical principles. At issue were not railroads, much less the well being of the country. The polite said the objective was money plain and simple, and

Below: Henry Villard poses triumphantly on an engine that has been polished and decorated ready to celebrate the Last Spike ceremony on the Northern Pacific Railroad in 1883.

its accumulation in hitherto unimaginable amounts. Those with less tact or more candor called it greed. Said Oliver Jensen:

It was the roughest age in the history of American capitalism, those years just after the Civil War, and the place to see it in action was not the plains, plateaus, and passes of the West but an ugly little brownstone, five stories high, at 22 Broad Street in New York City. This was the crowded Wall Street branch of Delmonico's Restaurant, just a few doors from the Stock Exchange. Here was the home of 'corners' and thimblerigging, the place where booms and panics were engineered; up and down the adjacent streets were the main offices of the railway kings whose imperial power and imperious ways so impressed the historian James Bryce. Railroads were our first 'Big Business,' and the main concern of Wall Street. Anyone who doubted that need only step into Delmonico's lobby and watch the anxious men at the ticker tape, or look in the eating rooms and see the men of the hour. These were not the men who built railroads, to paraphrase Jay Gould's remark, but the men who bought and sold them.[14]

The financiers were engaged in high-stakes territorial battles for the control of railroads which combined winner-take-all financial manipulations with often deep personal disdain for one another. 'Commodore' Cornelius Vanderbilt had in his mind the control of the railroads running west from New York. By 1867 he had outmaneuvered his old rival Daniel Drew for the New York & Harlem Railroad, the Hudson River Railroad, and the New York Central Railroad, which would all be united into the New York Central System. Drew experienced heavy monetary losses in the Commodore's victories and sought a way to even the score. He enlisted as associates the equally rapacious Jay Gould and 'Admiral' Jim Fisk in what would become the 'Erie Ring' and waited with a plan.

CREATING THE IMAGE OF THE WEST

Above: *A CP train in Humboldt Canyon.*

The railroads made recreational travel to the far west practical, and popularized the idea of tourism by train to the scenic wonders along their routes. Railroad companies employed artists and photographers to capture and bring back images of beauty and amazement which inspired some actually to undertake the journey west and many others to the conviction that the goal of Manifest Destiny had been splendidly realized. These images depicted the relentless march of railroads across the frontier as the inexorable force of progress, and justified the national policy of western expansion. They continue to shape our visual attitudes about the west nearly 125 years later.

The *Pacific Railroad Surveys of 1853-55* contained a wealth of tantalizing and authoritative information about the vast open lands beyond the Missouri River. Noted landscape artists exhibited paintings of the Rocky Mountains, Yellowstone and Yosemite in the 1860s to popular acclaim, proving the appeal of western subjects.

Both the Central and Union Pacific Railroads hired photographers to record their progress. The best known of these, Alfred A. Hart on the Central Pacific and Andrew J. Russell on the Union Pacific, created a body of work which depicted both the physical building of the lines and the striking landscapes through which they were constructed. Russell had established his reputation as a photographer during the Civil War, and produced a series of photographs along the new route which celebrated the victory of civilizing technology over nature. Hart was a painter whose work for the Central Pacific included over 300 stereographic views of the route from California to Utah which were sold by the thousand for promotional purposes.

The pictures made by these and many other photographers were circulated widely, and were translated by painters and engravers into woodcuts and lithographs which could be reproduced in newspapers, guidebooks, and on advertising broadsides. In this way the railroads themselves influenced how the west was depicted to the rest of the nation, and reinforced the image of the west as the undeveloped outlet for America's expansionist energies.

Vanderbilt, fresh from his latest victory over Drew and eager to finish him off, began to purchase shares in the Erie Railroad. The Erie had been Drew's plaything since the 1850s as he pocketed millions from the manipulation of its stock. Vanderbilt planned to corner the Erie by buying the majority of its stock and tossing Drew out. But the more stock the Commodore bought, the more appeared for sale. Drew, Gould and Fisk kept printing fraudulent stock in an attempt to trap the normally wily Vanderbilt. Vanderbilt spent millions, and was no closer to controlling the Erie than when he started out.

Vanderbilt was furious. He was granted an injunction by a judge ordering Drew and his cronies to desist, but the Erie boys got a counter injunction from a judge in their camp. Vanderbilt's judge ordered that the Erie Ring be arrested, but they fled across the Hudson to Jersey City — and safely beyond the jurisdiction of the New York courts — with some $6 million Vanderbilt had paid for spurious Erie shares. The Erie Ring bought enough New York State Senators to pass a bill legalizing the phony stock they had sold, but then the unthinkable happened. Drew — probably at Gould's urging — proposed a compromise whereby the Erie would buy back the stock it had sold to Vanderbilt, but at a reduced price. The Commodore agreed and cut his losses accordingly, although the poor Erie ended up $9 million deeper in debt as a result.[15]

Vanderbilt taken care of, Drew, Gould and Fisk turned on each other. Gould muscled his way to the Erie's presidency and in late 1868 the phony Erie stock went back on the market. This time it was Drew who was caught short and bankrupted. Gould and Fisk then directed their energies to the national economy and attempted to corner the market on gold. The effort failed,

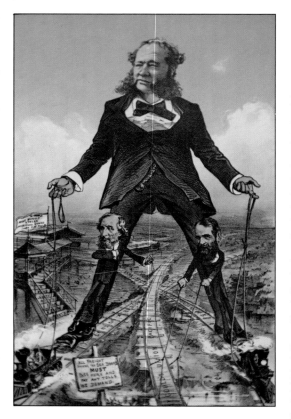

Above: *The 'Colossus of Roads', a satirical cartoon by Keppler published in* Puck *magazine in 1879, showing W. H. Vanderbilt (main picture), with Cyrus Field and Jay Gould controlling and manipulating the railroads.*

Below: *The roundhouse at Pittsburgh after the riots of 1877. Before order was restored, some $5 million-worth of damage had been caused to railroad and non-railroad property. Despite the public's disgust with the railroad barons, there was little sympathy for the strikers.*

but precipitated the infamous 'Black Friday', — September 24, 1869. Their plan was to buy all the available gold, and hold it until the reduced supply pushed the price up. To ensure that the federal government wouldn't release gold from its reserves to upset the scheme, they went so far as to hire President Grant's brother-in-law to let Grant in on the plan. Grant seemed to be in agreement, so Gould and Fisk thought, but dumped $4 million in gold from federal reserves into the market, dropping the price from $162.00 per ounce to $133.00 in 15 minutes. Thousands of small speculators were ruined, and the national economy experienced deep shock. Such was the power of railroad financiers in the 'Gilded Age.'

Fisk, for his part, when asked by a Congressional committee what had happened to the money owed to others and used in the attempt to corner gold, replied 'Gone where the woodbine twineth.'[16] Asked what the phrase meant, he said 'Up the spout.'

As railroads became the biggest businesses and the largest consumers of investment capital, they also ranked as the largest employers. Railroading was the great industrial occupation. Nearly 700,000 people, mostly men, were on the payrolls of the railroads in the early 1880s, and their wages accounted for about half of the railroads' operating expenses. It was estimated a few years later that each of these workers supported an average of three other people, meaning that more than five percent of the national population of 50,000,000 depended directly on railroad employment for support.[17] Tens of millions more depended indirectly on the railroads. The iron, coal and manufacturing industries and agriculture relied on the railroads for the transportation of raw and finished products. The railroads themselves became major consumers of coal and iron. Increasingly

standardized with 17,000 locomotives and 500,000 cars, railroads were a big market.[18] A mammoth and far-reaching network of interlocking businesses manufactured rails, track materials, locomotives, freight and passenger cars, bridges, water tanks, brakeman's lanterns, station stoves, signaling equipment and literally everything else necessary to build and run a railroad.

The manipulative tendencies of some railroad managers during the Gilded Age extended to their dealings with workers, and an adversarial relationship developed between management and labor which was to become a defining characteristic of the railroad industry. In 1877, after raising freight rates in the east, four major lines — the Pennsylvania Railroad, the New York Central & Hudson River Railroad, the Erie Railroad and the Baltimore & Ohio Railroad — set up a rate control pool, and then, to increase profits, decided to cut their workers' pay by ten percent. Other companies, representing over half of the total railroad mileage in the country, agreed to take the same action. The stage was set for the first national strike.

In June and July wages were cut on the Pennsylvania, the New York Central, the Erie, and other lines. Workers complained, but felt helpless to do anything. It was a different matter when the pay cuts started on the B&O. Wages had been reduced late the previous year, and since the company was still paying dividends to stockholders it seemed doubly unfair to cut wages further. In protest, trainmen at Martinsburg, West Virginia, refused to handle freight trains. The company brought in strikebreakers and militia to protect them, and the inevitable friction spread. Trains stopped at Grafton and there was a fight at Wheeling. Pent-up tensions flared and in a flash nearly every railroad that had participated in the cuts was

struck. For a week hardly a train rolled anywhere in the country.

Violence occurred at many places: Baltimore, Chicago, St. Louis, St. Paul, Omaha, and San Francisco; but it was in Pittsburgh on the Pennsylvania Railroad that the clashes between strikers and militia reached a bloody pinnacle. An incendiary mob of strikers and supporters estimated at 20,000 confronted some 10,000 militiamen and civil officers, with tragic consequences. Union Station, a hotel, the company's offices and the roundhouse were burned. Freight cars were looted, private businesses and residences were plundered and put to the torch. In the end, 24 people died, thousands more were injured, 100 locomotives and 2000 freight cars with their contents were destroyed, much of Pittsburgh was in ruins — and the strike was broken.

The railroad strike of 1877 did not result in the ten percent cut being restored on most lines, and many participants ended up in jail or on secret blacklists which prevented them from ever working on another railroad. (One method devised by employers to prevent blacklisted men working again involved writing the employee's supposed letter of recommendation on secretly watermarked paper. Managers thus knew not to offer the former striker a job.)

The period of western expansion concluded as railroads entered a 'Golden Age', which was to extend from the early 1880s until just after the completion of the last transcontinental railroad — the Western Pacific — in 1910. During

Below: *The station at St. Williams, Ontario, on the Grand Trunk railway, in the late 19th.C. The Grand Trunk — built as a main 'backbone' line, to which other lines would connect — was the most important railroad to be established in Canada between 1850 and 1860.*

this period the industry itself would experience considerable expansion and standardization. Railroads would literally go everywhere, and the nation would become, for the first time, dependent on a single form of transportation as the foundation for its industrial strength and social vitality. The great era of the railroad had arrived.

Notes

[1] Hubert Howe Bancroft, *History of California, vol.VII* (San Francisco: The History Company, 1890), p. 534.
[2] Hubert Howe Bancroft, p. 568.
[3] George Kraus, *High Road to Promontory* (Palo Alto: American West, 1969), pp. 135-6.
[4] Oliver Jensen, *The American Heritage History of Railroads in America* (New York: American Heritage, 1975), pp. 92-93.
[5] Frederick E. Shearer, Editor, *The Pacific Tourist* (New York: Adams & Bishop, various eds.), p. 65.
[6] Charles Nordhoff, *California: for Health, Pleasure, and Residence* (New York: Nordhoff, 1872), p. 32.
[7] Frederick E. Shearer, p. 5.
[8] "Overland Diary — 1869." Excerpts from the diary of Cornelia E. Comstock,' in *Trains*, (May, 1969).
[9] 'By the Way of Council Bluffs,' the account of Robert Louis Stevenson's trip, in H. Roger Grant, Editor, *We Took the Train* (DeKalb, Illinois: Northern Illinois University Press, 1890), pp. 44-58.
[10] *The Railways of America*, (London: John Murray, 1890), p. 429.
[11] Alfred D. Chandler, Jr., *The Visible Hand*, (Cambridge: The Belknap Press of Harvard University Press, 1977), p. 90.
[12] Alfred D. Chandler, p. 90.
[13] *The Railways of America*, p. 448.
[14] Oliver Jensen, pp. 136.
[15] Oliver Jensen, pp. 136-142.
[16] *Webster's Guide to American History*, (Springfield: G. & C. Merriam, 1971), p. 259.
[17] *The Railways of America*, p. 448.
[18] *The Railways of America*, p. 148.

'Singing through the forests, Rattling over ridges, Shooting under arches, Rumbling over bridges;
Whizzing through the mountains, Buzzing o'er the vale, Bless me this is pleasant, Riding on the Rail.'

JOHN GODFREY SAXE (1816-87)

RIDING ON THE RAIL

THE TRAUMA OF CIVIL WAR and the opening of the West marked the beginning of a new era of railroading, for war and territorial expansion reinforced and magnified the centrality of transportation to 'the American experience.' These three agents — the West, the war, and the railroad — irreparably broke the old bonds of sectionalism. They made possible a new nation: *the* United States as a modern, singular entity, as opposed to *these* United States of antebellum thought.

The business of railroading — the very reason for all of the building, inventing, promoting, and excitement — was transportation. Railroads transported many things, including freight, passengers, mail, and the raw material of economic development. They also transported intangible qualities such as ideas, emerging American values, notions of progress, and powerful symbols of modernization. But most importantly, they transported people. Before the automobile, airplane, and bus, the railroad was the only reliable, all-weather, reasonably rapid means of travel available, and Americans took full advantage of their railroads.

The passenger trains of the mid-nineteenth century bore little resemblance to the trains of

the early 1900s. Within the span of 60 years, the railroad and its associated technologies had not only reinvented themselves several times; they had also, usually without conscious intent or strategic aim, dramatically altered the structure, pace, intensity, and even the quality of American life. The great differences between railroad passenger travel at the end of the Civil War and the beginning of World War I stand as entirely typical of the greater changes in American industry, culture, and society.

Many of the changes were obvious and incremental. Train speeds, which rarely exceeded 40mph in the 1850s, had risen dramatically by 1900. Some trains routinely exceeded 80 or 90mph, and the daring special runs in excess of 100mph delighted and awed an American public hungry for greater velocities. Passenger cars became bigger, safer and more comfortable, and the range of passenger amenities increased until, by the time of World War I, the relative level of comfort and service available aboard most long-distance trains equaled that of the finest hotels of the day.

Other changes were more subtle and far-reaching. The very fact that persons could rely on the railroad for fast, all-weather transportation permanently changed the ways that we conducted business, settled the wilderness, and built the cities of the United States. The 'annihilation of space and time' wrought by railroads epitomized a new mastery over nature.

By the middle of the nineteenth century, the coming of the locomotive almost universally was hailed as a sign of mobility, prosperity, and progress. The long freight trains that increasingly left canal boats and turnpike wagons in their dust warmed the businessman's heart, for they were concrete evidence of the growing wealth of the United States. Having a railroad nearby eased the isolation felt by so many towns and settlements stretching between the Atlantic Ocean and the Mississippi River.

Nothing captured the fancy of the average American so completely as the simple ability to go to the train station, buy a ticket, and board a train for somewhere. From the time that large numbers of Europeans began settling the coastal fringes of the continent through the present, Americans have cherished mobility. The railroad was our first efficient, widely distributed, relatively comfortable and comparatively speedy mode of transport. With astonishing rapidity, politicians, entrepreneurs, and engineers laced the country with a network of iron reflecting our real and imagined need to travel.

Americans had demonstrated an affinity for travel long before the railroad. Perhaps this had to do with who they were: most citizens were immigrants, descendants of recent immigrants, or at least aware that they had come originally from someplace else. People willing to leave a life and family behind to find opportunity, land, or a fresh start on an immense continent half a world away generally had few qualms about moving about once they got here. With few longstanding social customs and a relative lack of legal, religious, political, or cultural barriers to free movement, the United States practically invited its inhabitants to relocate as whim or economic necessity dictated.

When Americans did travel before the railroad, they preferred to go by water. Coastal sailing ships, slow but comfortable canal boats, and the new steamboats plying the inland waters linked most population centers. The alternatives to water were primitive roads, traces (little more than paths through the woods, actually), and a few 'improved' toll roads. Roads, and even the earliest railroads, linked existing waterways before it dawned on the country that a reliable transportation route could extend

Railroads in the US and Canada built relatively few stations before the Civil War — usually, passengers would wait in a nearby tavern or hotel, as in this 1865 scene (below). Within 20 years substantial depots such as the one at Stillwater, MN (bottom), were the norm.

civilization into the wilderness as well as connect established cities.

In 1888 Horace Porter reviewed the history of early railway travel for readers of *Scribner's Magazine*:

The railroad was a decided step in advance, compared with the stage-coach and canal-boat, but when we picture the surroundings of the traveller upon railways during the first ten or 15 years of their existence, we find his journey was not one to be envied. He was jammed into a narrow seat with a stiff back, the deck of the car was low and flat, and ventilation in winter impossible. A stove at either end did little more than generate carbonic oxide. The passenger roasted if he sat at the end of the car, and froze if he sat in the middle. Tallow candles furnished a 'dim religious light,' but the accompanying odor did not savor of cathedral incense. The dust was suffocating in dry weather; there were no adequate spark-arresters on the engine, or screens at the windows, and the begrimed passenger at the end of his journey looked as if he had spent the day in a blacksmith shop. [Porter continued that] The springs of the car were hard, the jolting intolerable, the windows rattled like those of the modern omnibus, and conversation was a luxury that could be indulged in only by those of recognized superiority in lung power.[1]

Until after the Civil War, most Americans made the best of travel in coaches — distinctly American accommodations that bore little resemblance to their European antecedents. After a decade of experimentation, railroads by 1840 had settled on the general style of coach still in use today: a long, open room with a center aisle and rows of double benches or chairs running the length of the car.

These early coaches represented applied American culture, or at least tangible expressions of existing and emerging democratic ideals. For example, European coaches of the nineteenth century, and even until recently, were composed of individual compartments seating perhaps six or eight persons. British coaches had no aisle at all, so that the passenger boarded the compartment directly from the platform, and remained within it for the entire journey. In form as well as idea, European coaches closely resembled the horse-drawn turnpike coaches from which they evolved. American coaches, by comparison, were very democratic vehicles.

Throughout the nineteenth century, European travelers on American railroads (and steamboats) reacted with amusement or disgust to the seemingly haphazard way that men and women, blacks, whites, and Native Americans, rich and poor, sophisticated easterners and rustic westerners, traveled together. Railroads in Europe generally segregated passengers by social standing. First class was strictly for the 'better classes': nobility and clergy, military officers, landed gentry, well-off merchants, in general anyone with a claim to status as either a 'Lady' or a 'Gentleman.' Second class carried the middling sorts in reasonable comfort at somewhat lesser fares. Third class was for the mass of humanity: farmers, factory workers, peasants, and anyone with just a few francs or pence to spend on transportation. Third class accommodations sometimes lacked windows, toilets, and even roofs. Often they were crowded, always they were noisy, and writers of the day commented on the traveling habits of the lesser folk with a curious mixture of envy and disdain.

In contrast, throughout the nineteenth century American railroads sometimes segregated passengers on the basis of sex, sometimes by race or ethnicity, and sometimes on the basis of ticket prices and the quality of accommodations. They sold first, second, and third class tickets, but with a different — and often changing — set of criteria for class distinctions. With certain exceptions, in America first class simply meant the best accommodations, available to anyone with the cost of the ticket. Third class, when it was mentioned at all, commonly referred to 'emigrant' cars, providing one-way transportation at extremely low fares for hundreds of thousands of recent immigrants.

A comparison of the percentages of travelers in first, second, and third class accommodations and what they paid for the privilege confirms the essentially democratic nature of railroad travel in the New World. In Great Britain in the 1880s, an estimated 84 percent of all railway passengers rode in third class, which by then had been improved with such amenities as

Below: *The map shows the extent of the railroad network in the US in 1860 and 1870 (railroads constructed between 1860 and 1870 are shown by dotted lines). Prior to the Civil War, most railroad development took place in the east; after the opening of the UP and CP transcontinental in 1869, the network expanded to connect nearly every part of the nation: the 35,000 miles of track in use in 1865 had more than quadrupled to 156,000 miles by 1888.*

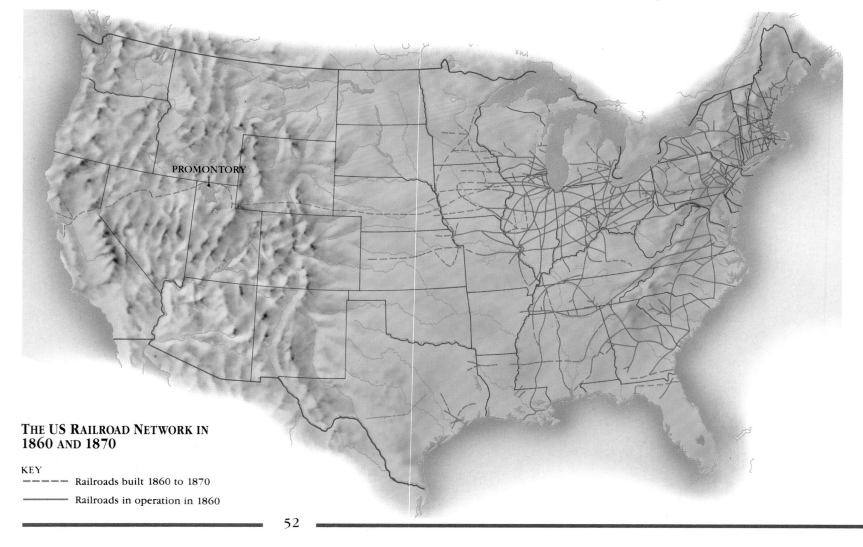

PROMONTORY

THE US RAILROAD NETWORK IN 1860 AND 1870

KEY

----- Railroads built 1860 to 1870

——— Railroads in operation in 1860

benches, roofs, and sometimes crude heat. Ten percent of the passengers purchased second class tickets, while a mere six percent rode first class. The figures for Germany were similar, except that only one percent rode first class.

In the United States, 99 percent of seats sold were first class, with a minuscule ½ percent each identified as second and third class accommodations. First class coach fares in the United States averaged a little over 2 cents per mile, as opposed to 4½ cents in Great Britain. A sleeping car berth cost two to three times more per mile in Europe than it did in the United States.

Of course, what passed for first class coaches in the US ranged from the luxurious to the austere. But the essential point remains: Americans were self-consciously averse to European notions of social class, and that was reflected in the way they built and operated their railroads. 'We have no second class cars for the inferior classes, because all our citizens rank as gentlemen and every man has his own coat of arms,' boasted the magazine *Scientific American* in 1852. Not mentioned, of course, were African-American chattel slaves, Native Americans, and certain recent immigrants.

Therein lies an important truth of both railroad and American history. The technology, style, and practice of railroading mirrored the society which created it. Railroads changed America, but Americans invested in their railroads all of those various notions, prejudices, strengths, and weaknesses which characterized the nation as a whole. 'The railroad system of

Above: *PRR Passenger coach No. 3556 represents state-of-the-art railroad travel in 1886. The car was entirely of wood, with sprung seats, oil lamps, and stoves at each end.*

Below: *Elaborately painted ceiling-liners were fashionable in the mid-nineteenth century. The craftsmen applied their creativity to the full, using a variety of colors and distinctive motifs.*

the United States, with all its excellences and all its defects, is thoroughly characteristic of the American people.'[2]

As society's attitudes toward race, gender, and ethnicity changed, those changes manifested themselves on the railroad. African-Americans, both as free hired labor and as owned or hired slave labor, built many railroads in the south, yet they are rarely considered in railroad history. They experienced the same discrimination on the trains as they did in hotels, restaurants, and other public facilities. During reconstruction, African-Americans usually won the right to occupy any seat on any southern train that they pleased. After the 1896 Supreme Court decision affirming the doctrine of separate but equal accommodations, those same railroads created 'Jim Crow' cars to enforce segregation. Women, immigrants, and Native Americans experienced all forms of discrimination on the railroad, gaining access and establishing rights in direct proportion to their successes in the larger society.

Yet despite the overall complexity and changing nature of American society, nineteenth century railroad travel and accommodations may be characterized in a relatively few ways: local or long distance, coach or parlor/sleeping car, and at times, according to race or gender. Then as now local coach passengers predominated. By definition, these short-distance travelers commuted to work or school, rode to the next town, or made their trips without leaving their region.

In the late nineteenth century, the texture of

local travel varied little throughout the country. It was one reason people had to give thanks for their railroads even as they resented the magnates and profiteers who seemed to be looting the farmer, worker, and passenger. On a local train, even one with a modest average speed of 15mph, a citizen could ride in an hour the distance it might have taken a day to cover before. Railroads made the next town on down the prairie accessible for shopping, commercial transactions, socializing, or starting a new life if the old one did not suit.

Americans liked their freedom even then, and showing up at the train station at train time was all it took to buy a ticket and climb aboard. If the ticket office was not open, or if the prospective passenger simply flagged the train down, the Conductor was empowered to conduct the Company's business and sell tickets. Passengers likewise could get off pretty much where they pleased, with proper notice to the Conductor.

Long distance travelers might ride hundreds or thousands of miles over many different railroads. They faced an entirely different set of concerns, beginning with the purchase of tickets. Some railroads handled 'through' tickets, enabling the agent to write a ticket valid for the whole trip over several railroads. The originating company would apportion the fare, and the connecting railroads were expected to honor the tickets. Unfortunately, the literature of the day is rife with tales of fouled-up tickets and petty fights between railroads, for which passengers paid a price of inconvenience. Whether traveling to resettle, for business, or for the increasingly common pleasure trip, these hardy souls faced conditions that often suggested the medieval concept of Trial by Ordeal.

Conditions aboard the cars which were tolerable for short-distance travel might be miserably uncomfortable during long trips. Comfort and speed varied according to the season, the region, the political and cultural climate of the moment, local custom, the relative prosperity of the railroad, and to the whim of the conductor and skill of the engineer. In a country as large and diverse as the United States, passengers enjoyed a sometimes bewildering variety of accommodations. By the 1850s, some railroads had attained a high level of comfort and service, while well into the twentieth century other railroads offered primitive amenities and wretched service.

On the eve of the Civil War, the railroad had attained a reasonable state of perfection, which would remain at about the same level into the 1880s. The classic 4-4-0 locomotive — known as the 'American' type — had reached a size and form familiar to us today from Currier & Ives prints and movies. Coaches carried 40 to 60 persons, and passenger trains on well-built railroads might reach 40 or 50mph. Many railroad companies were beginning to use the telegraph for railroad messages and dispatching. Specialized and somewhat uniform railroad operating rules had come into widespread use, and the American traveling public by and large knew how to purchase a ticket and navigate the increasingly confusing array of connecting and competing railroads.

Thanks to a superbly researched account of the North Carolina Railroad by historian Allen Trelease, we know a great deal about how one of the railroads linking the north with New Orleans and the south operated.[3] A train trip on the NCRR in 1859 is representative of train travel for much of the country for the middle four decades of the century.

New Orleans, at the receiving end of an immense line of waterborne commerce stretching 1000 miles or so through the heart of the continent, had grown from a swampy backwater at the conclusion of the War of 1812 into a cosmopolitan mercantile center. By the late 1850s, an all-rail route extended from Boston and New England southwestwardly to the Mississippi Delta, replacing a slow and sometimes dangerous ocean route and an equally slow and perhaps more dangerous, river, stage, and railroad route.

The NCRR carried a mix of local and through passengers. It connected with several other railroads at both ends of its line, offering travelers from the north and south a variety of routes. Like most of the railroads of the north, the NCRR was built to a gauge of 4ft 8½ in.; it connected on the north and east with other railroads of similar gauge. The western connection at Charlotte was built to the 5-ft gauge common in the south. Many railroads had been

Below: A Danville & New River Railway mixed train near Axton, VA, in 1883. The D&NR was built to a 3ft gauge in the early 1880s.

important link with the outside world.

The bay window was a feature of many railroad stations, for it permitted the agent/operator a better view of trains approaching from either direction. Often these offices were open long hours: many were manned 24 hours a day.

The small-town railroad depot was a significant place for most Americans — and for most Canadians as well. Simply put, the depot was a gateway. If you grew up in a rural town, the depot was probably where you made your first departures of discovery into a wider world. Later, it was where you picked up that long-awaited order from the Sears & Roebuck catalog, or received the freight shipment of a new farm implement. It was where, on holidays, you met visiting friends or relatives, and, afterward, saw them off. It was where you departed on long-anticipated journeys, either long or short, on travel or on business. The depot was a gateway, and therefore it was a place you remembered for the rest of your life.

The office shown here is a recreation of a typical rural depot office of about 1915. One of the exhibits at the Railroad Museum of Pennsylvania at Strasburg, PA the office has been equipped with (among others) these authentic items: ticket holder and tickets; ticket validator and ticket stamp; telephone (on scissors arm) and telegraph keys (on window ledge and desk); train order forms and train sheet (log); hoops for passing train orders to engineers; roll-top desk with agent's report book, copy of the *Official Guide* and *Book of Rules*, first aid kit, lamp and flag, and station clock (on the wall). Last but not least, there is a spittoon on the floor.

built to different track gauges, sometimes with good reason and sometimes on the whim of the railroad's promoters. In contending with the need to transfer all freight and passengers from one train to another at Charlotte, the NCRR was by no means alone.

Sometimes in these early days, cars 'ran through', or railroads published joint schedules which allowed passengers to board one car and remain ensconced as that car or train traversed a number of different railroads. Usually though, each time a railroad terminated, whether in a big city such as Philadelphia or a small town such as Goldsboro, North Carolina, the passenger and all of his baggage had to be unloaded from one train and reinstalled in the train of the next railroad to be ridden. Sometimes that entailed a wait of several hours or even a day for the connecting train.

For the antebellum traveler between New York and New Orleans, the whole trip by train might take anywhere from three to five days, which was considerably faster than the weeks required if the inland route or the coastal ships were used. Depending on how the presidents of the half-dozen or so railroads comprising the route were getting along with each other at the moment, and what kinds of through-car agreements were in effect, the traveler might have to change trains four to seven times. That did not count the ferry connections across the Hudson, Delaware, and Susquehanna rivers or the short steamboat connection between Washington, DC and Acquia Creek.

On the NCRR, passenger trains attained speeds of 20 to 25mph, but the railroad greatly preferred the more modest speed of 15mph or so. To be sure, some trains in the more populous northeast rocketed along at 40mph, but these were on well-maintained, relatively wealthy railroads that were often in competition with steamboats or other railroads. For the vast majority of railroads in the country, a top speed of 30mph and an average speed of half that was considered respectable at this time.

A passenger or mail train traveling the line from Goldsboro to Charlotte in 1859 might have taken ten to 12 hours for the 223 miles; a mixed train (passengers and freight) took twice the time. A passenger might alight at any of the 25 major stops along the way, but the crew usually would stop at any point to pick up or discharge a passenger. By then, the term 'flag stop' was part of the vocabulary. Too, the train would have required several stops for wood and water for the locomotive, at least one stop to change the crew, and probably additional stops to switch tracks, take sidings for other trains, and for miscellaneous causes such as wandering cattle on the tracks, to pick up messages, to avoid work crews, or for breakdowns.

The trip in one of the NCRR's 17 coaches might well have been pleasant for the first hour or so, but contemporary writers noted how quickly the monotony of railway scenery and the discomfort of the seats began to manifest themselves. Plush, well-padded seats in railroad coaches evolved slowly throughout the nineteenth century, and usually were found on the finer trains on the wealthier railroads. Some observers likened an all-day railway journey to sitting in a church pew for 12 hours.

Railway travel acquired a distinctive code of manners based partly on traditional notions of

Of all of the experiences one may have traveling by train, a breakfast, lunch, or dinner in the dining car is one of the most memorable and durable. The sheer novelty of a meal at 60mph or more rarely failed to make an impression.

The idea of providing meals aboard long distance passenger trains is almost as old as the idea for an American railroad system; Benjamin Dearborn proposed some sort of meal service for passenger trains in his 1819 memorial to Congress calling for a network of railroads. As early as 1835, Richard Imlay built a prototype passenger car with a buffet at one end, and a number of railroads offered meals aboard moving trains for special parties in the 1850s.[1]

A few eastern railroads outfitted crude 'refreshment cars' in the 1860s. Sometimes they were nothing more than a rough counter in an old baggage car serving food equally as bad as that found at railroad eating houses. During the Civil War, some hospital trains for wounded Union soldiers featured cars with a kitchen at one end and dining area at the other, presaging the later full dining car. It was George Pullman, however, who did the most to bring the modern dining car into existence. In the same fashion as sleeping cars, he took the idea of meals aboard trains and refined it into a marketable service.

Pullman first installed a small kitchen in a few of his sleeping cars, renamed them 'hotel cars,' and began offering surprisingly varied and complete meals to first class passengers in 1866. Two years later, he built the *Delmonico*, the first full dining car and quite self-

Above: *A Canadian Pacific dining car of about 1900. Such cars were stocked from strategically located commissaries, which often included a butchery and bakery.*

Left: *A Fred Harvey menu from the Santa Fe's* California Limited *draws on the romance of the Spanish Mission era. It dates from about 1911. Before Fred Harvey set new standards for others to copy, passengers were forced to grab what food they could when trains stopped at stations — as depicted in this 1884 print (above).*

consciously named after the New York restaurant of the same name. While offering meal service was not especially profitable for Pullman, he showed the way. Throughout the rest of the nineteenth century, railroads across the US and Canada adopted a variety of means by which to offer food to patrons traveling the increasingly long passenger train routes.

By the 1890s, dining car service had fully flowered, and would change relatively little in the ensuing seven decades. Usually dining cars lost money; railroads believed it to be in their best interest to subsidize the service as a way to lure first class passengers. Thus only the best, or at least best-patronized, trains offered dining cars at all, while lesser trains provided snack bars, lunch counters, or some similar level of accommodation. Dining car meals were not cheap, with prices approximating those of good restaurants. For most passengers, that was beyond reach, and generally only Pullman and parlor car passengers partook of full dining car meals.

The cuisine varied as to region, and most railroads strove to match the level of service, food, and ambiance to be found in the better big-city hotels of the day. That meant damask tablecloths triple-plated silverware, cut flowers, and hotel-style institutional food. Some railroads offered 'trademark' dishes and most had seasonal specialties, but they all

strove to provide a pleasing, varied, high-quality culinary experience. In his book *Dining by Rail*, Jim Porterfield concludes that railroads consistently managed to attain a standard of excellence in both food and its presentation.[2]

The car itself was a marvel of planning and space utilization. Food for 400 meals was stashed in various lockers, iceboxes and closets, along with as much liquor and wine as local tastes — or laws — demanded. Railroads stocked their fleets of as many as a hundred dining cars from commissaries that were strategically located in major cities along the routes.

Service was crisp because as many as

Below: *Pullman dining car* Isabella. *Pullman symbolically named his very first diner the* Delmonico — *for the high-class New York restaurant of the same name.*

several hundred people might desire to dine in a 40-seat car; almost always there were multiple seatings. According to railroad custom, patrons wrote out their own orders to avoid misunderstandings. The Steward handled the bill and seated passengers.

Today, travelers who are old enough to be able to do so invariably recall the glorious days of superior food, impeccable service, and gracious dining aboard the great trains of times past. For many, nothing indeed was finer than dinner in the diner.

Notes
[1]White, John H. Jr. *The American Railroad Passenger Car* (Baltimore: The Johns Hopkins University Press, 1978).
[2]Porterfield, James D. *Dining by Rail: The History and the Recipes of America's Golden Age of Railroad Cuisine* (New York: St. Martin's Press, 1993).

propriety, and partly on the hard realities of freewheeling American behavior. For example, 'no lady of genuine breeding will retain possession of more than her rightful seat in a crowded car . . . It is not required of a gentleman in a railway car to relinquish his seat in favor of a lady, though a gentleman of genuine breeding will do so.'⁴ Of course, away from Boston, Philadelphia or Charleston, persons of good breeding tended to be relatively scarce. Foreign travelers wrote of the often-boisterous conversations, the ubiquitous newspapers, squalling children, card games, and the quantities of food produced from hampers and pockets to be consumed enroute. For food was one of several inconveniences which were of little consequence when railroad journeys were short, but which were exacerbated in proportion to how long passengers might have to be on a train.

The NCRR was entirely typical in its practice of making meal stops at whatever town or facility was passed at or near the customary breakfast, lunch, and dinner hours. Jim Porterfield's lively history of railroad food service, *Dining by Rail*, provides some details:

> These early eating stops were nearly always described as terrible. The bitter black coffee may have been brewed only once a week. The ham could be dry, salty, and tough. Hard-cooked eggs were stored for an indeterminate period of time in limed water to keep them from discoloring. Fried eggs may have been cooked in rancid grease and certainly were served on stale bread. Here also one found leaden biscuits — their nickname, 'sinkers', giving a clue as to their quality — and something which earned the euphemism 'rail-road pie'. The recipe was thought to be to take two crusts of cardboard and fill them with thickened glue.⁵

The custom, as scathingly reported by contemporaries and recounted by Porterfield, was depressingly the same thoughout the country. At intervals of between 15 and 50 miles,

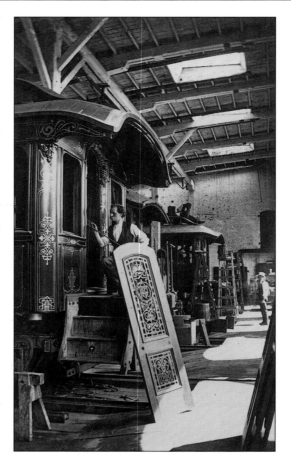

the train would stop at a town, station, or some windswept place which offered what was commonly known as a 'railroad eating house.' Passengers generally were allowed 20 to 30 minutes to eat. At places where competition between eating houses existed, proprietors or their minions loudly beat gongs to attract attention. The same gongs called passengers' attention to the fact that the train was soon to depart, usually causing a minor stampede as passengers attempted to stuff their pockets with food, wolf down a few mouthfuls, and sprint for the train.

Overnight accommodations for railway travelers were likewise problematic. Early railroads borrowed from turnpikes and canals the practice of locating inns or public houses along the line, where travelers could pause for a meal or a night's sleep. Their quality varied according to their owner's reputation and temperament, the contract with the railroad, and the relative prosperity of the region. For example, travelers on the Baltimore & Ohio on the all-day trip between Baltimore and Frederick in the 1830s might lodge and breakfast at the Three Tuns Tavern in downtown Baltimore, lunch at the inn at Sykes Mills 30 miles distant, and enjoy evening repast and lodging at any of several public houses in Frederick. The trip of almost 60 miles would have taken all day, whether hauled by horses at 7mph or by a primitive locomotive at 12mph. Still, that was twice or three times what constituted a good day's travel by road.

By mid-century, the 'railroad hotel' had become a fixture of the neighborhoods surrounding railroad depots in big city and small town alike. Some, especially in the larger cities and towns, were quite respectable and vied with the best hotels of the day in terms of room decor, food, and amenities. Others offered inexpensive rooms in which several adults might share a bed, and in which the 'furniture' was nothing more than a straw bed and a chamber pot. Nevertheless, railways called into being thousands of hotels across the country, and many millions of Americans experienced their first night away from home in connection with a railroad journey.

Sometimes that overnight stay was aboard a sleeping car, that curious but legendary translation of the 'hotel on wheels'. George

Pullman did not invent the sleeping car. The idea had originated in the 1830s, and dozens of relatively crude cars were in operation when Pullman became interested in the business in the late 1850s. Pullman did have capital, imagination, and a ruthless business instinct that sensed the immense profits to be made by providing the increasingly wealthy train travelers with decent overnight sleeping accommodations. Pullman was a visionary and entrepreneur, not an inventor.

His competitors were an assortment of cranks, cons, sincere creators and like-minded businessmen looking for a monopoly. Nearly 40 sleeping car companies operated between 1857 and 1910; some were run by the railroads themselves, while others bore such names as the 'Rip Van Winkle Line' and the 'Crescent Safety Parlor and Sleeping Car Company.' All eventually ended up as part of George Pullman's empire, which embraced car building, sleeping car operation, dining and parlor cars, and dozens of subsidiary businesses. 'Pullman' soon became synonymous with travel by train.

By the mid-1870s, a journey by Pullman Sleeping Car had acquired most of the characteristics which would define Pullman service until the advent of Amtrak in 1971. Pullman entered into contracts with individual railroads to provide sleeping car, and sometimes dining and parlor car service, over certain lines of railroad. Pullman Palace Cars would be included in the regular passenger trains, and their operation would fall under the direct control of the Conductor and railroad officials. For hauling the Pullman car, the railroad got a cut of the Pullman's revenues for that particular line, in addition to the regular fare for transporting the sleeping car passengers. What went on inside the car was George M. Pullman's business alone, for all he had to sell was service.

In turn, Pullman got a ready source of customers and access to the railroad's network

Below: An early Harvey House in Kansas. The 'Harvey Girls' were kept in strict line, and were expected to live in company dormitories.

of suppliers, agents, offices, and connecting railroads. Railroad ticket agents could sell a Pullman ticket to anywhere Pullman cars ran, and by the 1890s, that was pretty much the entire country. Pullman strove to offer reliable, first class service that varied but little from railroad to railroad, car to car. He pioneered modern notions of customer service, name brands, and product differentiation. From the moment a passenger entered a Pullman sleeping car until the final parting at the platform, the passenger was a guest of the company and was treated well. Of course, the passenger paid a premium price for this service, based on the railroad's per-mile transportation charge and a stiff Pullman accommodation charge that might be several times the railroad fare.

The cars themselves were the finest examples of the carbuilder's art, with decor borrowed from the latest fine hotels and restaurants. Inlaid wood, japaning, French polishing, carvings, tapestries and plush upholstery typified Pullman Palace Car interiors. Cars had 'sections': facing double seats which made up into an upper and lower berth. The idea for the sleeping car was borrowed from shipboard accommodations, as was some of the terminology, such as 'galley,' 'berth,' and 'saloon.'

A typical sleeping car might hold 20 berths, or fewer berths and a galley for the preparation of food. Some Palace Cars were indeed self-contained little hotels, from which a passenger did not need to venture until reaching the destination. Being aboard was likened to being on a ship. The passenger was expected to mix with his or her traveling companions, but the Pullman Conductor expected, and usually enforced, a high level of manners and civility. The Conductor was also the first line of defense against the various tramps, robbers, card sharps, and assorted vultures who tried so assiduously to prey on the passengers.

In the evening, the Porter would make down the berths in some predetermined order. Usually it took only a few minutes to fix each one. The seats made the lower bed; the upper one folded down from the ceiling like a shelf. Bedding —

FRED HARVEY'S EMPIRE

Some men made their railroad empires in finance, others in technology; some worked on a grand scale with raw materials or industrial might. Fred Harvey made his millions on the railroad serving inexpensive meals to appreciative customers one trainload at a time.

Harvey immigrated from England as a teenager and worked his way through the restaurant and railroad businesses in the mid-nineteenth century. After a string of business failures common to that rough-and-tumble era, Harvey hit upon the right idea in the right palce at the right time: a series of high-quality eating houses on the Atchison, Topeka, and Santa Fe Railroad. His restaurants would serve only good food, at reasonable prices, in clean, comfortable surroundings. And he would employ attractive young women of good morals and pleasant disposition to serve it. James Porterfield notes that Harvey 'boasted of never using canned food . . . paid the Harvey chef at Florence, Kansas, twice as much as the town's next-highest paid resident, and coordinated menu planning in Kansas City to insure that no guest . . . encountered the same selections at different stops along the way.'[1]

Harvey's first restaurant, in Topeka, Kansas, was such a success that 53 additional facilities followed, all run from his Kansas City headquarters. In addition, Harvey came to operate Santa Fe's dining car service, and the railroad heavily promoted both the Harvey Houses and the dining cars. Porterfield regards Harvey as one of the inventors of the modern fast food industry, but many people know more about the 'Harvey Girls.'

At first, Fred Harvey and the railroad made much of the fact that the women hired as waitress staff were carefully screened, closely supervised, and ensconced in supervised dormitories. In the last quarter of the nineteenth century, such paternalistic behavior toward women was common, and indeed enhanced the restaurant's stature. Harvey recruited women from all over the United States at a time when the west served by the Santa Fe Railroad was still wild and 'dangerous.'

Until the decline of railroad station restaurants after World War II, and the ending of dining car service on the Santa Fe in 1971, millions of travelers enjoyed a Fred Harvey meal. Porterfield estimates that 20,000 of the 100,000 women who served as Harvey Girls ended up marrying customers, which surely made Harvey and the Santa Fe one of the greatest civilizing agents in the west. To this day, the very name 'Fred Harvey' conjures images of Gibson Girl waitresses and good food.

Note
[1] James D. Porterfield, *Dining by Rail: The History and the Recipes of America's Golden Age of Railroad Cuisine*, (New York: St. Martin's Press, 1993), p. 25.

clean sheets, blankets, and pillows — were stowed in various places about the car. Heavy curtains separated the berths at night, and presumably the noise of the train obviated any loud snoring. In the morning, the Porter reversed the procedure, making the car into a comfortable day arrangement.

From the earliest days, Pullman employed African-Americans as Porters. They were paid poorly and expected to supplement their wages with tips. Indeed, Pullman almost regarded them as inside contractors who would succeed or perish according to the quality of service they rendered. Passengers traditionally settled up with the Porter on the platform at journey's end, although a strategically presented tip earlier in the trip could engage the Porter's more earnest attentions. In the raw and less-developed parts of the country, the arrival of a train with Pullman cars at some jerkwater town was often the only tangible contact the residents had with the prevailing mores and customs of the sophisticated East and the *nouveau riche* West. The depot and the Pullman car jointly symbolized escape and the 'good life.'

Between the end of the Civil War and the beginning of World War I, the railroad depot played a central role in the economic life of thousands of cities, towns, and even tiny settlements across the United States and Canada. During that time, the railroad in North America assumed its greatest physical reach and perhaps the zenith of its importance. Accurate figures are difficult to compile, but railroads built between 85,000 and 100,000 stations, freight houses, shelters, telegraph offices, and other structures which in one way or another provided public access to the railroad network. Railroads built perhaps another 30,000 roundhouses, shop buildings, interlocking towers, and other buildings, in the process creating one of America's greatest architectural legacies. Even today, there are almost 1500 rail-related structures in the National Park Service's National Register of Historic Places.

Stations varied along a continuum that ranged

from massive terminals in cities such as New York, Chicago, and Los Angeles — each terminal virtually a city unto itself — down to one-room depots in the remotest corners of the land. In between were substantial facilities in mid-size cities, which also might include railroad division offices and which perhaps served two or more railroads as a 'union station.'

By far the most common were the rural depots, spaced anywhere from a few to a few hundred miles apart on main lines and branch lines alike. As described by Roger Grant and Charles Bohi in their history of the country railroad station, 'In the not-so-distant past Americans universally viewed the railroad station as an important community building . . . Unquestionably, it served as the community's gateway to the world.'[6]

The small town train station has become something of a cliche, but like many cliches it conveys an accurate, if incomplete, picture. The depot was indeed the heart of many communities, for the railroad both practically and symbolically connected the town with the rest of the world. Before the massive expansion of the telephone network in the 1920s, news traveled via telegraph, telephone, mail, magazines, newspapers, and word-of-mouth — most of which arrived at the railroad station first. Many railroads operated their own telegraph and express businesses, but even after the functions were consolidated into allied companies such as Western Union Telegraph and the Railway Express Agency, the depot was still where one went to send or receive messages, pick up packages, and gossip.

The folks who hung around the station were known as loungers, hangers-on, or loafers. Sometimes they constituted an informal meeting group, in much the same way as gatherings that took place in saloons and general stores. By

Below: *The South Carolina Railway's depot at Ladson, SC. The depot was actually built at Summerville, SC, sometime in the 1880s, but was later moved to Ladson on flatcars.*

A BAGGAGE ROOM OF THE 1870s

Everything traveled by train. Baggage of every sort accompanied passengers — trunks, baskets, boxes, satchels, parrots in cages — and every other kind of object was shipped as express. Parcels, bees, catalog deliveries from Sears and Wards, fine wines, even bodies in iced caskets, were transported in the baggage car which ran at the head of most long-distance passenger trains.

Horace Porter described how baggage and express were handled in the nineteenth century:

The transportation of baggage has always been a most important item to the traveller.

The earlier method, of allowing each passenger to pick out his own baggage at his point of destination and carry it off, resulted in a lack of accountability which led to much confusion, frequent losses, and heavy claims upon the companies in consequence . . . the difficulty was at last solved by the introduction of the system known as 'checking.' A metal disk bearing a number and designating on its face the destination of the baggage was attached to each article and a duplicate given to its owner, which answers as a receipt, and upon the presentation and surrender of which the baggage could be claimed. Railways soon united in arranging for through checks which, when attached to baggage, would insure its being sent safely to distant points over lines composed of many connecting roads. The check system led to the introduction of another marked convenience in the handling of baggage — the baggage express or transfer company. One of its agents will now check trunks at the passenger's own house and haul them to the train. Another agent will take up the checks aboard the train as it is nearing its destination, and see that the baggage is delivered at any given address.

The cases in which pieces go astray are astonishingly rare . . . [The workings of the system] are so perfect . . . that an American cannot understand why it is not adopted in all countries.[1]

Note

[1]Horace Porter, 'Railway Passenger Travel,' in *The Railways of America*, 1890.

whatever name, railroad lore is rich with photographs and accounts of people gathered at the station, whether or not a train is due or recently departed. The telegraph operator was constantly in touch with other stations and often with faraway cities. The mysterious clicking usually conveyed routine railroad messages and telegrams, but often it warned of the approach of storms, floods, bad guys, celebrities, or big news. Hanging around the station was also one way to pick up skills leading to a railroad job. Too, then as now the population harbored a certain number of persons who simply liked trains. In a small prairie town with little else to do but watch the corn grow, the railroad depot was an exciting place indeed.

People regarded the railroad depot (or train station — the distinction matters little to the average citizen) as a public building belonging to the community, no matter what the railroad company might have thought. Frequently towns agitated for improvements to the station, partly to enhance local service and partly as a form of civic boosterism. Visitors might form their first impression of a town from the railroad station and its surrounding neighborhood, and communities (and railroads) sometimes installed parks and gardens at the station, often tended by the stationmaster and his staff. The size, style, construction, and degree of ornamentation of

a station often indicated how prosperous or important the town was. A brick station in the latest style was something of a status symbol for a forward-thinking town.

Few types of American architecture are as immediately recognizable as the train station. After about 1850, the form of the small station became fairly predictable. If it were a new railroad or a new town, the station might be in a local store or hotel. The first railroad-built structure would usually be an inexpensive wood one- or two-room building big enough for the agent and a few passengers. Later the railroad might erect a more permanent structure made either of wood or the favored local building material. Often local architects designed the town's station; otherwise, the railroad's architect or a firm on retainer might make the standard plans, to be built by railroad employees or contractors.

Busy stations might have a large agent's office, a freight room for express and freight shipments, and one or two waiting rooms. Before 1900, especially in more civilized parts, stations had separate men's and women's waiting rooms and

toilets. In the south after the advent of 'Jim Crow' laws, stations were built or modified with rooms for white and 'Colored' travelers. At truly busy locations, the station might have separate buildings for freight and express and perhaps warehouses as well.

Station agents sometimes needed an inducement to take a post on the railroad in the middle of nowhere. Or the railroad may simply have wanted to keep the agent handy in case he was needed. In those instances, stations had living quarters built in, customarily on the second floor. The agent and his family would live there free, or for a nominal rent, for as long as the railroad employed him at that point. Savvy agents ran a telegraph line into their quarters so as not to miss important transmissions.

No matter how grand or humble the depot, the agent was the railroad's man on the spot. By virtue of his mastery of the telegraph, his regular (and relatively large) paycheck, his power to transact business, and his pivotal role in promoting or retarding local commerce, the agent enjoyed a considerable amount of respect and power. He was one of the best informed men in town, and if he was smart and ambitious, he might go on to bigger things.

Richard Warren Sears, who went on to establish the mail order catalog house of Sears, Roebuck & Company was but one example (see

Chapter 5 for the full story). Other soon-to-be-famous individuals who got their start on the railroad in one capacity or another included inventor Thomas Edison, oil man John D. Rockefeller, steelmaker Andrew Carnegie, and labor leader Eugene V. Debs. These men were, in the words of historian Daniel Boorstin, 'go getters.'[7] They would likely have made their mark in any age, but their successes illustrate how useful and pervasive railroading was in the nineteenth century in the United States.

Nowhere was that more apparent than in the business of promotion. Just as the needs of the railroads accelerated the development of steel-making, civil and mechanical engineering, the creation of machine tools, standardization, uniform timekeeping, modern business organization and dozens of similar fields, railroading also helped create the new fields of public relations and advertising.

The railroad industry was the nation's first big business. But it was never a unified cartel or collusive entity, despite the anguished cries of populists, reformers, and government regulators. Certainly the railroads were guilty of many abuses of the public trust, and they did exploit the traveler and freight shipper whenever possible. But competition — often ruinous, hostile, to-the-death-or-bankruptcy competition — defined the entire industry. What cooperation there was, as with through passenger ticketing or the interchange of freight cars, was by competitive necessity, not altruism or concern for the welfare of the customer.

Railroads early on resorted to advertising to lure passengers, and to a lesser degree, freight to their lines. The first public timetables were printed in the newspapers of the 1830s, often with a wood cut of a steam train to capture people's attention. Individual timetables appeared by the 1840s, often in the form of trade cards and printed broadsides. Over the next 20 years, railroads gradually established the principles of railroad promotion by advertising frequently, issuing free passes to newspaper editors, sponsoring press trips, and by slowly developing into one of the country's largest customers for maps, printing and photography.

One of the most noteworthy early press trips took place on the B&O Railroad in 1858. The year before, the B&O had opened a through route to St. Louis from the Atlantic seaboard, and it was anxious to lure new business to the line. Aware of the value of good press, the B&O put together a special train of six cars, including a dining car of sorts, a baggage car fitted out as a photographic laboratory, and several parlor and observation cars. It invited noted artists, writers, and editors of the day for a free trip through the rugged Allegheny mountains to Wheeling, on the Ohio River in what is now West Virginia. The guests were free to stop the train wherever and for however long the party aboard wished, with the particular hope that the guests should feel free to make accurate and flattering portraits of the B&O's scenery, route, and service. They did, of course, greatly enhancing the railroad's public stature.

In the 1880s, most large railroads began hiring publicity agents, who generally worked in the passenger traffic departments. These fellows never let a fact get in the way of a good story as they laid the foundations for modern public relations and advertising. Some railroads touted

Above: *Vacation travel soon became a major source of revenue for railroads: when the 'New Florida Short Line' was opened in 1893, the participating railroads hoped to cash in on Christmas holiday traffic from the north.*

their scenery, as the traveling public had little to do but watch the passing landscape. Others crowed about their modern cars, steam heat in coaches, new dining and sleeping cars, or the superior quality of their railroad eating houses. The railroad with the shortest route between two points never failed to raise that point in ads, timetables, posters, and maps. Likewise the railroad with the best track, or cleanest coal.

Passenger trains were inherently dirty, as steam locomotives discharge soot and cinders. One railroad, the Delaware, Lackawanna & Western, burned anthracite in its locomotives. This hard coal made little smoke, less soot, and few cinders, suggesting a long-running adver-

tising campaign featuring the fictitious railroad traveler 'Phoebe Snow' (see Chapter 6).

Maps, too, preoccupied railroad traffic departments. In the late nineteenth century, navigating about in the United States could still be a hit-or-miss affair. The local passenger station, with its office copy of the *Traveler's Official Guide of the Railway and Steam Navigation Lines in the United States and Canada*, was the best bet for finding the shortest, cheapest, and easiest way to get from here to there. That guide, still published today, listed every known railroad and steamship schedule with such rigor as to be indispensable. Its maps were often the most accurate ones available to the public at a reasonable cost. By the 1850s, many map and printing houses were issuing their own regional or national railroad maps. Some were quite good, offering the traveler a fighting chance of planning a trip effectively. Many included railroads which had not yet been built, roads, and steamboat routes.

Railroads themselves issued maps of varying creativity and reliability. Some accentuated the virtues of their routes — easy curves, good connections — while representing competing railroads in somewhat less favorable light. Others elaborately described the healthfulness of the climate, scenic wonders, suitability for agriculture, or other attributes real or perceived. An 1896 color panoramic map from the Kansas City, Pittsburg & Gulf Railroad has Uncle Sam 'showing his children, who live in the treeless, blizzard-swept plains of the North and Northwest the NEW SOUTH in all her beauty and freshness.'[8]

Railroads increasingly demanded full color and better graphics for their material, challenging the presses of the day. Maps and advertisements could be quite large, and highly prized as wall decorations. By demanding ever more complex, cheaper, larger, more technically difficult advertisements, maps, and timetables from the printing industry, railroads spurred the development of many new techniques and inventions. This was but one of the many ways that railroading leveraged and accelerated the growth of the economy. A business which required several million timetables and advertising pieces per year by the 1890s was bound to have an effect rippling all the way down to the wood pulp industry.

The need for timetables implies a system of train operation based on time, which indeed the railroads had been perfecting since the 1830s. But in this case the railroad industry had to invent new notions and perceptions of time for the American traveler. Before the railroad, time was a local, individual, idiosyncratic and rather disorderly concept. Noon was whenever the sun was directly overhead wherever you happened to be. For every 15 miles a traveler might move to the east or the west, the time changed by one minute, plus or minus. Noon in New York was several minutes behind Boston's noon, and ahead of noon in Philadelphia, Baltimore, Washington DC, and Richmond, which themselves differed on when noon was.[9]

Left: *Railroads advertised the scenic wonders, history, and recreation available along their lines in an attempt to entice tourists to their trains — as with this SP poster of 1908.*

A flexible, local, almost impressionistic system of time was sufficient for a nation of farmers and artisans who generally worked for themselves and at their own pace from early morning until dark. When 20 miles was a good day's travel by stage coach or canal boat, and when a 'close' connection meant hours and some connections took days, uniform and accurate time was of little consequence to all but mariners dependent upon it for navigation. Railroads and later the telegraph completely changed the structure and meaning of time in the United States. For even a modest-sized railroad to run effectively, train crews adhered to an elaborate set of train schedules and operating rules. This required the use of reasonably accurate timepieces and some means by which to ascertain and distribute the correct time to all points on the railroad.

Furthermore, the needs of the railroad to run 'by Time' required the traveling public to adhere to 'railroad time.' Such railroad-generated time often was at odds with local time. The Pennsylvania Railroad, for instance, used Philadelphia time for all of its operations east of Pittsburgh, and Pittsburgh time for all operations west of that city. Other railroads serving Philadelphia and Pittsburgh used their own official railroad times, which made coordinating schedules difficult at best. In places such as Chicago, where dozens of railroads met, the situation was chaotic. Train stations had multiple clocks set to different times to help travelers make sense of the apparently random comings and goings of hundreds of trains each day.

As part of a larger movement toward some level of standardization throughout industry and society, railroads in the early 1880s discussed various proposals for dividing the country up into 'time zones,' arbitrary boundaries within which all railroads would hew to a common time. The railroad industry was not attempting to impose its will on American society; it simply wanted this common-sense system so as to rationalize scheduling and decrease the risk of accident. In 1883, under the general leadership of William F. Allen of the industry group The General and Southern Railway and Time Convention, most United States railroads formally agreed to the division of the country into the now-familiar four time zones. The idea itself dated back to the 1830s and had antecedents even earlier in maritime navigation, but it took intensive lobbying by Allen and the railroad industry to make it finally happen.

Fifty years after the more conservative elements of society had denounced high speeds (20mph), steam locomotion, and operating trains on the Sabbath as contrary to the will of the Creator and hazardous to the health of the human organism, a chorus of the same voices arose denouncing railroad standard time as contrary to tradition, the will of God, and the rights of the people. In his history of time in America, Michael O'Malley quotes a newspaper editorial from Ohio, a center of opposition to railroad time: 'Let the people of Cincinnati stick to the truth as it is written in the moon and the stars.'[10] Indeed, it took Congress until 1918 to adopt as standard for the United States the railroad system of time. By then, virtually the entire country was already using it.

November 18, 1883 was 'the day of two noons'. Most newspapers and most people understood and supported the idea of standard time, if only because they had had so much difficulty with different railroad timetables all referring to different 'times.' Because nothing quite like 'regulating time' — which many people thought was directly linked to the motion of the universe — had ever been attempted, there was widespread curiosity and apprehension as to just how stopping the sun was to be accomplished.

Allen and the railroads coordinated an elaborate set of orders for train dispatchers, conductors and crews instructing them to obtain the 'new noon' from telegraph stations or other reliable sources. And despite the fears of the uninformed, natural cataclysm did not attend the moment. Some trains stopped for a prescribed time; thousands of railroad men reset their watches and proceeded according to existing schedules, and life for the railway passenger became immensely easier and considerably safer.

The public debate as to railroad safety had grown increasingly strident as the nation reeled from the accelerating 'progress' of society following the Civil War. The pace, intensity, and rate of change of American life increased dramatically between 1865 and 1915, perhaps more so than any other comparable period in human history. The railroads were central to that process of modernization, and the comparative safety of the railway traveler was an unreliable but very highly visible indicator of that process.

Before the Civil War, passenger train speeds were relatively low, and traffic levels were such that keeping trains out of each others' way was not too difficult. The system as a whole, comprising iron rails, 30-ton locomotives, wooden passenger cars, and leisurely schedules, operated in a sort of equilibrium. To be sure, railroad accidents killed and maimed people. Their causes were the familiar broken axles, rotten ties, excessive speeds, recalcitrant cattle, and human error. But the number of spectacular wrecks with high loss of life was relatively low and apparently within the realm of public acceptance (just as Americans today tolerate tens of thousands of deaths by automobile accident).

The underlying conditions changed after the Civil War. The war itself had greatly speeded up the economy, the industrial base, and life in general. Americans had always seemed to observers to be in a hurry, and now they demanded of the railroads faster and faster trains, and more

Left: *The derailed cars of a GN passenger train, about 1905. Despite the impressions created by major wrecks with their loss of life, derailments usually produced few casualties.*

Above: *To satisfy the public appetite for spectacle, promoters in the years before World War I staged head-on collisions like this one at the California State Fair.*

of them. Railroad mileage increased from perhaps 31,000 in 1860 to almost 193,000 miles in operation by the turn of the century, effectively linking every point of importance on the continent with this vast, increasingly busy network of passenger, freight, express, and special trains.

As speed and traffic grew, so did the demands on the system as a whole, and railroads found themselves always trying to catch up with new technologies and increased maintenance. Iron rails which were perfectly safe for light passenger trains failed when subjected to bigger, faster, heavier trains. Increasingly fast and frequent schedules taxed the abilities of crews and railroad management to keep the speeding trains safely separated. Bridges quickly became obsolete as the heavier locomotives threatened to pound them to pieces.

Railroads were a new and evolving technology throughout the nineteenth century, and railroad passengers assumed some of the risks associated with any complex new system. Major

accidents captured the public's imagination, but minor ones were much more common. One, or indeed several, passengers might be seriously injured or killed in a derailment without seriously arousing public indignation. Often, storms washed out the roadbed or landslides covered the tracks with debris, which then derailed the train. Passengers might be crushed between the cars or thrown beneath the wheels in derailments, injured by flying glass or luggage, or suffer any of hundreds of types of injuries. Sometimes the railroads would make restitution. At other times, injured passengers or the executors of their estates would sue the companies, alleging negligence. An immense body of railroad law arose from these actions, much of which helped to shape our present

Below: *After 1900, automobiles replaced cows as a major hazard to trains. This wreck — typical of thousands to come — occurred near Geneva, NY, in December, 1916.*

notions about liability.

One of the most dramatic, and most illustrative, railroad accidents took place on the Lake Shore & Michigan Southern Railroad on December 29, 1876. The overnight *Pacific Express* was westbound, with over 200 passengers aboard for Chicago and points west. A tremendous snowstorm was blowing in off Lake Erie as the train approached the northern Ohio town of Ashtabula. The surviving enginemen described plowing through two feet of snow at 12mph with little visibility.

As the two locomotives and 11 cars crossed the relatively new iron bridge over the Ashtabula River, the bridge gave way. The lead engine managed to break the coupling and make it to the other side. The second locomotive plunged backward into the shallow river 76ft below, along with the first few cars. Momentum carried the rest of the train into the gorge. Each succeeding car fell on top of those before it, creating a horrible scene of shattered wood

TIME AND THE RAILROADS

Time works well as a method for controlling the movement of trains only if there exists some reliable way to quantify, tell, and distribute that time. In basing an entire system of operation on time, railroads necessarily also became expert at the various ways one may control and convey it.

Steamboats passed each other wherever they happend to meet, but railroads had to closely coordinate the movements of many trains. This led to the adoption of complex rules governing where each train on a given line was to meet other trains, how long they were to wait, and so on.

The public, at first bewildered by the profusion of individual 'railroad times,' adopted the *Official Guide* as the traveler's Bible. Listing every train schedule in the country, the *Guide* brought order to the nation's passenger train network. It also helped foster the tradition of railroads as the guardians of accurate timekeeping.

Underpinning the entire system were the watches and clocks themselves, along with detailed instructions as to how to use both time and time pieces. Railroad clocks and watches were precision instruments. By 1900, a half-dozen or so American companies were producing 'railroad-grade' pocket watches.

Certain employees, such as engineers and conductors, were required to carry an approved watch. The railroad's time service department kept track of the type, accuracy, and condition of every watch used on the system. Railroad men quickly adopted the watch as a badge of distinction, and the watches themselves became family heirlooms.

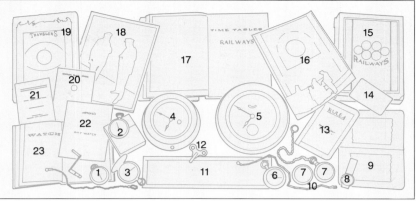

1 Gold pocket watch by Elgin National Watch Company.
2 'Howard' railroad chronometer.
3 'Railway Timekeeper', by Joseph Johnson.
4 Brass locomotive cab clock, made by Seth Thomas & Sons, New York, 1880.
5 Locomotive cab clock made by McGrane.
6 Elgin silver pocket watch.
7 Waltham 21-jewel pocket watch and cover.
8 Gold 'railroad approved' Bulova Accutron watch.
9 Pages 14-15 from *Rule 4: Change of Time Table*, 1910.
10 Pocket watch chains.
11 Sign that would have been hung under a station's clock.
12 Clock winding key.
13 *Rule 4: Change of Time Table* booklet, 1938.
14 Employee's Card Certificate, issued by D&RGW's Time Inspection Service, 1942.
15 The *Official Guide*, 1901.
16 Cover of the *SP Bulletin*, June, 1928.
17 Title page, *Official Guide*,
June, 1877.
18 Cover of the *SP Bulletin*, August, 1923.
19 Cover, *Official Guide*, January, 1878.
20 SP *Time Service Regulations* booklet, 1949.
21 SP Time Service Bureau booklet issued to watch inspectors, 1939.
22 1880s advertisement for watches able to 'keep a standard and changeable local time.'
23 1872 American Watch Company advertisement for its 'Railroad Watch.'

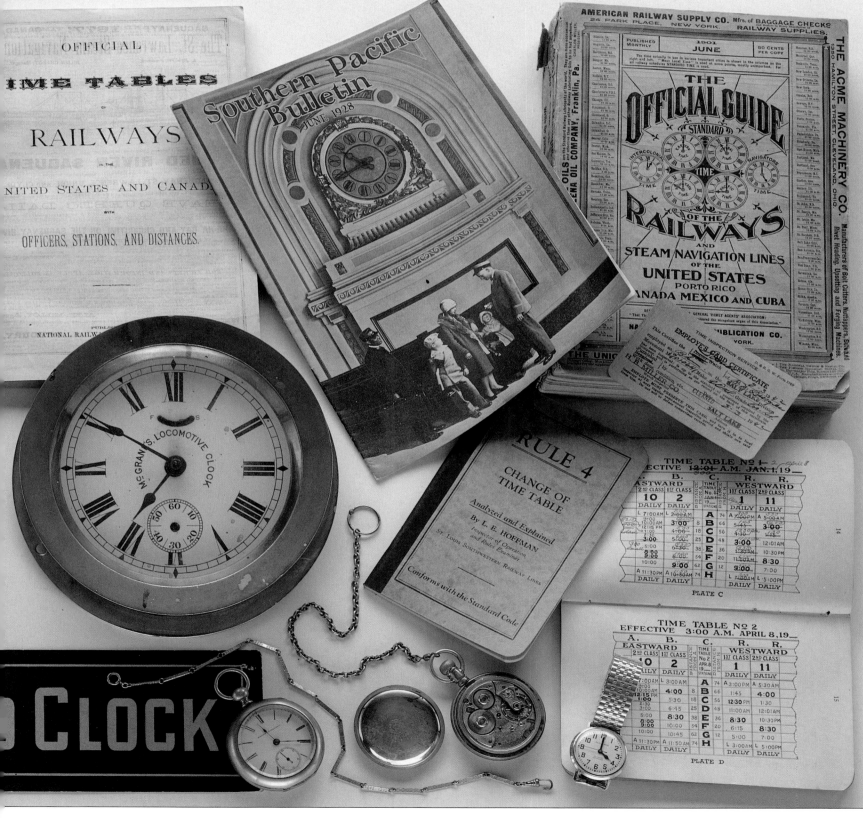

carbodies and trapped passengers. What happened next was too typical of wrecks of the day, when serious accidents turned tragic through happenstance and stupidity.

The town responded quickly, sending two fire engines and a number of men to assist the passengers. Many were railroad men, as Ashtabula was a railroad town on the LS&MS. Yet rather than immediately extinguishing the small fires caused by overturned stoves in the wrecked passenger cars, the firemen were told to help extricate the injured. The confusion at the scene must have been horrific: 200 injured passengers, 11 wrecked cars at the bottom of a ravine, and men and women frantically trying to save themselves and others in the middle of a raging snowstorm, at night. Then the fire spread.

Flames rapidly engulfed the dry, varnished wood of the coaches and sleepers. Many injured passengers were trapped in the wreckage and burned to death. Indeed, the coroner could not even establish with certainty how many had perished, as the entire train was so thoroughly consumed by fire. The commonly accepted figures are 80 dead, 100 seriously hurt, and several million outraged.

This was the flagship railroad of Cornelius Vanderbilt, who himself died but four days later. Vanderbilt's imperious ways had already earned the railroad industry a great degree of public enmity, and the Ashtabula Disaster fixed in the public's mind that railroads were wilfully negligent and completely indifferent to safety. In this case, that was true. The bridge, although of iron, had been incorrectly designed and shoddily maintained. This was neither an Act of God nor the consequence of individual carelessness (although the railroad's chief engineer committed suicide just after the inquest), but rather the result of a string of mistakes and collective negligence.[11]

Until World War I, other spectacular wrecks fanned the public's ire. Some resulted from cars telescoping into each other during derailments, others from collisions, boiler explosions, and derailments ascribed to excessive speed. The railroad commissions of various states and the United States Congress all took note, and passed a series of bills intended to increase public safety and make the railroads more accountable. Yet the railroads were not alone in presenting the traveler with hazards. In 1865, one Mississippi River steamboat explosion alone resulted in 1400 deaths. Inland steamboat explosions and sinkings occurred every few days, claiming 20, 40, or as many as 200 lives. Shipwrecks caused thousands of deaths, as did factory accidents, coal mine explosions, tenement house fires, and natural disasters. Railroading and society in general became steadily safer in the early twentieth century. Now, travel by train vies for status as the safest mode of travel.

This safer train travel was part of a larger process of modernization. Throughout the late nineteenth century, railroading underwent successive technological revolutions which made trains safer, more comfortable, and vastly more efficient. This transformation illustrates the process by which a complex technological system such as a railroad shapes, and is in turn shaped by, the people who use it. Sometimes

Below: *Passengers at St. Paul Union Station, about 1910. Before the 'automobile age', just about everybody depended on the railroad for most of their long-distance mobility.*

customers demand more of a technology than it is capable of producing, at least until some new material or gizmo or process comes along to fill the need. Americans got to be awfully good at inventing and exploiting new technologies. The railroad's embracing of steel illustrates this point.

Steel had been known as a material for a thousand years, but it was difficult and expensive to make. In the 1850s, Bessemer in Great Britain and Thomas in the United States perfected new ways of making large quantities of inexpensive steel from molten iron. Because of the availability of railroads to carry coal, iron ore, and limestone cheaply, it was possible to build steel furnaces large enough to realize economies of scale. In turn, railroads quickly became the steel producers' major customers, for railroads were voracious consumers of steel for rails, boilers, cars, wheels, pipes, buildings, and parts. The railroad made it possible to produce cheap steel on a large scale; railroad demand for steel spurred the rise of the modern steel industry and helped lower the cost of the metal to the point that it became more efficient to use steel than to use iron, wood, stone, or other traditional materials.

Steel rails lasted longer, and although initially more expensive they were more economical than the wrought iron rails they replaced. They were generally stronger, too, and the widespread introduction of steel rails in the 1870s permitted faster passenger trains. Faster trains required larger, more powerful locomotives, which in turn required heavier rail and more steel for boilers and wheels. It was also thus with cars. Better track and bigger locomotives meant that it was possible to operate

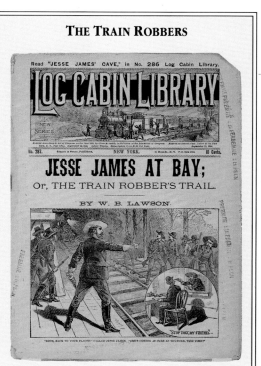

fire. Railroads converted from candles to tallow and whale oil, and then to rock oil — kerosene — as soon as that cheaper fuel became popular in the 1860s. But it still shed a dim light, made noxious fumes, and caused its share of fires. At about the same time, inventors were adapting compressed coal gas to railroad passenger car use, followed after the Civil War by illuminating systems which utilized 'Pintsch Gas.' Julius Pintsch had been a tinsmith in Berlin who experimented with compressed petroleum gas as a source of lamp fuel for European railroad cars. His system was a success, and it predominated on American passenger trains for almost 30 years. The gas burned cleanly, safely, with little odor, and it provided much more light than even the best oil lamps. As in American hotels, businesses, and homes, the prevailing tendency was to push the night back with as much artificial light as could be mustered. Even then, we wanted to squeeze more into the day than daylight would permit.

In 1881, following closely on the heels of Edison's successful demonstrations of the incandescent light and centralized electrical generating system, railroads experimented with electric lighting aboard trains. At first, steam-powered dynamos in the baggage car provided current for incandescent lamps strung throughout the train. The New York Central Railroad's crack train the *Twentieth Century Limited* received a new electric lighting system in 1902, but it took most railroads until World War II to convert fully to electric lighting. After about 1910, most new cars were built with electric lighting, just as most new homes in cities were wired for electricity.

Other inventions were fully as important. The

Above: *Train robbers such as Jesse James were often romanticized by the press.*

THE TRAIN ROBBERS

For 75 years or so, railroad travelers in the United States contended with one more highly-visible, and for the most part, annoying hazard in addition to those offered by nature, the railroad, and the food: the train robber.

The first real train robberies took place near Seymour, Indiana in 1866, when armed men robbed the Adams Express car of several thousand dollars. Ten months earlier, thieves had rifled an unguarded express car enroute from New York to Boston of $700,000. That, however, was a burglary. Shortly thereafter, the country experienced an ebb and flow of railroad robberies which did not subside until the turn of the century. In the process, a combination of sympathetic news reporting, hostility to railroads, and the popular culture's need for mythical characters created a new breed of 'romantic' hero: the James Gang, Butch Cassidy and the Sundance Kid, the Dalton Brothers, and others.

In fact, the methods of these outlaws were simple and often brutal: stopping or derailing trains, stealing the contents of safes and mail cars, robbing the passengers at gunpoint, and escaping into the wilderness until captured, killed, or the time came for the next job. These hard characters sometimes murdered the train crews. Railroads and the government spent millions of dollars to track them down. Allen Pinkerton's American Detective Agency and the special agents of The Wells Fargo Express Company were just two of the outfits engaged in the fight.

A combination of improved methods of shipping valuables, stronger cars, and more effective law enforcement finally put an end to this line of work. The attention which train robberies received from the press, however, guaranteed that they would remain part of the lore of the West.

Above: *A letter written by a disgruntled passenger giving details of a watch stolen from her during a hold-up while she was traveling on a train near Oakland, CA.*

longer, heavier passenger coaches, sleepers, parlor, baggage and express cars. Because these cars were larger and operated at higher speeds, they had to be substantially stronger than the cars of the 1860s. This meant the increasing use of steel for underframes, structural parts, and running gear (the assorted wheels, brakes, and assemblies that allow cars to stop and go with some predictability). Related to this somewhat circular process in turn were the development of brakes, couplers, and all sorts of ancilliary systems. (See Chapter 4 for further details.)

As the steel rail, air brake and automatic coupler boosted the speed and efficiency of passenger train travel, several pivotal inventions of the 1880s and 90s similarly increased passenger comfort and safety. Coal and wood stoves were at best unsatisfactory and at worst grave dangers in the case of accident. By the 1870s, a handful of railroads were experimenting with the use of steam from the locomotive to heat the cars. The principle was simple: pipe a small quantity of the steam that the locomotive is already producing back through radiator pipes in the cars, obviating the need for the cursed stoves. The only problem, and that was easily overcome, was to deliver the steam at low pressure so that passengers had little risk of being scalded should a pipe burst. By 1900, steam heat was common. Its adoption provided an even, easily regulated heat and no doubt prevented multiple repetitions of the Ashtabula horror.

The oil lamps carried on all passenger cars were another source of annoyance, soot, and

Right: *Rube Burrows (1854-1890) was one of a few criminals who specialized in robbing trains. When shot, his body was propped up in a coffin against the train to be photographed.*

Pullman Company claimed to have invented the diaphragm and vestibule, which enclosed the space between passenger cars and permitted safe passage from one car to the other. But like so many other railway developments, the vestibule had been conceived decades earlier; all Pullman did was perfect and market a workable version. Still, the vestibule and diaphragm did make individual cars into one unit, giving rise to the concept of the passenger train as a 'hotel on wheels' through which the passenger could move about freely.

Mundane matters assumed greater and greater importance as the nineteenth century closed. Cars began carrying water tanks to supply fresh water for drinking, cooking, and for the new-fangled flush toilets that began to show up in first class cars in the 1890s. Until then, and persisting well into the twentieth century, toilets aboard trains were nothing more than 'dry

Above: *The 'Adams Windsplitter' resting near Annapolis Junction, Maryland, in May, 1900. The design of the coaches eerily presaged the streamlined trains of 40 years later.*

hoppers,' or closet-like rooms resembling outhouses. One of the reasons that commodious washrooms were provided at most large train stations was that washing and toilet facilities aboard the trains were so limited. And in the days before air conditioning and diesel locomotives, soot and cinders rendered the most hardy traveler begrimed and uncomfortable after a day aboard a train.

Cold drinking water seems to be a peculiarly

Below: *By 1900, railroad waiting rooms were somewhat formal affairs. The B&O stations at Youngstown, OH (left) and Washington, DC (right) were typical of the period.*

American passion; water fountains to this day are rare aboard European trains. Until about 1900, water aboard American passenger trains was either sold by the glass (with everyone using the same glass) or provided by the railroad in a water cooler at one end of the car. Again, all used the same glass, although reformers made attempts to require paper cups and wise travelers carried their own container. Joseph Lister proposed a theory in the early 1870s that diseases were caused by microorganisms. It took two decades for the traveling public to appreciate fully Lister's 'germ theory' and cease the communal use of cups, towels, spittoons, bedding, water, and who-knows what else aboard passenger trains. By World War I, good hygiene had come to the passenger train.

Most essential qualities of railroad travel improved incrementally throughout the period between the Civil War and about 1915. The form

Above: *Railroad passengers of the 1860s would have been amazed by the advances in speed, comfort, safety and size embodied in this NP passenger train at the turn of the century.*

of the car did also. The truly revolutionary change, and the one which completes the evolution of the passenger train from its stagecoach origins to the modern era, was the use of steel. All of the preceding developments took place in or on cars of wood, which was the material of architecture most familiar to Americans. Highly decorated, painted and varnished passenger cars were crafted, not simply made in a factory. Or at least that was a view of the day, which applied as well to ships, early automobiles, and buildings. Nevertheless, railroading made the transition from wood to steel passenger cars.

The reasons were compelling. Wood cars, weighted down with all of the modern amenities, were both heavy and dangerous. In wrecks, even the best-constructed wood cars suffered terrible damage and caused loss of life. As cars got longer and larger, the challenges of designing and maintaining them became daunting. A number of railroads and car builders experimented with steel passenger cars after 1900. Finally, the construction in 1906 of the Pennsylvania Railroad's Hudson River Tunnel from New Jersey to Manhattan provided the impetus for the perfection of the all-steel car. Pennsy did not wish to risk a fire involving wood cars in the new tunnel. By designing a new style of steel car that was more crashworthy, and longer lasting, the PRR showed the way for all other railroads. By the 1920s, most wooden cars had been replaced throughout the country by steel ones.[12]

The net results of these incremental improvements were both strikingly obvious and quite subtle. A traveler on an American railroad in 1870 would have experienced speeds, sensations, amenities, and a level of overall comfort quite similar to those of the previous thirty years. To be sure, there had been progress since the introduction of the first crude coaches, and the alternative was still a bone-jarring ride in a stagecoach, a roundabout journey by water, or walking. Yet the trip would still have tried the patience and endurance of all but the hardiest souls.

A traveler on the railroad today would feel quite at home aboard a train dating from the eve

of World War I. There have been significant improvements in details, and air conditioning ranks as a welcome advance. Nevertheless, the differences would be more of style than of substance or comfort. Respectable mainline passenger trains of 1915 had steam heat, carpeting, good windows, bathrooms, nice seats, and strong, safe steel carbodies. They went about as fast, featured electric lights, and lacked none of the major amenities of today (except that cool air).

Yet our 1870 traveler would feel as though he had been transported to another planet had he been placed aboard that 1915 train. Our modern traveler, who could easily adjust to passenger trains of 1915, would feel as though consigned to the Dark Ages if hoisted aboard a train from 1870. The point is this: travel by rail changed completely between 1870 and 1915, much more so than during railroading's first four decades and more even than the past eight decades. In those 45 years, the United States evolved from a contentious, somewhat backward, primarily agrarian wilderness nation to an industrialized world power filling the continent. Railroads, and railroad passenger travel, played a large part in the modernization and development of both the United States and Canada.

The same processes which reshaped North America also revolutionized passenger train travel. A combination of new technologies, new perceptions of time, speed, and distance, the demands of the traveling public and competition to open the continent and create wealth made the train of 1915 so different — and, hopefully, better — than that of 1870 so as to be almost unimaginable to our intrepid carpet-bag-toting traveler. Millions of Americans had their first restaurant-style meal in a railroad dining car. Railroad travel introduced millions of others to such novel technological wonders as electric lights, flush toilets, central heating, and instantaneous long-distance communication: the telegraph and telephone. Just as the

needs of a restless people striving to fulfil their Manifest Destiny called into being a complete network of iron highways, railroading introduced an entire continent to the fruits, both sweet and bitter, of modern industrialization.

The jet airplane and the newest high-speed railroad technologies stand in stark contrast to the traditional passenger train; they are the ways for the future. For two centuries, life in the United States has been defined by an adherence to certain principles of democratic organization, faith in technology, and by change — nothing else. Traveling the line of railroad in the nineteenth century was no exception.

Notes

[1] Horace Porter, 'Railway Passenger Travel,' *Scribner's Magazine* (September, 1888).

[2] Charles Francis Adams, Jr. *Railroads: Their Origin and Problems* (New York: G. P. Putnam & Sons, 1878), p. 116.

[3] Allen Trelease, *The North Carolina Railroad 1849-1871 and the Modernization of North Carolina* (Chapel Hill: University of North Carolina Press, 1991).

[4] Richard A. Wells, *Manners, Culture and Dress of the Best American Society* (Springfield, Mass.: King, Richardson & Co., 1894), pp. 151-152.

[5] James D. Porterfield, *Dining By Rail: The History and the Recipes of America's Golden Age of Railroad Cuisine* (New York: St. Martin's Press, 1993), p. 7.

[6] H. Roger Grant and Charles W. Bohi, *The Country Railroad Station in America* (Sioux Falls, South Dakota: The Center for Western Studies, 1988), p. 3.

[7] Daniel J. Boorstin, *The Americans: The Democratic Experience* (New York: Random House, 1973), Part One.

[8] Andrew M. Modelski, *Railroad Maps of North America: The First Hundred Years* (Washington: Library of Congress, 1984), pp. 136-137.

[9] Michael O'Malley, *Keeping Time: A History of American Time* (New York: Viking Penguin, 1990).

[10] Ibid.

[11] Robert B. Shaw, *A History of Railroad Accidents, Safety Precautions, and Operating Practices* (The author, 1978).

[12] For an authoritative history of the passenger car, see John H. White's *The American Railroad Passenger Car* (Baltimore: Johns Hopkins University Press, 1978).

WORKING ON THE RAILROAD

IN THE 1820s, THE FEW COMMON-CARRIER railroads that existed were seen as a superior kind of toll turnpike — a low-friction, more nearly all-weather pathway over which draft animals could haul their owners' wagons on a first-come, first-served basis. The development of the steam locomotive engine changed this. Only a well-capitalized enterprise could afford to acquire and maintain a fleet of locomotives to haul trains of carriages or wagons. Inevitably, these more specialized wagons also had to come under the ownership or control of the railroad.

As was quickly demonstrated when the heavy steam engines either destroyed the lightly constructed roadways or were themselves pounded to pieces by the early stone-block trackage, common ownership of vehicle and guideway was necessary if the new railroads were to operate efficiently. The recognition of this would allow the first real advance in overland transportation in some 3000 years to come to fruition.

In size and geographic scope, the steam packet lines which had only

Below: *New York, Ontario & Western 2-6-0 No. 101 at Sidney, New York, circa 1905, with crew. It is fitting that the latter appear somewhat jaundiced-looking, because the railroad they worked for was nicknamed the 'old and weary' or, alternatively, simply 'the old woman' by passengers and locals alike.*

recently begun to revolutionize coastal and inland water transportation could furnish some organizational guidance for the management of the new enterprise. Technically, however, a whole new spectrum of innovations had to be devised, perfected and accommodated within the enterprise. In retrospect, it is amazing that in a period of about two decades this innovation was essentially accomplished in North America and Europe, with differences between the railway hardware details, and operating practises on the two sides of the ocean outweighed by their similarities; even the distance between the rail ('gauge') in due course became standardized at precisely the same 4ft 8½ in.

Many of the occupations of those working on the railroad were little different from those in the mechanic trades — some trades were ancient, with others flowering only as the industrial revolution was riding its tide of invention in shop and factory. For example, building a freight car body involved the same carpentry skills as erecting a house or barn, and the newly important boiler-making techniques involved, in the main, developing skills that were already in existence. Running something as long, heavy and jointed as a train, however, brought into being a number of distinctly new occupations.

Two factors necessitated the development of these new operating occupations: first, for the first time in history, the stopping distance of a land transport vehicle exceeded the sighting distance of its driver. Second, the vehicle's operating speed outran the available methods of communicating that it was on its way. These

Wm. Buchanan's No. 999,
New York Central Railroad 4-4-0, 1893.

The artworks show three 'tall and handsome' steamers, and an interloper: No. 999, designed by Wm. Buchanan, was the first vehicle to attain 100mph; the 'Ten-Wheeler' No. 382 carried Casey Jones to fame in 1900; The 'Pacific' 4-6-2 became the most numerous passenger locomotive type; but the little electric presaged a new era.

considerations were particularly important in America, where most lines were single-tracked and unfenced, and operated by night as well as by day. (Not surprisingly, the bell and headlight — never considered necessary in Britain — were among the first additions to locomotives in the United States.)

Although the two factors mentioned did not apply to maritime operations in the same way, it is still logical to trace the development of the organization of the train crew back to navigational roots. The steamboat's propulsion gear was in the charge of an 'engineer' who obviously was too far below deck to be concerned with steering the vessel; topside was the captain, responsible not only for the course of the steamboat's journey but for the handling and security of its lading.

With the track doing the steering, the locomotive engineer essentially must control the motion of the train; who or what was aboard the train remained the province of the ship captain's descendant, the 'conductor.' Who was in charge, then? Legendarily settled on at least one occasion by fisticuffs, the question has been codified almost from the beginning of railroads in the Book of Rules governing the operation of trains: this states that the conductor is vested with 'the general direction and government' of the train, with all other employees on the train required to obey his instructions, unless they 'imperil the safety of train or persons, or involve violations of rules.' If in any doubt as to the safety of proceeding, the conductor is required to

Above: *SPRR Conductor's badge; SP Freight Brakeman's badge; SP Locomotive fireman's badge; Pullman Attendant's badge. The fireman's badge is relatively rare, as engine crews did not often wear badges: mainly, they were worn by those employees who had to mix with the passengers.*

'consult with the engineer' and 'be equally responsible with him' for the safety and proper movement of the train.

To this day, the responsibilites of the conductor are similar to those of the captain and purser on a steamboat — making sure that all the people on the train have tickets ('waybills' in the case of freight), or have paid their fares. Also responsible for the conduct of trainmen throughout the consist, the conductor is still likely to be addressed as 'captain' and his 'All aboard' retains a somewhat nautical flavor.

Apart from dealing with demanding passengers, freeloaders, only marginally competent trainmen and a myriad of often conflicting company rules, how did the conductor fare physically while getting his train over the road? In passenger train service, he benefited along with his passengers as the design of the cars improved: the earliest cars, which had stagecoach type bodies running on flanged wheels, gave a rough ride. The later eight-wheeled cars, boasting such amenities as windows and even stoves were surely a good deal more comfortable. The early development of open saloon coaches (as opposed to the cars with separate compartments favored in Britain) also enabled the trainman to move from car to car to check tickets and take fares, which was much easier than getting in and out at stations.

In freight service, it was a different matter in the earliest days; the first recorded reference to a 'conductor's car' on a train was in the mid-1840s; it spoke of a converted box car equipped with windows, a desk and a supply of chains, tools and other emergency essentials for keeping the train in action despite difficulties. The term 'caboose' appears to have been borrowed from its earlier use as the name for a cookshack mounted on the deck of a ship. By the 1850s the caboose had become a stove-heated vehicle equipped to serve as a train crew's sleeping and eating quarters at their away-from-

Casey Jones' No. 382,
Illinois Central Railroad 4-6-0, 1896.

A Great Northern 'Pacific' type 4-6-2, 1909.

home terminal; sometime in that decade the first elevated cupolas appeared, providing an excellent vantage point for keeping tabs on the condition of the train ahead. The caboose also acquired a variety of both official ('van' in Canada, 'cabin car' and 'way car' on various US roads) and highly unofficial ('crummy,' 'brain cage,' and 'hack,' for example) nicknames.

Equipped with a handbrake that was accessible while the train was in motion, the caboose was the most effective way of stopping a train during the early period when few freight cars were equipped with their own brakes; aside from the caboose, only the engine and perhaps its tender could help retard a train's momentum. Indeed, some cabooses were weighted to try to help them stop trains more efficiently — the only problem being that, by the time the rear-end crew had heard the whistle call for brakes, the caboose had usually already experienced a pretty fair collision with the cars ahead as the slack in the link-and-pin couplers ran in with a crashing bang.

If, during the early days of railroading, traveling in a caboose was often fraught with danger, what of the working conditions of the engineer and his fuel-stoker, the fireman?

From the beginning, the steam locomotive had been an ungainly affair, with little provision made for the comfort or convenience of its crew. Early engines, for example, were open to the elements; but as speeds increased to 30 or 40mph what had been a cooling breeze at slower speeds demanded at least some sort of windshield. At first, this consisted simply of a

metal bulkhead with a couple of glassed portholes. By 1850, though, American locomotive builders had developed this into a well-proportioned wooden cab affording protection not only from wind but rain, snow or hail as well. For another 70 years or so (until the Canadians fought their winters with a completely closed vestibule connection between

engine and tender) the rear wall of this little house consisted mostly of an opening through which the fireman reached his fuel, so the heat of the boiler might not have made it thoroughly

Below: *Close cooperation between the fireman and engineer was essential if the locomotive was to be run with maximum efficiency.*

First electric locomotive for a main line road, B&O, 1895, built to haul trains through a tunnel in Baltimore.

cozy in the coldest weather. Controls were located so the engineer could keep his hand on the throttle while perched on his seatbox with a clear view ahead. The fireman also had a seat on which he could rest a bit between sessions of flinging wood or coal into the firebox.

Although the 4-4-0 'American' locomotive (which, by this time, was a virtual standard for both freight and passenger service) was a simple, reliable machine, running it was no casual matter. Until the adoption of the steam injector in the 1860s, maintaining the correct water level in the boiler required expert planning; the crosshead-pumps worked only when the engine's wheels turned, so more than a short delay might involve the tedious business of uncoupling the engine from the train and running it back and forth to prevent the boiler water level from becoming dangerously low.

The degree to which an engineer might be expected to take part in major repairs to his locomotive would vary from master mechanic to master mechanic, but all adjustments between stops would be his responsibility. The general understanding was that the fireman would take care of all running maintenance above the running board — principally, wiping down the boiler jacket and the considerable amount of brass brightwork adorning the locomotive and its ornate headlight and fancy bell-bracket — while the engineer kept the machinery below lubricated and adjusted. Assigning each locomotive permanently to its own crew limited the engine's operating hours and mileage, but for 30 years or so this was considered to be the best way to insure reliability and longevity from each iron horse.

Naturally, as the driver of the only thing in the country that could move faster than a trot and haul more than a wagon load, the engineer acquired a certain cachet with people in his area, the more so since many could admire his aplomb close up from time to time as he rushed past on his lofty perch. But the engineer did need some real skills, for throughout its 120 years of dominance the steam locomotive remained a somewhat individualistic beast. The best crews could make better time, run farther

before taking water or do the job using significantly less coal.

What of the role of the man on the left-hand side of the cab — the fireman? At the peak of its demands upon a human body, when the steam locomotive had grown to a size and power fully demanding his maximum shoveling capacity (about two and one half tons per hour over any sustained period) few occupations demanded such a combination of brains and brawn. Few also could be as affected by the cooperation, or lack of it, between two co-workers. Not only did the best engineer do the job with less coal by skillful manipulation of throttle and other controls, but by helping the fireman anticipate changes in demand he could allow full boiler pressure to be maintained without blowing energy away through the safety valves.

In between shoveling enough coal to keep the white-hot firebed at a correct and even depth over an area of up to 70sq. ft, the fireman somehow had to find time between scoops to see all signals and call them out to verify the engineer's observations. With the application of mechanical stokers to all locomotives 'with more than 240,000lb weight on drivers used in fast or heavy service' (as was mandated by Federal regulation following World War I), most of the brawn was eliminated.

One occupation originating centuries before the first railroads, and that has survived through both the iron horse and diesel eras, is that of the hostler. In the days of the stage coach the hostler was responsible for taking care of the horses at inns on stage coach routes. With the coming of the iron horse he carried out similar duties — banked fires had to be tended, water had to be kept in the boilers, and tenders had to be fueled and filled during the hours between engine assigments. (Today, with most trains being pulled by a multi-unit assemblage of diesel engines, the hostler is kept busy arranging,

Below: *A local pulls into Ellicott City station, on the B&O, sometime in the late 1880s. The baggageman waits on the platform, ready to load freight for destinations down the line.*

sized station . . . The agent at a small station has a great multiplicity of duties to perform. He must sell tickets, be a good book-keeper, and a faithful switch-tender. He generally must be a telegraph-operator and must be vigorous physically. He . . . should be a peer of the businessmen of his town . . . The practical difficulties that most beset him are those incident to doing everything in a hurry. People who buy tickets wait until the train is about to start before presenting themselves at the office. Then the agent has a dozen other things to attend to . . . Just as the train reaches his station the train dispatcher's click is heard on the wires, and he must drop everything and receive a telegram in which an error of a single word would very likely involve the lives of passengers. At a very small station the checking of baggage devolves on the agent, his overburdened back being thus loaded with one more straw. He is in many cases agent for the express company, and so must count, seal, superscribe, and way-bill money packages and handle oyster-kegs and barrels of beer at a moment's notice. Women with wagon-loads of household effects to go by freight, and shippers of car-loads of cattle, for which a car must be specially fitted up, [must be dealt with] just as the . . . station-man is receiving a telegram with one side of his brain and selling a ticket with the other . . . It is not every day that a small station is enlivened by this sort of excitement, yet it is common, and is familiar to every station agent.'[1]

Note

[1] From B.B. Adams, 'The Every-Day Life of Railroad men', in *The Railways of America*, 1890.

connecting and checking out suitable loco-motive consists.)

Now, how about the occupation most affected by the maturing of railroad technology — that of the brakeman? In moving hordes of people and tons of freight over a railroad line safely, the stopping distance becomes more important than the horsepower available to get up to speed. The earliest braking systems consisted of the caboose and a series of hand brakes on the cars — plus, of course, the brakemen to wind them up when the engineer whistled to give the 'down brakes' alarm.

On passenger trains the brake wheels on the end platforms were reasonably accessible, though of course nothing prevented ice from making things dangerously slippery. But even at the modest speeds of the middle years of the nineteenth century, with perhaps only one brakeman for each two cars, a stop could be agonizingly leisurely.

On a freight train the situation was consider-ably worse; the brake wheels were located on top of the freight cars and they could be tightened effectively only by poking a hickory club through the spokes of the brake wheel to give extra purchase. The brakeman had to move from car to car via a narrow running board atop each car, leaving a gap to be jumped between cars — which might be considerably higher or lower than each other. And on grades or approaching points where a stop might be expected (a junction or crossing of another railroad, for example), the brakemen were required to 'deckorate' the cars — to tie down as many cars at once as their number, including the conductor — made possible.

'On a spring morning in the canyon scenery, when I'm enjoying the breeze and the view, I wonder why anybody would want any other job in the world,' reminisced one old western brakeman. 'Then I would remember finding a flat car in the way on a December snowstorm and climbing down with my lantern and brake club and the thought would go away.'

Complicating the brakeman's job was the lack of standardization of the type, position and security of the ladders, steps, platforms and handrails needed to reach the brake wheel and running board in the first place. Many of these items were fixed to the wooden car body with lag screws, which lost their grip if rot developed around their threads, as it often did.

With so much left to be desired with such a braking system, inventors rallied round with dozens of proposals for actuating brakes throughout a train automatically. Most of these schemes envisioned tapping the momentum of the car (created when it collided with the car ahead when the locomotive's steam brakes were suddenly applied) to tighten that car's brake shoes against its wheels; several different forms of this 'buffer brake' were built and tested, but George Westinghouse's compressed-air brake easily carried the day. His 1869 version, in which air from the locomotive's pump flowed through a pipe to push a piston on each car, worked well in short passenger trains and was quickly adopted by the more progressive lines.

It was only after a successful 1887 test of his 'automatic air brake' that air braking for long freight trains was accepted as the way forward. With the automatic brake, air is pumped from the locomotive to an airline connecting all cars

BATTLING WITH THE SNOW

Snowfighting on the railroad, even today, is a rugged, cold, tedious, and dangerous job. Keeping the line open, 24 hours a day, and irrespective of weather, is essential.

Railroads like the Union Pacific, Great Northern and others operating across the northern prairie had to face winter head-on, with sheer brute force. 'I used to spend six or seven months out of every 12 in ceaseless battle with snow' wrote E.W. Hadley in 1897. He was a superintendent on a section of mainline stretching from Minnesota through the Dakotas. It was his job to keep the railroad open despite gale-force winds, subzero temperatures, and drifts 20ft deep.

A closed railroad line made no money; by the 1880s, railroads would go to great lengths to keep traffic moving. More urgently, entire trainloads of passengers might perish if trapped for too long in a blizzard miles from civilization.

The main tools available to Hadley and his counterparts on hundreds of railroads in snow country were the 'bucker' plow, stout locomotives and strong men. A superintendent such as Hadley would select the most powerful locomotives at his disposal, with the most experienced crews. Four, six or sometimes eight locomotives would be coupled together behind a bucker

plow. Often, a second train composed of a 'pull-out' engine, commissary, and bunk cars carrying hundreds of men for shovel duty would follow closely behind. When the plow train got stuck in some massive drift, the 'pull-out' engine would come up behind and pull the stuck train loose.

The plow itself was the railroad equivalent of a battleship. Most were homemade in railroad shops and customized to suit local conditions; some were commercially built. Eastern plows tended to be anemic in comparison to western ones. They had massive frames of timber, heavy trucks — the wheel assemblies underneath — and great curving iron plow blades to the front. Most acquired supplemental iron blades for scraping the rail free of ice and plowing the snow from between the rails. None had springs; all were wretchedly uncomfortable for the crews.

Snowbucking was as simple as it was dangerous. When the train reached a drift or a small valley — called a cut — filled with snow that the locomotives simply could not push through, the bucker plow train backed up several miles, and stopped. When the conductor on the plow signaled the lead engineer to go ahead, he opened the throttle and signaled with his whistle for the engines behind him to do likewise. The idea was to

Above: *As the CP's line went through the Sierras, they had terrible problems with snow: by 1869, the CP had covered more than 30 miles of track with snowsheds like this.*

Left: *A UP snow crew digs a train out of a snow drift on 'Laramie Plain' in the 1870s. Crews were often away from home for a week or more; cases of frostbite were common.*

hit the drift with as much power as possible.

If the crew was lucky, the train would hold to the rails and momentum would carry it through the drift. If it stalled, the train would back or be pulled out and try again.

Crews who were unlucky, who misjudged the drift, or who hit ice or hidden obstructions would wreck their trains and often perish. In a few cases, bucker trains disappeared into drifts and stalled with no means of escape. Their crews died of exposure before they could be rescued. In other cases, plow trains making a run for the snow collided with other trains hidden by the blizzard or the snow cover. Snow-train duty separated real railroaders from dilettantes.

Hadley tells of bucker trains consisting of an immense Congdon plow, faced with wood and shod with steel, shoved by two of the largest locomotives of the day, racing into snow-drifts at 65mph. By having his men cut trenches in the drift beforehand, the snow boss could often ease the plow's way through the drift. Nevertheless, whenever the plow became stuck, the men still had to dig it out by hand so that it could be pulled back for another run. Crews on snow duty might be out for a week before seeing their homes again. They might spend months at work with only brief respite.

An amateur inventor finally provided the decisive weapon for this campaign against nature. Several schemes had proposed harnessing the power of the steam engine to some sort of giant auger or Archimedean screw. None had been successful. It fell to a

Canadian named Orange Jull to propose not one giant auger to be pushed into the snow, but rather two sets of giant fan blades rotating in opposite directions. The first set of blades cut or scooped the snow from the drift and flung it backward. The second set of blades caught the snow and impelled it out of a chute and to the side of the railroad.

Jull patented his contraption in 1884. After tests on the Canadian Pacific Railway near Toronto, The 'Rotary Snow Plow' went into commercial production and was a great success. The Union Pacific Railroad bought the first commercially produced rotaries, and they were made into the 1950s. Several are still in service on western railroads.

The rotary was as complex as the bucker plow was simple. Inside a wooden (later steel) housing was a boiler and machinery similar to a normal locomotive's. The cylinders drove a series of gears that powered the fans. The rotary plow pilot controlled the machine from a little compartment atop the front

Below: *A steam rotary plow on the GN about 1900. Rotaries used two sets of blades to chew through snow at a steady 6 to 8mph.*

Above: *When 'snowbucking', the engine (or engines — as many as eight would be used) and plow would back up, then take a run at the drift at high speed.*

portion, just behind the blades. An engineer and fireman made the thing run.

Its power went to the fans, so the rotary plow had to be pushed by another locomotive like any other plow. But because the rotary cut the hard snow into powder and threw it clear of the track, only one locomotive was needed to push it into drifts.

Instead of ramming impacted snow masses at high speed, the rotary patiently chewed through them at a steady 6 to 8mph. Think of a massive Cuisinart turned on its side and placed on railroad tracks: impressive, and awfully dangerous to be in front of. A January 1890 newspaper report on the progress of a Jull Excavator (a modified rotary plow devised by Jull) as it cleared a UP line to Oregon described how the machine encountered a herd of cattle trapped by the snow, 'scattering beefsteaks all over the landscape.'

Contributed by John Hankey.

in the train and stored in a tank on each car. To apply the brakes throughout the train the engineer *reduces* pressure in the train airline; a simple valve on each car then shifts, allowing air in its car's own reservoir to apply the brakes. In the 1887 version the brake on the fiftieth car would apply in two seconds. The later versions still braking today's freight trains contain several additional features speeding and smoothing brake application and release, but the fail-safe characteristic remains the same; if the train breaks in two, a hose bursts, or air is lost in any way, the train will be brought to a stop.

Westinghouse succeeded in getting the brakeman off the car tops, since the handbrake now only needed to be used to hold cars parked on sidings or in yards — or did he? For communication is another vital facet of railroading; the engine whistle allowed the engineer to call for brakes and let the crew at the rear end know when he was about to start the train, but passing the word in the other direction was another matter. On passenger trains, the conductor could ring a bell in the cab by pulling on a cord strung, car by car, throughout the train — this inelegant system was rapidly superseded, with the introduction of air braking, by providing a second air line. This second air line enabled the conductor to blow a whistle in the cab by pulling a cord in each car vestibule.

On freight trains, however, the brakeman could still only signal with flags or lanterns. The only way to pass a signal from end to end of a long drag wrapped around a curve in the woods was to have enough brakemen on top of the cars, stationed so that each one could see his neighbor. So, the roof-top running boards and ladders to reach them had to be retained until walkie-talkie radio communication became universally available in the late 1960s.

Designated the 'flagman' on passenger trains, and known as the rear or 'parlor' brakeman (because he got to ride in the caboose) in freight service, was the employee charged with the all-important responsibility for protecting his train consist from any *following* train. Whenever a train fell behind schedule, or came to a stop, the flagman had to walk back on the track far enough to provide warning of his train's presence in time for a train running at maximum authorized speed to stop short of a rear-ender. His warning devices included a red flag or lantern, fusees (red flares capable of burning for five or ten minutes, even underwater) and 'torpedoes' which, when run over, made a bang big enough to be heard over the loudest noise. When his train prepared to move, the parlor brakeman could leave a fusee and two torpedoes clamped to the rail for protection while he clambered back into the caboose.

Like so many things in life, rear-end flag protection was most unpleasant when most needed — in rain, snow and fog and on descending grades where adequate warning might require going back on the track a mile or more. Once block signaling had been introduced there was theoretically no longer any need for flagging, but the procedure was generally retained as an extra safety measure. Naturally, 'drawbar flagging' — in which the flagman chose to define an adequate distance as being a few feet from the rear coupler — was frowned upon.

As the brakemen were being brought down

Above: *A print of a brakeman of the 70s, battling to turn down the brakes in freezing conditions, captures the dangers of the job. The invention of the air brake saved many lives.*

off the running boards, what was going on in the caboose? Most noticeably, it had sprouted a cupola so the trainmen could keep a good watch over the train ahead — particularly for 'hot boxes', one of the most hazardous defects to occur to a car en route. If an axle bearing failed, the friction generated would heat the axle box enclosing it until the oil-soaked wool waste with which it was packed would burst into flames. If undetected, a few more miles of travel would so overheat the axle that it would break off, with disastrous results: the size of the resulting pile-up would be determined only by the speed of the train. Visible night or day by flame or smoke, most hot boxes could be found in time — a tell-tale pungent smell, noticeable even on the back platform of the caboose when the train was passing through a cut, also alerted the brakeman to this danger.

As freight cars increased in size, there came a time when the cupola's height was no longer much help; some roads thus substituted side bay windows located at floor level. Meanwhile, agreements with the unions meant that new amenities were steadily being provided — better bunks and heating, even refrigerators and toilets later on. And just as locomotives had ceased to be assigned to a single crew years before, so the resplendent new cabooses were now put into pool service, with only a few on the most local services still serving as living quarters, with through-run crews moving into railroad-provided quarters 'ashore' at their away-from-home terminals.

If the parlor brakeman or flagman played a vital role when the train was underway, before the train actually ventured out onto the main line its cars had to (and, indeed, still must) be assembled in order and coupled together. This was, and remains, primarily the province of the switch or yard crew. The crew's chief also came to be called the conductor but his 'field men' are still known as switchmen or 'snakes,' on account of the 'S' contained in their union's emblem. Because road brakemen also had to make many couplings, a badge of their experience was at least one missing finger. 'Wouldn't hire a man with all ten of 'em' was the remark of many a trainmaster or yardmaster. The cause of the missing fingers was the infamous 'link-and-pin' coupler.

Above: *One of the first freight trains on the Central Pacific running round Cape Horn, with all three brakemen — head, swing and parlor — ready to 'tie them down' if necessary.*

Below: *Caboose interior, about 1900. The 'rear end' crew of conductor and two brakemen lounge for the camera in their well-appointed caboose, complete with coal-fired caboose stove.*

Above: *Sheet music for the song praising the engineer's heroism.*

Far simpler than the British chain and buffer system (which used spring buffers to keep the cars apart), the link-and-pin coupling required that the single oval link be held up as the cars came together, allowing it to enter a cavity in the approaching drawhead. The pin was then dropped into a hole in the drawhead, completing the coupling. Theoretically this system was safe if the link was held up with a stick rather than the fingers; but usually, that was far too much trouble.

The universal use of such a primitive and hazardous system prompted numerous inventors to try to come up with a coupler that would allow cars to be connected without requiring a man to be between them. The most widely accepted systems were those based on a patent issued to Major Eli Janney in 1863: Janney's idea was to have a coupler with a swinging 'knuckle' that engaged its mate with a clasped-hand action, locking as a key dropped behind it. A lever extending to the side of the car unlocked the knuckle (if the slack was pushed in) to provide for uncoupling from a safe position. Installation of this coupler, which was far stronger than the old type of link, was eventually made mandatory under the federal Safety Appliance Act of 1893.

The work of a switch crew has changed relatively little over the years compared to that of the road crews; in 'flat switching,' groups ('cuts') of cars or single cars are still kicked at low speed to coast into the desired marshalling track, where they join other cars headed for the same destination. An able crew can control a car so it couples with the others on the track at less than the 4mph impact speed at which some damage to lading may occur.

Almost extinct in the yard, however, are the 'car riders' who used to accompany each cut coming off the 'hump' — in a yard in which gravity is used to roll cars into their appointed tracks. It is said that the first such hump yard went into operation in 1853; since 1924, ever more sophisticated automatic car retarders operated from a yard tower have taken over the job of making sure that each cut reaches its coupling point at a safe speed.

Communication capability within the train is one essential for efficiency with safety — even more crucial is communication with trains as they move over the line, and this has brought into being the remaining 'operating' crafts: dispatchers, operators, towermen.

Early railroads in already fairly densely populated areas such as southern New England, the

THE MOST FAMOUS RAILROADER

Who is the most famous railroader? No question, Casey Jones:

> Come, all you rounders, I want you
> to hear
> The story told of a brave engineer;
> Casey Jones was that rounder's name,
> On a high ten wheeler he rode
> to fame.

Close examination of Jones' very well-documented life and death confirms that he was, if anything, a finer and more highly skilled man than depicted in folklore. Nicknamed for his hometown of Cayce in Kentucky when he apprenticed as a telegrapher on the Mobile & Ohio, he learned Morse with amazing speed, because that was the only way to take a first step toward his real goal: driving a locomotive on the Illinois Central.

One exploit can serve to illustrate Casey's reputation with the management. At the age of 30, with only three years' 'whiskers' as an engineer, he was tapped to run shuttle trains in Chicago carrying passengers for the World's Columbian Exposition. Centerpiece of the IC's exhibit at the fair was No. 638, a 2-8-0 ranking as one of the largest and newest engines in the world and slated for service on Casey's home division in Mississippi. At his request, he was authorized to drive this gaudily decorated engine home across four intervening divisions, where it would be assigned to him and his fireman.

On what was to be his farewell trip to the promised land in 1900, Casey may indeed have misjudged the situation at Vaughan, Mississippi, brought about by a burst airhose immobilizing a freight in his path, but he did manage to brake No. 382 and its train to an impact speed well below that theoretically possible. He thus preserved intact his record of never having caused the death of any passenger.

THE ENGINE CREW

'An aristocracy of labor,' said several historians about railroad crew members. In the steam age, the most exalted of these aristocrats were the engine crew: engineer and fireman.

No tool of the trade was more important than the coal scoop (never a shovel). The fireman's skill in 'placing his shots' on the huge, roaring firebed was akin to a baseball batter's skill; without fine accuracy in maintaining an even fire, boiler pressure dropped. The firehook — to rake down lumpy spots in the coal bed or to pull out clinkers — was rarely used by top firemen.

The 'hickory stripe' style of bib overall shown here became popular in the 1920s; engine crew caps cut like the one at top-center were common, often made of leather. Engine crew members *never* wore 'uniforms.' Engine crews were a fiercely independent lot, and individualism in caps, jackets, and styles of overall was prized. Lunch boxes varied, too: an early nineteenth-century engineman or conductor might carry a small one like that shown; the box or bag soon grew larger to also accommodate overnight clothes and a virtual library of fat employees' timetables.

Crews often had to make repairs to the engine enroute, and basic mechanic's tools were essential. Signal devices included lanterns, flags, rail torpedoes (for setting an audible warning), and fusees. 'Trademark tools' of the engineer were the long-spouted oil can, for running-gear oiling, and the handful of cottonwaste for wiping up. And the broom? Good firemen kept 'a clean deck,' free of spilled coal.

1 Engineer's or fireman's cap and goggles.
2 Drinking cup.
3 Engineer's or fireman's cap.
4 Employee's Book of Operating Rules.
5 PRR (Pittsburgh Division) employee's timetable.
6 Train orders ('Form 19's').
7 Conductor's lunchbox, Cumberland Valley RR.
8 Red flag.
9 Oil can.
10 Inspection torch.
11 PRR signal lantern.
12-16 Monkey wrench; adjustable wrench (for square nuts); alligator wrench; 'S' wrench; spud wrench. All used for making adjustments and repairs enroute.
17 Double burner torch.
18 Fusees. Flares that, when lit, burned very brightly. Either held, or placed on the ground. Used as a warning device.
19 Torpedoes. Used by the brakeman or flagman to warn following trains of danger ahead. They were strapped to the rails, and exploded with a very loud bang when run over by a train's wheels.
20 Engineer's 'hickory stripe' overalls.
21 Gauntlets.
22 Cotton waste, used to clean levers and gauges.
23 Precision-made engineer's watch.
24 Tallow pot.
25, 26 Square-head hammer and coal pick.
27 Fire hook.
28, 29 Engineer's oil cans.
30 PRR scoop.
31 Signal lantern.
32 Broom for sweeping locomotive's cab.

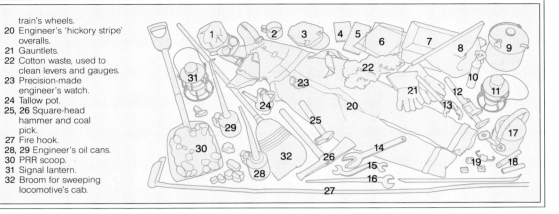

Hudson River valley and eastern Pennsylvania and New Jersey were likely to be built as double track lines in anticipation of heavy traffic (trains being both short and slow, from the early days it could be expected that carrying even modest tonnage would result in a line full of trains in each direction). Before long, however, single track became more the norm and trains could 'cross' (meet each other) only where there was a passing siding. This made a timetable necessary to establish meeting points, and these points had to be inviolate since there was no way to pass the word that a train was running late, or even not running at all.

Fortunately Samuel F.B. Morse came along to develop a telegraph system that could send words over the wire. In 1844 the message 'What Hath God Wrought?' was sent over a line between Washington, DC and Baltimore (not the first words sent by telegraph, certainly, since sections of the line were tested as completed), and by 1848 the main stem of the Erie Railroad was equipped with the telegraph, with operators handling messages at all stations.

In one of the best-documented technological breakthroughs in history, Erie Railroad Superintendent Charles Minot safely advanced his train two stations against a delayed train coming the other way by sending the first train order. In sending the order by telegraph (thus insuring that the late train would observe a new meeting point), and in then moving to a new point, Minot broke new ground: within a few

Below: *Harris Ellis, depot agent at Solway, MN, photographed sometime between 1907 and 1913. The hoop on the wall was used to pass train orders to passing trains.*

years a system of operation by timetable and telegraphic train order was in extensive use. (Minot, incidentally, had to move the train concerned himself, as the regular engineer refused to risk bending the rules.)

Ever since that time, the dispatcher has been a central figure on the railroad. Responsible for ever-lengthening segments of line as technology has changed, each dispatcher directly controls all train and work-equipment movements on his track by supplementing the scheduled authority of the timetable with train orders to accomplish the work of the day and to prevent anything happening that threatens to stem the desired

Above: *No. 8 roundhouse at Armstrong, Kansas, probably in the 1880s. The engineers pose by their lovingly polished engines with a highly proprietorial air.*

flow of traffic during his eight hours. Since the dispatcher inherits any delayed trains from the previous shift and from the other divisions or connections feeding him traffic, it has never been a job for anyone unable to handle surprises. To those crews who naturally like to feel as if theirs is the only important train on the railroad, the dispatcher is of course referred to as the 'delayer.'

From the late 1840s, right through to as recently as the 1970s, the operator or telegrapher has worked closely with the dispatcher. The 'brass pounder' (as the telegrapher was called) copied the Morse code of the dispatcher's precisely formatted orders through as many carbons as necessary to address each of the conductors and engineers whose trains would receive orders at his station. Telegraphed back to the DS, who would underline each word on his original as it was verified by the retransmission, the order could then be put into effect by completing it with the initials of the Superintendent, in whose name all orders were (and still are) issued. If an order was a 'Form 19' order permitting a train to pass his station without stopping, the operator would pass the written form to the train's engineer and conductor with an 'order hoop' as the train sped past — no job for anyone inclined to flinch.

As traffic levels and train order office locations varied, the op's job could range from being frantically busy to dangerously boring. At an isolated siding in the desert, train order activity might be the whole story, with even main-line traffic passing only at long intervals: in such a case, the op had to fight to stay awake. At the more typical small-town depot the operator had different problems to contend with. First, he was also likely to be the stationmaster, ticket agent, baggageman and express agent as well as the op. As if that wasn't enough, he would also have to act as the Western Union telegrapher, handling that company's affairs. (The Western Union had its own lines, separate from the dispatcher's wire, though carried on the same poles and crossarms.) In short, he not only had to run the depot, but also served as the

Above: *African-American Elijah McCoy, in the 1870s, improved a device used on locomotives for metered lubrication. His patented form of lubricator was preferred by engine crews.*

community's most valuable (because fastest) link with the news of the outside world. Exhaustion was the more likely problem in such situations. In any case, ability to handle the dots and dashes thrown at him by the fastest telegraph sender — requiring the development of the distinctively fast but legible handwriting style that came to be prized as the 'telegrapher's fist' — made the operator's calling worthy of

Below: *The conductor and his attendant check passengers onto a train. The conductor was in charge of the movement of the train, the welfare of passengers, and the collection of fares.*

the greatest respect from the beginning.

Part of the dispatcher's problem in anticipating delays has always been in knowing where his trains actually are as opposed to where they are supposed to be. Only as the operator actually reported a train as it left, or passed through, his station (putting it 'On Sheet' as the dispatcher logged it on his train sheet from the message) was a point on a train's progress safely determined. Since the next 'OS' point might be many, many miles away, particularly at night when some offices might be closed, the dispatcher who knew each engineer's capabilities so well that he could predict whether each train would do better, worse or as well as called for by the book in getting to a meeting point, was a jewel to be cherished.

With Alexander Graham Bell's invention at hand in the early twentieth century, train dispatching began to be transacted by telephone rather than by telegraph, although for many years thereafter fluency in the Morse code remained a requirement, because telegraph messages had a chance of getting through if the phone lines were down. The same read-back confirmation process is required for telephone dispatching; with the rate of transmission still limited by the writing speed of the operator, orders may not get through any faster, but at least train crews could now use wayside telephones to contact the dispatcher.

On lines busy enough to justify its considerable cost, the demise of the operator as the intermediary between dispatcher and train crew was predictable as soon as Centralized Traffic Control (CTC) was introduced in the late 1920s. By clearing signals and throwing switches directly from his desk, the dispatcher could

authorize train movements by signal indication, keeping track of trains' progress by OS indications fed back to his control panel. Not only were his commands transmitted almost instantaneously, the CTC machine itself contained interlocks which canceled any dispatching errors, such as clearing opposing train movements into the same track.

More than half of US mileage failed to rate CTC, however, remaining 'dark' (unsignaled) territory or being protected only by Automatic Block Signals (ABS). ABS prevented trains colliding, but train orders were still required to handle meets and passes. Train-orders and order hoops only finally passed into railroad history in the mid-1980s, though, when Direct Train Control (DTC) or Track Warrant Control (TWC) systems were developed. These allow train crews (by now mostly riding on the head end of cabooseless trains) to receive and repeat back orders by radio.

While the story about the early statute decreeing that two trains approaching a railroad crossing at grade must both stop, and that neither may proceed until the other has passed is probably purely legendary, trains were (and still are) required to stop at rail junctions unless they are protected by interlocked signals. After some false starts by various inventors, in 1856 the British company Saxby & Farmer devised an effective interlocking machine that gave greatly improved crossing protection. These machines, interlocked with the track switches, prevented setting switches and signals in conflicting routes at junctions. These devices were rapidly exported to the United States, where a multitude of interlocking towers sprang up to allow trains to roar through junctions and over crossings at track speed.

Manning these installations were the towermen, of necessity strong of arm and back — clearing a 'distant' semaphore meant moving the 1000ft or so of pipe which connected the semaphore to the 6ft lever in the machine. The levers and their locks were interconnected by means of an assembly of locking bars with dogs and tappets so arranged that all lever movements involved in setting up a route and clearing its signal must take place in the correct sequence. All opposing signals had to be at stop, all derails open (so that there was no possible advantage

in 'running a red') and all switches locked before the signal allowing passage at the speed appropriate for the curvature in the route could be cleared. Saxby & Farmer machines deserved their reputation for reliability and ruggedness — a few still remain in service, even though domestically produced electro-pneumatic power systems began to relieve the towerman's physical burden by the 1890s, and all-electric relay interlocking machines had taken over by World War II.

When the ability to control interlockings remotely over a single pair of wires was established in the late 1920s, the number of towers began to shrink drastically; towermen were kept busy by consolidating those not eliminated by CTC. Working alongside them in doing this would have been the signalmen, allocated to the Communications & Signals (C&S) department, and who were responsible for maintaining the railroads' electrical systems and for carrying out any necessary electronic engineering work.

The very nature of railroad operations has, from the earliest days, dictated that for most of the time train crews, operators and towermen must operate with no direct supervision. The result has been a quasi-military system of rules and orders interpreted and enforced, almost entirely *in absentia*, by the first echelon of supervision. For conductors it was and remains the trainmaster or yardmaster; when it comes to how the locomotive should be handled, the road foreman of engines represents the motive-power department; operators of course receive train orders from the dispatcher while handling the business of telegraphy.

None of these bosses can be present much of the time in caboose, cab or depot — the trainmaster's principal job is to arrange train schedules to move the traffic with the available motive power and crews, assuming the yardmaster will let the trains in or out of his yard. Adherence to the operating rules has to be the principal manifestation of effective supervision; the rules examiner can find out whether the trainmen know and understand them, but there

Below: *Section gang at Ponca City depot, Oklahoma, in the latter part of the 19th.C., on the Santa Fe. In the southwest, many section gangs were composed of Mexican-Americans.*

trains was involved. Nineteenth century section crews were labor-intensive and often employed 20 or 30 gruff, muscular 'Gandy dancers' to remove old crossties, replace worn rails and re-build culverts. Unlike with most other aspects of railroading, their basic tools, such as spike mauls, bolt wrenches and ballast forks, have changed little, while larger items of equipment have radically altered the craft of maintaining track. Today, only the placing of fish plates and tie plates, the bolting of sections of ribbon rail, and the grooming of the roadbed are done by hand.

1 Water can and cup.
2 Handcar.
3 Pickaxe.
4 Ballast shovel and fork.
5, 6 Spike puller bars.
7 Bolt wrench.
8 Spike maul.
9 Rail tongs.
10 Tie plates and spikes.
11 Gauge bars.
12 Crosstie and rail.
13 Rail bolts, fish plates.

Above: *A portrait of a typical small-town wheel shop. Cast-iron car wheels wore quickly and needed frequent replacement. The man at left carries an inspection hammer.*

Below: *Canadian Pacific backroom staff in 1911. Keeping accounts and checking the bills was not glamorous — but it was vital to the survival of the railroads as businesses.*

will always be somewhat of a cat-and-mouse game in finding out how well the rules are being put into practise.

From the beginning of railroading in the United States the 'non-ops' not directly involved in transportation have been in the majority, roughly in 60/40 proportion to the railroaders operating the trains themselves. Billing freight, ticketing passengers, and accounting for the

results has required about the same number of employees as those engaged in maintenance of way and those keeping the fleet of locomotives and cars in trim.

Mechanical department craftsmen include the boilermakers, blacksmiths, pipefitters, sheet-metal workers and machinists whose work is basically that of the metal-working trades in manufacturing or construction, as is that of the

carpenters and electricians. Unique to the railroad industry is the work of the carman, trained specifically to make the car inspections and minor repairs in yards and stations, overhaul and test air brake equipment and dismantle and reassemble cars in the shop. Most popularly known as 'car tonks' for whacking car wheels and listening for the dull sound that indicates a crack, the carmen are the most numerous of the equipment-maintenance craftsmen, also taking care of such diverse matters as skillfully reupholstering coach seats.

Throughout the history of railroading the shop forces of the railroads themselves have maintained a 'we can build (and, often, improve) *anything*' attitude. As technology advanced to the point where a more formal education was advantageous, railroads recruited mechanical and industrial engineering graduates. To provide a grounding in the business, however, the graduates were enrolled as special apprentices who were rotated through a year or more of assignments to the greasiest aspects of locomotive or car maintenance with no guarantee that they would progress to management positions in the organization — though most did, properly chastened, make it.

The real heroes may be the track crews. Massive as railroad track may seem to be, during most of railroad history the heaviest individual item (a standard length of rail) could be lifted and put into place by a gang of eight to ten men with no tools more sophisticated than a pair of tongs. Once the heavy earthwork in building the line had been completed by an army of contractor's men using horsedrawn scrapers,

Below: *A tower man at work, about 1900. The introduction of interlocking machines vastly improved the safety of operations at railroad junctions.*

blasting powder and shovels, the track could be maintained, renewed and even upgraded by installing superior gravel ballast and heavier steel rail — and this could all be done by a small; well-organized crew of section hands and an occasional ballast-train visit.

The resulting Maintenance of Way (M of W) organization therefore rapidly stabilized as a crew of trackmen and their foreman; this crew would be assigned to keep their four to ten mile 'section' of track in shape. Some of the work involved 'lining' the rails — shoving the rails sidewise to eliminate kinks, a matter of coordinated, all-hands pulling and leaning on lining bars — which inspired some of the best work chants and songs. Vertical irregularities were reduced by jacking the rails and tamping the ballast, a process whose bodily motions prompted the trackman to be called a 'gandy dancer.' In the wide open spaces, company housing was customarily provided for trackmen and their families, with all necessities delivered by supply train in extreme cases of isolation. Section gang foremen in turn received direction from roadmasters and their assistants.

The 'ops' personnel may have always kept the railroads in action, but equally important from the earliest days have been those agents and clerks behind the scenes: without them, there would have been no traffic to haul and no revenue to keep the railroad in business. As will be seen in the next chapter, railroad non-ops personnel not only had to devise new accounting methods and administrative systems to cope with the demands of the United States' first big business; they also recognized the importance of promoting the railroads and their services and, in a real sense, established the promotional and advertising industries that are such an ever-present part of life today. Non-ops were in the front line of the railroad revolution.

*'Great cities of importance are reached along its way . . .
We reach them by no other than the* Wabash Cannon Ball.*'*

FROM A TRADITIONAL SONG.

THE NATION'S ARTERIES

THE WORD 'REVOLUTIONARY' is overworked in contemporary conversation (and even in contemporary writing), but it is the correct term to use to describe the impact of the railroad on American society late in the nineteenth, and into the twentieth centuries. Indeed, the railroads' influence was so pervasive and America's adoption of railroad technology so eager, that it produced what justifiably can be called the 'steamcar civilization.' The railroad industry helped lay the foundations for the modern American economy, and pioneered many of the systems by which it is organized: advanced methods of finance and management; ways of regulating labor relations and competition; and it opened up new fields of operation for financiers, bankers, and speculators. The expanding network connected manufacturer and consumer and, as the services offered became more dependable, enabled inventory practise to be changed, aided in the rise of the factory system, and offered huge new opportunities for wholesalers. (Indeed, the industry also provided an impressive market in its own right.) In short, the railroad (and its ally, the telegraph) were at the center stage throughout the years when the United States was extending its agricultural frontiers to the farthest corners of the West while simultaneously undergoing a transformation that would

see it become a powerful and vibrant urban and industrial nation.

During the tumultuous years from 1865 to America's involvement in World War I, the nation's population nearly tripled, from 35,700,000 to 103,400,000. At the same time, the American rail network increased by a factor of seven — to 253,626 miles — while gross operating revenues rose spectacularly — thirteenfold, from $300 million in 1865 to approximately $4000 million in 1917. In fact, American trackage exceeded that of Europe even before the turn of the century.

In 1865, America's railroads had not been integrated; nor had they been efficient. System-atization soon followed, however. An early example of how this occurred is provided by the Vanderbilts, who skillfully stitched together a collection of roads to form the New York Central System. This reached from New York City to Chicago and eventually tapped Boston, Cincinnati, and St. Louis with main routes. The Vanderbilts typically plowed money back into plant and demanded a high degree of efficiency

from their operations. Not surprisingly, the managers of the Vanderbilt roads dutifully guarded their respective service areas against encroachment by competitors. In the so-called 'trunk line region,' only the Pennsylvania Railroad afforded any significant competition, although the Erie and a few other pretenders plied the same region.

In the west, a similar pattern emerged as the Southern Pacific forged a crescent-shaped route structure stretching from Portland through San Francisco, Los Angeles, Tucson, San Antonio and Houston to New Orleans. Led by the irrepressible Collis P. Huntington, the SP survived the Panics of 1873 and 1893 and, by 1900, encompassed an operation of over 14,000 miles. This system was particularly attractive to Edward H. Harriman, who came to control the Union Pacific — with which the SP was connected at Ogden as partner on the historic Overland Route — and Harriman successfully pursued the SP when Huntington died. 'We have bought not a railroad, but an empire,' Harriman exulted in 1901.

At first, the country's great roads constructed their primary arteries to link established cities, or to enable them to make claim to substantial undeveloped areas, which they could develop and market later. Competition on routes was cutthroat. A fleshing out process followed later, with the opening of secondary lines and branches. These were built to open up farm land, to access stands of timber, to serve mines and quarries, to outflank pretenders, to make territorial claims, or to achieve a combination of these aims.

The scope of the railroads' plans varied from the humble to the expansive. In northwest Iowa, the Milwaukee Road built a short spur simply to reach some lakes of surprising beauty in the otherwise predictable landscape of the prairies: the Milwaukee's managers had the business vision to recognize that the development of

Below: *The depot and grain elevators at Bottineau, North Dakota, circa 1917. As here, so in the rest of the US — the local economy depended on the railroads, and vice versa.*

resorts among the lakes would result in a healthy flow of lucrative passenger traffic from points near and far. In the same region, the Burlington, Cedar Rapids & Northern's promoters dreamed fruitlessly of pushing that road to the Black Hills of Dakota Territory; they had to settle instead for western termini at Watertown and Sioux Falls. In North Dakota, meanwhile, the Great Northern threw down a series of branches, resembling the teeth of a comb in pattern, all in order to hold a broad territory near the Canadian border against penetration by other railroad companies. In Oklahoma, a local road — soon to become part of the Missouri, Kansas & Texas — inched northwestward, determined to complete its grand design: a 500-mile line that would enable it to funnel locally grown wheat to mills in Texas. Farther west, the Great Northern and SP tilted for advantage in much of Oregon, while the SP and the Sante Fe wrestled to win dominance in Arizona. West Texas and New Mexico would see the final burst of railroad expansion when the Santa Fe, Rock Island, Frisco, Fort Worth & Denver, and even the tiny Quanah, Acme & Pacific sparred for new market areas during the 1920s.

The early transcontinentals had built ahead of demand, and had suffered accordingly. The Union Pacific, for example, went bankrupt in its early years. The fleshing out process, however, often occurred in response to local demands — as was the case with the evolution of Minneapolis as a flour-milling center. As the United States became industrialized, and as its economy matured, farmers responded to the nation's new wealth by increasing production. More land was put under the plow, mechanization was introduced, and entrepreneurs built

larger and more efficient processing facilities. With these developments came a corresponding requirement for additional transportation — not simply to tap newly opened farmlands, but also to move produce and other items to distant markets. Thus, Minneapolis had become the country's premier flour-milling center by 1882 in large part because its processors had access to a marvelous system of trunk railroads and allied branches. Indeed, when the Minneapolis millers realized that the Chicago-based roads threatened their business, they determined to circumvent Chicago altogether by sponsoring the construction of the Minneapolis & St. Louis and, later, of the Minneapolis, St. Paul & Sault Ste. Marie railroads.

The evolution of the steel industry was similarly dependent on the development of rail services. As late as 1867, the US produced a mere 2600 tons of steel, but that rose to 930,000 tons in 1879, and in 1901 United States Steel became America's first billion-dollar company. Steel production eventually spread to centers in Indiana, Tennessee, Alabama, and even Colorado, but the center of steel remained Pittsburgh and its environs — astride the main line of the mighty Pennsylvania Railroad and

Below: *Following the completion of the first transcontinental in 1869, the US embarked on a frenzy of railroad building; some 77,000 miles of track were placed in service in the 1880s alone and — despite a severe economic depression — 31,000 miles were added in the 90s. By 1900, the nation boasted more than 195,000 miles of railroad. The network was to reach its greatest extent in 1916, when over 250,000 miles of track were in existence.*

also served by the Baltimore & Ohio and by various smaller carriers, all of which were more or less dependent on steel traffic to earn their keep. As demand for steel grew, Pittsburgh looked afar — to ranges in Michigan, Wisconsin, and Minnesota — for high-grade ore. Rail lines were then built to gigantic docks on Lake Superior and Lake Michigan, where the ore would be shipped to the south shore of Lake Erie, for the final leg of the journey by rail to the hungry furnaces at Pittsburgh.

The story of copper was much the same. Thanks to the innovative work of Thomas Edison, George Westinghouse, and various other tinkerers and inventors, the demand for copper rocketed as the nation's homes and businesses raced to install electricity (all the cords were made of copper in those days). The problem, though, was that the domestic copper ore deposits were located far from the manufacturing plants and the urban markets — in the states (or future states) of Montana, Utah, Arizona, and New Mexico. Fortunately, rails had already been pushed through these areas by the major carriers, so it was not an overwhelming difficulty to build more track to the mines. The scenario, then, was the same: the railroad industry 'grew up' with copper, just as it did with flour milling and steel.

If the 'smokestack' industries needed railroads in order to grow and mature, so the railroads needed basic industry in turn — and not simply for the traffic they generated but also for what they produced. Steel, after all, was required for rails, locomotives, cars, even for the cutlery in the dining cars. And copper was used in signaling systems, then for telegraphs and finally for telephone wires — as well as for the wires

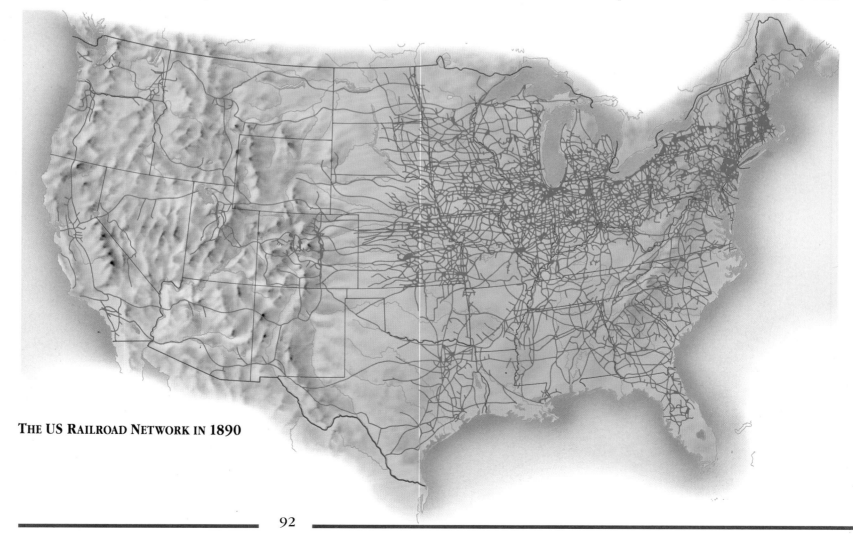

THE US RAILROAD NETWORK IN 1890

Main Slip and Dock No. 1, Conneaut Docks, Pittsburg & Conneaut Dock Co., Conneaut, O.

Hulett Automatic Unloading Machine, Conneaut Docks, Pittsburg & Conneaut Dock Co., Conneaut, O.

Ore Train, Bessemer & Lake Erie R. R.

Left: *In 1901, US Steel — who produced these photographs showing how ore was transported via ship and rail to the smelters — became the nation's first billion-dollar company.*

used to transmit electrical energy to the shops, depots and the companies' general offices. Then there were timber products — required for ties (at the rate of 3000 or more per mile), bridge piling, dimension lumber for depots and other structures, not to mention wood for constructing thousands of cars. Locomotive fuel — coal — was moved by the trainload to all points of the railroad compass. 'Fuel' for draft animals during the construction era was another essential commodity; 600,000 bushels of oats for horses were stockpiled at Minot in 1887 for the push into Montana Territory by a predecessor of the Great Northern. In short, the railroad industry was a prime consumer of materials and goods and thus, in still another major way, dominated the burgeoning American economy.

The railroad industry also became a monumental consumer of labor. Rail employment stood at 163,000 in 1870, but mushroomed to 1,018,000 in 1900 and to 1,700,000 in 1916. As the United States entered World War I, roughly four percent of the nation's gainfully employed were working in the railroad industry. Even then, this figure does not include those employed by locomotive works, car foundries, and other railroad suppliers.

Construction of rail lines reached a frenzy during the 1880s when 11,568 miles were built in 1882 alone; another 12,983 were added in 1887. For the decade, a staggering 76,733 miles of track were placed in service. As 1890 dawned, the country boasted mileage of 163,597.

Despite the Panic of 1893 — which resulted in a five-year depression of monstrous proportions — another 31,929 miles were added during the 1890s. As the new century dawned, the statistics showing the expansion of the previous decade were impressive: by comparison with 1890, there were 25 percent more locomotives in service in 1900, 32 percent greater investment in road and equipment, and passenger miles traveled had increased by 35 percent. Even more impressively, ton miles had increased by a walloping 86 percent.

The railroad was now very big business. The estimated total wealth of the United States in 1900 was $90 billion; of that total, railroad assets made up about $12.5 billion — with an even higher market value of their securities. At the same time, the total capital and surplus of all domestic banks and loan and trust companies was $1.6 billion. Only agriculture exceeded the rail industry in the amount of invested capital and in the value of annual business.

The size of America's railroad operations were also impressive on an international basis. Of the 490,000 miles of railroad in operation around the world at the beginning of the century, two-fifths was in the United States.

The vast territory of the United States in large part explains the size of the network; railroads, after all, could militate if not conquer the tyranny of distance. There may no longer have been a definable frontier line in the United States

Left: *Logging engines at work in British Columbia, around 1920. The railroads consumed vast quantities of materials.*

STEAM LOCOMOTIVE BUILDERS

There were dozens of locomotive manufacturers in the early years. In the 1850s, leading firms were Baldwin, Norris, and Rogers. Other companies included Niles, Mason, and numerous small machine shops. The Baldwin Locomotive Works in Philadelphia, begun by jeweler and abolitionist Matthias Baldwin in 1831, became the biggest such firm by 1900, constructing engines in all sizes and gauges for railroads all over the world. In 1901, eight other builders consolidated to form the American Locomotive Co. (Alco). By 1905, two more companies had joined Alco, including the Montreal Locomotive Works. Eventually, Alco's largest plant was at Schenectady, NY. Smaller independent firms, such as H.K. Porter, Lima (pronounced 'Lye-muh'), Climax, and Heisler, built small industrial engines — the latter three firms specializing in low-speed 'geared' locomotives for logging duty. Some railroads built their own locomotives, notably the Pennsylvania, the B&O, the Southern Pacific, and others. In 1916, the Lima Works changed the competitive scene. New owners took over, hired a brilliant young design engineer (William E. Woodard), and began fielding their 'Super-Power' locomotives in 1925: 2-8-4s, 2-10-4s, and — ultimately — the highest-horsepower steamers ever, the 8000hp 2-6-6-6s for the Chesapeake & Ohio. Lima also controlled some important locomotive-parts firms, such as the Superheater Company (Elesco) and Franklin Railway Supply. Upstart Lima carved out a solid niche as one of the 'Big Three' locomotive manufacturers.

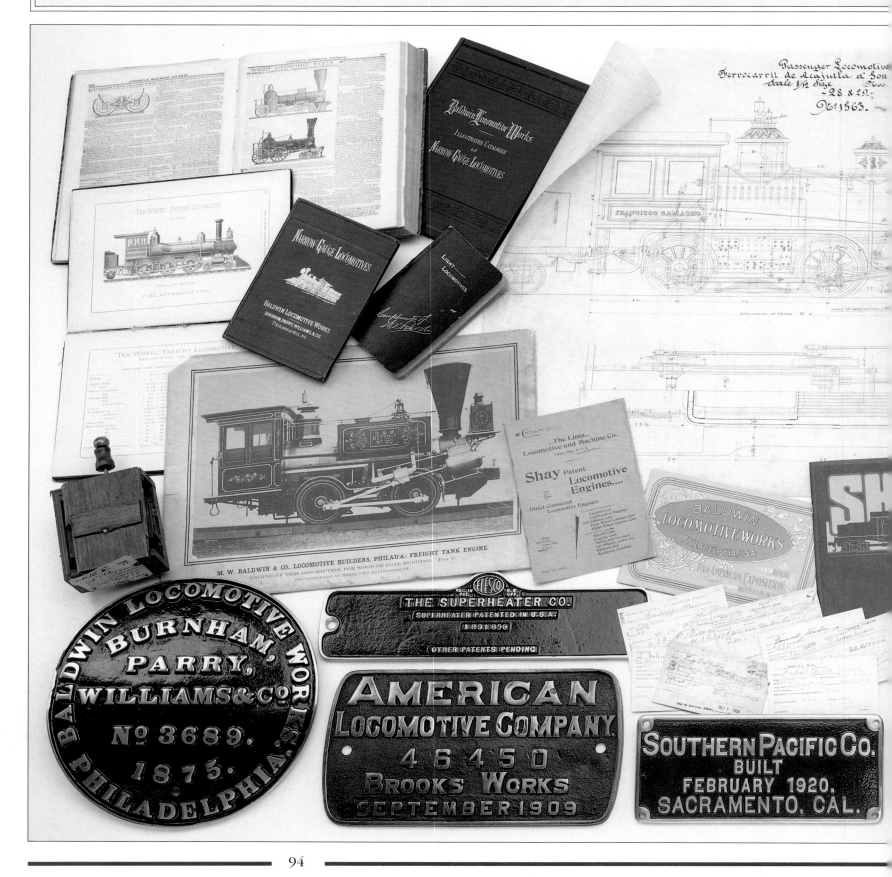

1 The *American Railroad Journal*, April 8, 1848.

2, 5, 6, 7, 9, 11, 13, 14, 19, 23, 29, 30, 31 Locomotive builder trade catalogs, 1885-1947.

3 Ink-on-linen drawing for two locomotives built for export to the Ferrocarril de Acajutla a Sonsonate (El Salvador) by Union Iron Works, San Francisco, 1881.

4 A patent model made by Samuel M. Vauclain of Baldwin to illustrate a design for cylinders and valve gear.

8 Metal paperweight model of a C&O Railroad 2-6-6-6 locomotive.

10 *Manual de la Locomotora*, published by the American Locomotive Company, 1917.

12, 15, 16, 18, 21, 25, 26 Builder plates, affixed to locomotives to show maker (or rebuilder) and date.

17 Special catalog produced by Baldwin for the Panama-Pacific Exhibition, San Francisco, 1915.

20 Employee record cards from the Southern Pacific

Railroad's Sacramento shops, 1900-1920.

22 Special catalog produced by Baldwin.

24 Patent plate produced by the Superheater Company (a firm controlled by Lima).

27 Builder photograph of Baldwin locomotive No. 30 built by Baldwin for Detroit & Mackinac Railroad.

28 Patent model made by Andrew J. Stevens in 1863 to demonstrate a design for slide valves for steam locomotives.

by 1900, but clearly there were huge chunks of the domain, particularly in the west, that remained lightly populated. These regions, especially if they had agricultural potential, attracted entrepreneurial carriers, large and small, which soon moved to lay their respective claims. Yet the sparse population of these territories meant that the carriers had to employ every ounce of their energy and ingenuity to bring about development adequate to justify the expense of construction in the first place. The trunk roads, as they had pressed westward, had long since developed sophisticated methods to persuade people to settle the lands their lines passed through. For the railroads recognized that they needed hard-working persons to open up the land and to make it productive. The Illinois Central, for example, pioneered a colonization program in the 1840s and 50s which was later adopted and perfected by the Burlington, Union Pacific, Northern Pacific, Sante Fe and others. Such carriers missed no opportunity to advertise the character of the country through which their lines passed, or were projected to pass. Neither did they miss the opportunity to craft innovative ways of bringing prospective and committed settlers to those regions. 'One man will be passed free one way,' promised the Burlington, 'with one or more cars of settlers' goods' destined for 'the land of opportunity unlimited' — which was defined, predictably, as that company's trade territory. The Missouri Pacific reminded inter-

ested settlers that along its lines were 'thousands of acres of rich agricultural land, that need only the hand of intelligent farmers to bring about their rapid development.' Even the obscure Iowa Central offered 'one fare plus two dollars for round trip' tickets to 'homeseekers' points in Iowa, Minnesota, South and North Dakota, Manitoba and the Canadian Northwest.'

Carriers typically looked to already established areas nearby as well as to the northeastern states as prime recruiting areas. Many also focused on northern and western Europe, where political and economic upheaval meant that a substantial portion of the population was living in poverty, or danger, or both. For thousands of such Europeans, the United States offered much better opportunities than the old country. The timing of the European troubles could not have been better for the railroads, and they seized the moment. For example, the Great Northern, the Northern Pacific, and the Soo Line — all three serving a broad expanse from the lakehead at Duluth/Superior to Montana — actively recruited Norwegians, Swedes, and Germans whose strong work ethic had impressed the managers of these properties.

Many people who 'went west' did so to take land and engage in farming. Many others settled

in the towns and cities that sprang up in the wake of the railroads' expansion. Townsite development was promoted by the railroad companies, by subsidiaries of those railroads, or by outsiders who usually had the tacit support of the carrier involved. Bismarck and Mandan in North Dakota were creations of the Northern Pacific and a syndicate; Gate and Knowles, Oklahoma, owed their inceptions to a subsidiary of the Wichita Falls & Northwestern; and Narcisso and Roaring Springs, Texas were established by subsidiaries of the Quanah, Acme & Pacific. Calculated efforts were made by the railroads to populate these townsite projects. 'A new town every week,' boasted Thomas A. Way, townsite agent for the Minneapolis & St. Louis in 1907, when that road opened new lines in eastern South Dakota. A new town meant an immediate need for hotels, cafes, implement dealerships, banks, and hardware stores. 'Crops excellent, farmers rich, large territory,' promised M&StL's Way. 'Will sell you a lot and guarantee results.'

The continuous campaign to 'open the country,' to 'make productive' a huge hinterland, belied powerful ties to entreports in the rear. For example, Thomas Way's M&StL was born to serve Minneapolis interests — initially flour milling but eventually a broad constituency of manufacturers, wholesalers, bankers and retailers who proudly considered themselves 'the Greatest in the Whole Northwest' and who earnestly dedicated themselves to any proposal that would expand or tighten their hold on the

Above: *The front cover of the Sears, Roebuck catalog of Spring, 1899. Whether the latest style of dress or furniture, Sears would deliver it to the remotest house by railroad within days.*

domain of Minneapolis. Railroads were worthy tools of such urban economic imperialism.

Minneapolis was merely one example of this symbiotic relationship that existed between urban centers, outlying areas, and railroads. The archetypical example was Chicago. A mere handful of souls lived outside the gates of Fort Dearborn in 1831 but, by the end of the century, Chicago's population stood at an astonishing 1.7 million — three-quarters of whom were foreign born. The Chicago experience demonstrated a curious reality: even as rural and agricultural expansion continued, the country was becoming increasingly urban and industrial.

This development was driven by the revolutionary impact of the railroads. Even before rails had reached Chicago from the east, entrepreneurs at that place had thrust iron arteries toward the Mississippi River. In amazingly short order, Chicago became the nation's — nay, the world's — rail transportation hub. The prefix 'Chicago & . . .' defined much of the national web. Indeed, roads with headquarters in Chicago — the Chicago & Alton; the Chicago & North Western; the Chicago, Burlington & Quincy; the Chicago Great Western; the Chicago, Milwaukee & St. Paul; and the Chicago, Rock Island & Pacific among others — all became premier carriers. And most of these railroad systems developed a classic hub and spoke pattern, with Chicago's primacy reflected in its position at the hub. The whole, meanwhile, reflected an integrated national economy, wedding city and hinterland to expanding national and even, increasingly, international markets.

To Chicago flowed grain, lumber and livestock — grain that had to be graded and stored, lumber that had to be dried and graded, and livestock that had to be slaughtered, packed, or dressed. Chicago, then, was a meeting-place where distant producers met distant markets through willing intermediaries — with rails providing the essential all-weather, efficient, two-way thoroughfare. City and hinterland grew together — tied together inextricably by steel.

Railroads also provided the 'glue' that bound the nation by means of a far-flung, comprehensive, and efficient postal system. Early in the railroad era mails moved aboard cars in closed pouches, but from August 28, 1864, en-route sorting of mail began between Chicago and Clinton, on the Mississippi River in Iowa, over Chicago & North Western rails. Railway Post

Below: *Hogeland, Montana. The railroads were responsible for developing many such new towns: for towns meant people, and people meant new freight and passenger business.*

Office routes soon proliferated, with hard-working government clerks handling mail aboard specifically designed cars in the consists of 'Fast Flyers' and humble locals. Even tiny hamlets benefited because non-stop 'exchanges' could be made as clerks 'kicked off' a locked pouch while a steel catcher arm on the RPO car snatched a waiting pouch from the trackside mail crane.

Letter mail was the exclusive province of the federal government, but packages and parcels were the responsibility of privately owned express companies — of which there were several early on, reduced later to just one: Railway Express. Express cars, or combination baggage and express cars, moved on passenger trains and, as with the mail service, this express service blanketed the country with a highly integrated system. In larger communities, the express companies had their own offices, but in small towns the 'depot agent' was also the express agent, and customers transacted business at the railroad office.

Railroads not only provided transportation services; they simultaneously served as the major arteries of communication. Passengers, crewmen, and even tramps moved quickly from one place to another taking news, views, and rumors with them. And newspapers from metropolitan centers reached the interior by means of the railroads' cars. But it was the trackside telegraph, with its ability to transmit any message at lightning-like speeds, that captured the fancy of the American public. Those who could read Morse code — the telegraph operators — were held in special awe not only for their particular talent but also because they were the first to know important

Below: *A Canadian National Express local freight delivery. In the US, the Railway Express Agency was able to deliver packages to almost any destination quickly and cheaply.*

SOUTH DAKOTA HOMESEEKERS'

EXCURSIONS

Via Minneapolis & St. Louis Railroad

$7 to **$10** Round Trip From Most M. & St. L. Stations in **MINNESOTA**
To Stations Conde, S. D., and West and North

$10 Round Trip From Most M. & St. L. Stations in **IOWA**
To All Stations in South Dakota

$15 Round Trip From M. & St. L. Stations in **ILLINOIS**
To All Stations in South Dakota

Tickets on Sale each Tuesday, February to November, 1926.	RETURN LIMIT 15 days in addition to date of sale.	STOPOVERS Stopovers will be permitted in both directions at all stations in South Dakota.

Your Opportunity To See The Wonderful Farm Land Bargains in South Dakota.

Descriptive Literature and Further Information on request to the Undersigned:

C. C. LAKE, Agricultural Development Agent,   W. K. ADAMS, Division Passenger Agent, Minneapolis, Minn.

J. A. LUCEY, Passenger Traffic Manager, Minneapolis, Minn.

14   15

As the railroads swept through the prairie country and across the plains toward the west coast, their promoters labored to recruit hard-working and reliable persons to open and make productive the new areas.

Both major and minor carriers created immigration and colonization departments, with each company predictably promoting its own area. 'Dakota Country,' the region that in 1889 became the states of North Dakota and South Dakota, provides an example of how the railroads went about populating an area.

In 1883, the Northern Pacific advertised 'Land for sale, ranging chiefly from $2.60-$4.00 per acre for the Best Wheat Lands! Best Farming Lands!' By 1899, the NP focused on central North Dakota where 160 acres of land could be had 'under the crop payment plan where payment is made by turning over to the owner one half of the crop each year.'

The country's second northern transcontinental, the Great Northern, in 1888 advertised its domain in Dakota and beyond as one abounding 'in pure water, an abundance of fuel, and timber along the streams.' By 1907, the GN pointed to the 'exceptional opportunities for young men,

men of energy, men of moderate means, and men of capital.' There were, GN affirmed, 'abundant openings for merchants, manufacturers, mechanics, professional men, and every man willing to work.'

The Milwaukee Road, which eventually also reached Pacific tidewater, was especially energetic in promoting South Dakota — 'The Last Best West.' Nowhere, said the Milwaukee, were 'crops more certain and markets more accessible.' Moreover, 'In no section are there better educational advantages, greater social opportunities, or more healthful climatic conditions.'

Another principal player in the area, especially during the great boom of the early 1880s, was the Chicago & North Western. '2,000,000 farms of fertile prairie lands to be had free of cost,' boomed the C&NW during those halcyon days. 'Central Dakota is now open to settlement,' C&NW enthused, because 'Indians have been removed and their reservations offered to those who wish to occupy them.' A flood of settlers followed. The C&NW's chief engineer reported in 1883 that every lumber yard had 'sold out clean' and that sidings were 'filled with boxcars in which immigrants are living.'

A bit player by comparison, the tiny

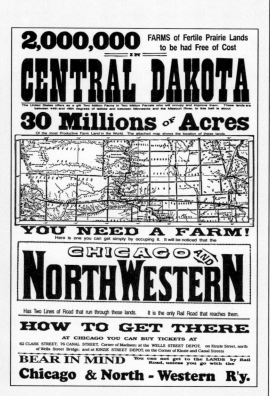

Left: *A Minneapolis & St. Louis Railroad poster of 1926 aimed at enticing potential settlers to come and view 'The Wonderful Farm Land Bargains' in South Dakota.*

Above: *Homesteaders loading their possessions onto a GN boxcar around 1910. Having opened up the land, the railroads needed such people to make it productive.*

Above: *A reproduction of a C&NW poster of 1870. Although each railroad differed in its approach, the bottom line was always the same: the promise of a new and fulfilling life.*

Minneapolis & St. Louis railroad was no less enthusiastic about the counties it served in South Dakota — 'one of the best watered and richest farming sections of the entire West.' Prosperity was assured. 'The farmers of this territory have grown rich. They have proved the character of this soil; they are all rich and contented,' said M&StL. All this development, of course, implied collateral opportunities in wayside towns. 'Fine openings for lumber yards, stores, banks, livery barns, implement houses, hardware stores and all lines of business opportunities. Come and get one,' admonished the road's energetic townsite agent enthusiastically.

Soo Line promoted North Dakota as well as Canada's Prairie Provinces. 'Get yourself a farm in the well known golden grain belt . . . This area can be as fertile as the land in Iowa which is now [in 1903] selling for $50 to $75 per acre . . . If you wish to become convinced of the possibilities of these opportunities visit this stretch along Soo Line.'

The carriers differed somewhat in their approaches. The NP and C&NW stressed agricultural advantages, the M&StL and Milwaukee pointed to the commercial possibilities, and the GN stressed the rewards that would come to those 'willing to work.' On the other hand, all the railroad companies were similarly motivated to 'settle up' the

country as quickly as possible with industrious persons who would build commerce, industry, and agriculture; who would make the virgin country blossom; who would make a rough-hewn part of the continent — much of it earlier blasphemed as the Great American Desert — a pleasant and prosperous place to live; and who would, in

the process, ship and travel by way of these very same railroads that had served up such a marvelous opportunity.

Opportunity. If there was a solitary word that the companies agreed on it was that one. And so they came in their thousands, full of optimism — lured by the railroads, and delivered aboard their cars.

Right: *A GN agricultural exhibition car of around 1910. The purpose of such cars was to prove the abudance and quality of the crops that could be grown in the area being promoted to settlers.*

THE MAKING OF THE CONSUMER SOCIETY

Prior to the completion of the first transcontinental railroad in 1869, life in rural areas and isolated communities throughout the west was hard and lonely. Farmers, ranchers or miners might hear little from the outside world for weeks on end. Obtaining machinery, equipment, and even many 'everyday' items, was difficult.

At the same time, getting western resources to markets and factories in the east and midwest involved arduous, expensive, and dangerous journeys by land or sea. Food supplies throughout the country were limited largely to what might be grown locally.

Within 50 years of the driving of the golden spike at Promontory, however, railroads had eased much of the isolation of the west. Newspapers, books and magazines from the east or Europe brought ideas and sophistication to the frontier. Pioneers were turned into consumers. Manufactured items, which once would have been considered luxuries, became readily available through catalog houses such as Sears Roebuck and Montgomery Ward. Goods were whisked by train from factory or warehouse to the customer's local freight or express office.

At the same time, the bounty of western mines, forests, and farms rolled eastward on the tracks of the Southern Pacific, Union Pacific, Atchison, Topeka & Santa Fe, Northern Pacific and Great Northern railroads. Likewise, the development of refrigerated railroad cars meant that fresh vegetables and fruit from the temperate valleys of California could grace New England tables even in the dead of winter.

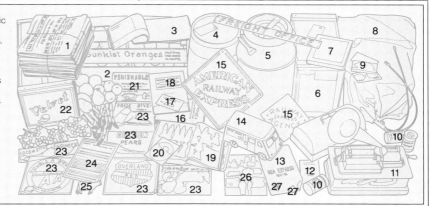

1 Copies of the *Sacramento Union*, March 24, 1918.
2 Sunkist orange crate, c.1920.
3 Virginia & Truckee freight dispatch log, with freight waybill, 1914.
4 Wooden keg, c.1910.
5 Milk can, c.1920.
6 Standard Oil crate, with labels.
7 Official Directory of SP Lines for 1897-8.
8 US Mail bag, early 20th.C.
9 Postcards from 1909 and 1901.

10 Cylindrical sound recordings, c.1910.
11 Edison phonograph, c.1910.
12 Union Pacific Express: information booklet on freight handling for conductors, 1944.
13 REA bag for carrying valuables.
14 Metal toy REA truck, late 1930s.
15 Express agency signs, hung outside offices.
16 Jeffrey Manufacturing Company Catalog, 1922.
17 Card advertising electric interurban freight service.

18 Baker, Hamilton & Pacific hardware catalog.
19 Facsimile of 1902 Sears, Roebuck catalog.
20 SP booklet promoting California fruit, 1908.
21 Perishable commodities notice for fruit car. .
22 'Velvet'-brand fruit crate.
23 Authentic fruit crate labels of 1920s.
24 CP freight rail tariff, 1876.
25 Enamel cow, used to promote milk.
26 Flyer promoting UP freight service, 1930s.
27 REA employee badges.

news. As with the express business, at first there were many telegraph companies in operation, but over time these fell by the wayside, leaving the field to Western Union. Again like the express companies, the telegraph companies maintained special offices in larger centers but relied on 'depot agents' in smaller places to 'send' and 'copy' messages.

It was to such telegraph offices that traveling salesmen — 'knights of the grip' — repaired to send the orders they had taken during the day. The evolution of railroads and telegraphy, metropolitan centers and outlying areas, and wholesaling the jobbing collectively provide an important case study of symbiosis. Typically, the salesman put out from his point of origin on a Monday morning and stopped off at a wayside place with his sample cases to contact prospective customers. Orders in hand, the salesman returned to the depot where he 'wired' them to his employer, bought a ticket to the 'next stop,' and (with his trunks safely deposited in the baggage car ahead) 'dusted the cushions' of the 'smoker.' Meanwhile, orders received, his firm dispatched goods that evening or next day by express or by freight in Less-than-Carload Lots (LCL), perhaps on 'trap' or 'package' cars that were routinely attached to local freights.

That pattern was substantially altered after 1912 when federal legislation allowed the Post Office Department to start up a domestic parcel post service — to handle packages in (subsidized) competition with express companies.

Below: *Freight cars for 'dry goods': an evolution. Left to right, top: Two wooden boxcars, 1857 and 1895, and a Pullman-Standard PS-1 steel boxcar, 1947. Left to right, bottom: Three hopper cars for coal, 1860, 1880 and 1897. Center: Covered-hopper car for grain or dry chemicals, this innovative one built of aluminum, 1965.*

This clearly benefited those firms engaged in 'direct mail' sales — firms which were to take increasing amounts of business from local merchants, and thus from jobbers represented by traveling salesmen. Sears, Roebuck & Company was an early direct mail company. Ironically, Richard W. Sears had originally been a railroad agent for the Minneapolis & St. Louis at North Redwood, Minnesota. In 1886, a jeweler at North Redwood refused a shipment of watches and Sears, instead of simply returning the parcel to the Chicago wholesale house from whence it had come, decided to buy the watches and sell them himself. Soon he was ordering more. By the end of the year, he decided to quit railroading and in 1887 he moved to Chicago where, with Alvah C. Roebuck, he laid the foundation of the famous company bearing their names. Sears & Roebuck catalogs offered just about every product imaginable, ranging from corsets to kerosene lamps. Orders came from near and far — a pattern accelerated by the institution of the parcel post.

The demand for rail services of all types grew exponentially as the nation's population increased and as its economy matured. In cities and even in larger towns, streetcar lines provided rapid transit. An elevated rail system was built in New York as early as 1867, but subways, such as that begun in Boston in 1897, awaited advances in electrical engineering. Those advances would also have important applications for street railways and would give birth to a new phenomenon — electrically powered intercity railroads or 'interurbans.' Beginning in 1889 with a seven-mile rural trolley line in Ohio, interurban mileage grew to a nationwide total of over 1500 miles a decade later. In 1916, the peak year, 15,580 miles of interurban railroad were in service across the country.

Railroads were not only agents of change; they also symbolized the changing nature of America itself. Many Americans celebrated these changes, seeing them as evidence of 'progress;' others saw the infrastructure of the new industrial giant as an abomination on the landscape. Certainly, by the turn of the century the United States was far from being the rural agrarian republic, populated with small farmers and shopkeepers, that Thomas Jefferson had dreamed about. It was, instead, a centralized urban and industrial state in which the builders, financiers, and operators of industry — especially the railroad industry — were perceived as villains, or at least as potential villains, by many if not most users and customers. Moreover, a majority of Americans early in the twentieth century had come to fear the power (or potential power) that had accumulated in the hands of a few. This was to lead to the testing of a traditional American value: the right of unfettered competition to operate according to the spirit of laissez-faire economics.

The fabled story of Cornelius Vanderbilt illustrates the point. Born to humble parents in 1794, Vanderbilt was worth $100 million when he died in 1877. He was the personification of the American dream — he achieved success by making the most of his talent, through single-minded determination, and, in doing so, seemed to prove that the United States was a land of unequaled opportunity for those who followed Horatio Alger's prescriptions. Yet, in forging the powerful New York Central system, Vanderbilt placed himself in an immensely powerful position throughout the great trunk road territory. And when his sons, William and Cornelius, as well as those who followed them, increased the power of the so-called Vanderbilt Roads still further, the situation struck fear in those who saw monopoly as the only end result of unrestrained competition — of 'survival of the fittest.' Elsewhere, the diligent work of Edward H. Harriman and James J. Hill to carve out efficiently run transportation dominions further alienated public sympathy. So, too, did creation of United States Steel, the country's first billion-dollar corporation, in 1901.

Below: *Unloading bananas from refrigerator cars in 1910 — supervized by a policeman (left) and two inspectors.*

THE PACIFIC FRUIT EXPRESS

The development of a large and profitable fresh fruit and vegetable industry in Oregon, California, and later in Arizona, hinged on the rapid evolution of the country's rail net. Interstate shipments of produce from California began in 1869 but amounted to a mere 33 tons. Nine years later the Southern Pacific convinced the Union Pacific and its eastern connections to handle not more than two cars of California fruit per day on passenger trains bound for New York City. Then, on June 24, 1886, the SP dispatched the first special fruit train from Sacramento; in the same year Boston received its first carload of California fruit.

As volume grew, so did the need for sophisticated equipment. Boxcars were replaced by ventilator cars, which were then replaced by refrigerator cars.

To promote sales of California citrus, the SP joined with the California Fruit Growers' Exchange in an advertising campaign in which each party paid an equal share. The two found other ways to assist each other. An experimental marketing campaign focused on the state of Iowa. 'Oranges for Health — California for Wealth' was the wisdom spread throughout that state before specially bannered trains arrived there with Sunkist lemons and oranges. Each train was accompanied by a messenger who, upon arrival at scheduled locations, had the news telegraphed ahead. A 50 percent increase in sales was the result for the growers, and a fine increase in traffic was the SP's reward. The promise of continuing and expanding demand was reward for both.

Production and consumption of western produce leaped. By 1916 over one billion oranges were shipped annually from California. Citrus, however, was not the only commodity rolling east to hungry markets. Strawberries, peaches, watermelons, apples, potatoes, pears, apricots, grapes, figs, cherries, onions, asparagus, and cantaloupe joined the parade — often in special trains. The rates were reasonable: $1 to $1.15 per hundredweight to Chicago, slightly more to the east coast.

To handle the mushrooming business in perishables more expeditiously, the SP joined the UP on an equal basis in forming the Pacific Fruit Express. PFE commenced operation on October 1, 1907, with a fleet of 6600 new refrigerator cars. PFE was charged with the responsibility for operating and maintaining cars and services for shippers on both roads. Although owned and operated in equal shares by SP and UP, PFE loadings were made mostly on the SP and then moved eastward to Ogden, Utah for forwarding by UP. Business was good. PFE handled 70,000 carloads of Pacific Coast perishables in 1913 alone. Four years later it was, sometimes, billing 300 cars daily.

THE BROTHERHOODS

In May of 1863, a small group of Michigan Central Railroad locomotive engineers established the Brotherhood of the Footboard, North America's first railroad union. Later known as the Brotherhood of Locomotive Engineers, the organization spread to railroads throughout the United States and Canada. Other unions based on occupation followed the B.L. of E., among them the Brotherhood of Locomotive Firemen, Brotherhood of Locomotive Firemen and Enginemen, Order of Railway Conductors and Brotherhood of Railroad Brakemen (later the Brotherhood of Railroad Trainmen). In addition to representing their members in disputes with the companies, they offered insurance and burial benefits. Ladies' auxiliaries were formed, and social activities became important aspects of membership in all of the brotherhoods.

In 1893, the dynamic labor leader Eugene V. Debs sought to create an association which would encompass all railroad employees, but his American Railway Union soon fell apart.

Eventually, most railroad workers attained representation through the craft and industrial unions of the American Federation of Labor. In 1922, its Railway Employees Department organized America's first truly national rail strike. Under the leadership of A. Philip Randolph, meanwhile, the Brotherhood of Sleeping Car Porters — composed almost entirely of African-Americans who worked for the Pullman Company — was formed in 1925. The story of the key role it came to play in national life is related in Chapter 6.

1 Minute book for July, 1894 meeting, Brotherhood of Locomotive Engineers, Sacramento Division. The meeting discussed the Pullman strike. A gavel (26) was used to call order at meetings.

2 Union 'blackball' box. A black ball dropped in the box was sufficient to deny somebody membership.

3, 4, 5 Union magazines from different periods.

6 SP 'blacklist book', for the period 1887-92.

7, 8 SP Division Superintendent's passes, issued to a newsboy to allow him to pass through the military lines during the Pullman strike.

9 A letter from the SP General Manager giving instructions about how to report damage to SP property during the 1894 Pullman strike.

10-14 Union constitution and rule books.

15 Brotherhood of Locomotive Firemen and Enginemen's Magazine, 1912.

16, 17 Brotherhood traveling cards, 1936 and 1898.

18 American Railway Union membership card, 1894-5.

19-23 Dance programs/ tickets, various annual brotherhood balls.

24 China made for the Ladies' Guild of the BLFE.

25-27 Membership and convention badges. All date from the late 19th.C.

28 Metal sign announcing union meetings.

29 Brotherhood lapel pins, buttons, and badges.

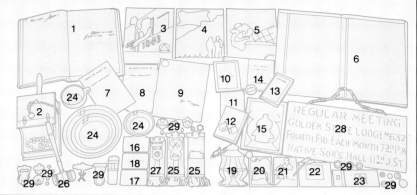

Early manifestation of public unrest came from the interior and reflected confusion as to the ultimate purposes of railroads. Farmers and small merchants hoped they would be providers of all-weather, reliable, low-cost transportation. Owners and managers, however, perceived railroads plainly as profitmaking ventures. A collision was not long in coming. Legislatures soon heard charges of discrimination and ruinous rates based on 'all that traffic will bear' and, beginning with Massachusetts in 1869, states set up regulatory agencies with varying degrees of power and oversight responsibility. The movement against laissez-faire was especially pronounced in the upper-Midwest where organized farmers, the Patrons of Husbandry or 'Grangers,' urged the introduction of legislation to limit maximum interstate rates. But most commerce flowed across state lines and thus was the province of the federal government. Grassroots forces soon focused on Washington, DC where, on February 4, 1887, a reluctant Congress passed, and President Grover Cleveland signed, legislation creating the Interstate Commerce Commission (ICC).

The Interstate Commerce Commission Act, however, seemed to be a toothless tiger with railroad companies prevailing in most litigation. Further campaigns to throttle carriers followed. The Elkins Act (1903) was designed to attack the practice of rebating (or 'kickbacks') and provided penalties for such; the Hepburn Act (1906) placed express companies and sleeping car companies under regulation, forbade issuance of free passes except for clergy, rail employees, and charity cases, and empowered the commission to set 'just and reasonable' maximum rates; the Mann-Elkins Act (1910) gave the ICC the right to change rail rates on its own initiative and to suspend rates proposed by carriers for up to ten months; and the Adamson Act (1916) gave railroad labor the eight-hour day.

Given that the railroads were the nation's first big industry, it is not surprising that they

Above: *'The Senatorial Round-House', an 1886 cartoon by Thomas Nast for* Harper's Weekly, *ridicules the Congressional railroad lobbies and their fight against Federal legislation.*

provided the setting for the first great industrial union movement. Initially, this movement only involved the operating crafts, which bound themselves into individual benevolent and protective societies — the Brotherhood of Locomotive Engineers, the Order of Railroad Conductors, the Brotherhood of Railroad Trainmen, and so on. The impetus to form such societies sprang from the dangerous nature of railroad work, and the insurance industry's determination not to sell life insurance policies to those employed in it. Thus the 'brothers' paid premiums and not dues. But these were not the

Below: *A mixed freight on the narrow-gauge Denver & Rio Grande around 1900: narrow-gauge operations proved very vulnerable to competition from trucks.*

only reasons: for, as the industry expanded, and as trains grew in length and tonnage, so the workers lost their individual identities among what became a huge pool of employees — which now had to be managed by means of a military-style organizational structure, with the railroad managers ('officers' of the company) overseeing 'the men.' Workers also complained of the long hours that had to be worked, with no overtime compensation; of the ever-present dangers of the job (and the low priority given to safe practice); of work cycles that reflected business cycles; and of the lack of any job protection.

The Great Railroad Strike of 1877 was not only the first great American industrial strike; it was also characterized by monumental violence. Public sympathy for the workers faded as it was to do over the course of the Pullman Strike of the 1890s. Meanwhile, the Brotherhoods began to amalgamate to form unions, the success of which flowered as the public became ever more willing to vote for legislation that would regulate the carriers.

The very railroads which had sparked such incredible changes in the fabric of American society were themselves to become, ironically, more and more the victims of change. The railroad industry was the first to be regulated collectively (and, as it unfortunately transpired, the first to be over-regulated, too). The labor movement also grew in power to challenge — and in some cases stymie — managerial prerogative, flexibility, and initiative.

The railroads had to come to terms with additional new realities. By 1900, the railway network covered the country, with only isolated pockets remaining for potential growth. Construction remained brisk in the first decade of the twentieth century — aggregating 47,093 miles — but in the second decade a mere 12,406 miles of new track were placed in service. There simply was little need to expand route miles much further. If demand required it, capacity

was added to primary corridors by double-tracking or triple-tracking.

Yet another change of profound proportions was the end of the era of heroic entrepreneurship. In the period following the Civil War and lasting into the next century, roads increasingly were clustered under the leadership of men such as the Vanderbilts (the New York Central and the Chicago & North Western), J.P. Morgan (the Southern & the Erie), James J. Hill (the Great Northern, the Northern Pacific, and the Chicago, Burlington & Quincy), and E.H. Harriman (the Illinois Central, the Union Pacific, and the Southern Pacific). But Harriman died in 1909, and Hill in 1916; and with them passed the era. Faceless bankers and professional managers were to take over, and they were often inadequate replacements.

The greatest change facing the railroads, however, was competition from other forms of transport. Completion of the Panama Canal in 1914 and growing public sympathy for government-funded improvements of inland water-

Above: *Boulder Creek, CA, depot staff (Agent Joe Aram second from right) with their specially decorated railcar, ready for the forthcoming parade to raise money for the war effort.*

ways cut into the intercity freight business while bicycles and interurbans took many short-haul passengers. But it was the evolution of the motor vehicle — automobiles, trucks, and buses — that provided the great competitive threat to the financial well-being of the country's railroads.

Ironically, many railroad managers supported the 'Good Roads Movement,' seeing in vehicular transport a means to effect an efficient intermodal hub-and-spoke system by which automobiles, trucks, and buses moved passengers and small freight to and from long-haul rail lines. They did not foresee that Americans would

Below: *USRA officials with Mikado 2-8-2s in 1918. The first ('Light') Mikado, a narrow-gauge type, was built for export to Japan. Many of the standard-gauge type were built for use in the US.*

develop a passionate love affair with the automobile. And they absolutely failed to understand the potential of trucks as competitive weapons. In any event, the new trend gathered pace and strength as states authorized tax-supported roadways and even trunk routes and, more importantly, when the federal government pledged itself to a national network of 'US highways' in 1916. Railroad owners and managers could grouse that various levels of government were aiding a campaign of unfair competition, but the impact of motor vehicles on the nation's carriers was not immediate. In fact, intercity travel by auto was negligible before 1920. Nevertheless, railroads before that time did note the impact of autos on short-haul traffic — the giant SP as early as 1914, and the tiny Minneapolis & St. Louis in 1916. What would happen in the future was clear to see for anybody who cared to analyze the incredible increases in the domestic production of automobiles: 4192 in 1900; 181,000 in 1910; and 1,905, 560 in 1920. Total production for the two decades amounted to 10,755,376. More ominous by far, insofar as the potential challenge to the railroads' revenues was concerned, was the domestic production of trucks — 841,396 — in the first 20 years of the new century.

As the United States entered World War I in 1917, railroad managers and owners had every reason to be nervous about the future of the industry. Revenues attendant to domestic as well as war activity were sure to be high, but against that hopeful sign loomed great difficulties — a hostile President in the White House, the heavy hand of regulation, militant unions, and burdensome competition. Matters were only to get worse. The huge amount of war traffic — plus war-clogged and inadequate port facilities on the east coast — resulted in an overwhelming congestion that stalled movement even in the interior, and created an artificial railcar shortage. At the end of 1917 the government responded by taking control of the nation's carriers,

ostensibly to provide overall direction. This action may or may not have been justified. Certainly, reviews of the United States Railroad Administration (USRA) and its director, William McAdoo, remain mixed. Duplicated services were rightly trimmed, but government-granted wage increases meant that labor costs, which ate up just 40 cents of every revenue dollar earned in 1917, were to swallow 55 cents of every dollar earned by 1920. Increases in government-authorized freight rates and passenger fares failed miserably to keep up with rising costs. In the end, the period of government operation may have been satisfactory from an operational point of view, but it was disastrous from a financial perspective. And owners and managers feared worse. By law, the carriers were to be returned to the proper owners within 21 months following the end of hostilities, but during and after the War, four big Brotherhoods aggressively agitated for the federal government to purchase the nation's railroads and manage them with a 15-man board made up equally of government bureaucrats, rail labor, and rail

managament. There was, after all, such a model readily at hand — the Canadian National Railway Company, a Crown Corporation owned by the people of Canada through the Canadian government.

There was much in the Canadian railroad experience that was similar to that of the United States. There was also much that differed. Canadians, like their cousins south of the border, saw in steam locomotives a means to overcome the tyranny of distance and 'conquer the continent' through reliable, all-weather, efficient transportation. But Canadians were much more willing to temper the tenets of laissez-faire economics than their American neighbors. Government thus typically played a greater role in Canada's rail history.

It was not possible, however, to disconnect events in Canada from developments to the south. Indeed, as discussed in Chapter 1, much of Canada's early strategy corresponded with the aims of entrepreneurs in Portland, Maine, and Boston, Massachusetts, who dreamed of roads linking those east coast American ports with the interior of the continent by way of Canada. But here again, if private British investors provided much of the finance for the resulting Grand Trunk, the road also benefited from government largesse. Canadians took the position that their circumstances were different from those prevailing in the US — that private enterprise was inadequate and thus government assistance was essential because Canada's distances were so great, its population so sparse, its other commitments so heavy, and its possessions so poorly integrated.

The Grand Trunk may have been the godfather of Canadian railroads but it was hardly the only contender for that title. There was an abundance of competition in eastern Canada, and once the Canadian Pacific had completed

its fabled route to the Pacific in 1885, the CP itself invaded the Grand Trunk's heartland. Retaliation followed as the Grand Trunk looked westward in turn, but presently another upstart was to appear — the Canadian Northern, which promised to make itself a serious candidate in the Canadian railroad stakes.

Canada treated herself to a splendid orgy of construction throughout much of the late nineteenth century and well into the next. Was there any justification for such a massive expansion of the rail network, given the lack of demand for it? Not likely. After all, the country still suffered from the handicaps of great distances, difficult terrain, harsh climes, and sparse population. Yet a range of many powerful forces — from bankers and promoters, to the government, and the Canadian people themselves — were passionately committed to railroads both as a means of transport and as instruments of social policy.

An outsized financial embarrassment was the predictable result of this passion. Plainly stated, Canada soon had more transportation capacity than it could support. Early in the century, Canada had a population of just over six million people, meaning that the Dominion could boast one mile of railroad for every 185 citizens. (By comparison, the United States at the time had one mile of railroad for every 400 persons.) Strikes, crop failures, the Panic of 1907, and obdurate government decisions regarding rates added to the sour stew. Financial failure for much of the Canadian mileage was followed by a rancorous national debate and mutual finger-pointing. In the end, on June 6, 1919, the government established the Canadian National Railway Company. Eventually, the entire Grand Trunk and Canadian Northern systems (as well as sundry other roads) were to come under CN's auspices. Bold was the aim of the new

enterprise: to consolidate these several roads and operate them as a publicly owned national system. Conspicuous by its absence from this family was the CP, which remained a Canada-wide, investor-owned system. The ensuing years would see the government-owned CN in head-to-head competition with the privately held CP.

The heated debate in the United States over the railroad question would not yield a similar pattern. Some elements of American society continued to urge outright ownership of the railroads by the federal government. USRA Director General McAdoo himself suggested five years of government control following the end of hostilities, and the Hearst and other major newspapers began to beat the same drum. Meanwhile, a consensus among owners and managers gradually took shape: railroads should not seek to escape regulation in matters demanded by the public but should, instead, attempt to bring about a more orderly system. The Esch-Cummins or Transportation Act of 1920 fell short of that, but at least the roads were returned to their owners as of March 1, 1920.

Esch-Cummins greatly increased the power and scope of the ICC Act. It also appeared to recognize new realities. For example, the new law directed the Commission to prepare a plan anticipating the consolidation of the nation's carriers into a limited number of systems. And, insofar as rail transportation was concerned, Esch-Cummins seemed to set aside covenants of the Sherman Antitrust Act of 1890 which mirrored a primary American value — unrestricted competition as the life of trade.

Owners and managers in 1920 faced a curiously fluid future. The past offered little guidance. Yes, railroads had transformed the United States into a mighty industrial and agricultural giant — as if by a mere wave of a magician's wand, as Ralph Waldo Emerson had observed. Rails had become, and for the most part they remained, the dynamic force defining American life. They were the glue binding the nation together; their great urban passenger stations seemed as temples where Americans worshipped sacred values — progress, prosperity, success. The population had increased by 68 percent between 1890 and 1920, but during the same period passenger miles per person had leapt by 138 percent, and ton miles per person skyrocketed by 223 percent. It all reflected the vibrancy of the American economy and the rails' centrality in that economy.

Yet that centrality was clearly under assault. Competitive forces — highway, water, and even air — were already nibbling the edges of the carriers' financial pie. Furthermore, some roads were overcapitalized in terms of traffic potential; other roads were captive to single industries or commodities or to the vicissitudes of nature. Owners and managers, if not the general public, eventually recognized a truth: the country had too many route miles. This became an even greater burden as competition increased, as labor consolidated its gains, as labor and government regulators stripped management prerogative, and as owners, managers, labor, and regulators collectively slipped into a counterproductive 'this is the way we have always done it' mentality.

Railroaders in 1920 could look backward with pride of accomplishment, but forward only with a profound uncertainty.

Above: *The care and attention to detail lavished on the front and towers (below) of the Southern Railways' Atlanta Terminal Station, built in 1910, symbolise the wealth, and confidence, of the railroads at the beginning of what would be their golden age. The architects clearly did not envisage that the building would be demolished within some 60 years.*

"The rails go westward in the dark . . . Have you seen starlight on the rails?
Have you heard the thunder of the fast express?"

THOMAS WOLFE

A GOLDEN AGE

DURING THE FIRST THREE DECADES of the twentieth century the North American railroad network reached its greatest extent; the last links in the system were placed in position; and the railroad's central place in the public consciousness, as a symbol of the new wealth and industrial might of the nation, was assured.

It was also during this period that the visible elements of the American railroad system — locomotives, cars, tracks, stations, signals, grade crossings — were developed throughout the continent to the extent that in the 1920s the term

'Standard Railroad' was coined; this indicated that what would have been regarded as a sophisticated level of development in an earlier period was to be regarded as the norm. Indeed, the Pennsylvania Railroad, busiest of the US systems, came to advertise itself as 'The Standard Railroad of the World,' even though few other lines chose (or could afford) to adopt all of the Pennsy's often unique locomotive, car, signal or right-of-way practises.

Although during this period passenger service continued to represent only a fraction of the railroad's gross revenues — and, at best, a

smaller proportion of its net income — it was the crack passenger train that was advertised and maintained as the symbol of any Class 1 railroad's overall capabilities and competitiveness. The care lavished on these 'Limiteds' has caused the era to be remembered as a golden age of railroading.

Perhaps the story should start with George H. Daniels, reportedly a patent-medicine salesman who, just before the turn of the century, brought his promotional talents to the New York Central as its general passenger agent in time to make a splash in anticipation of traffic to

You could even travel over the sea by railroad in the 20s! Here, the Havana Special *of Henry Flagler's Florida East Coast Railway pauses on the Long Key viaduct about 1932. The viaduct was built in 1908, and abandoned in 1935, after a hurricane blew parts of it away.*

Chicago for the World Columbian Exposition of 1893. A pair of impractically high-wheeled 4-4-0s ran miles on a slight downgrade west of Batavia, NY in 35 and 32 seconds respectively (about 112 mph) with light *Empire State Express* trains; Engine No. 999 (actually the slower of the two) became the most famous locomotive in the world. The more significant result of Daniels' superb piece of promotion was the designation of a 20-hour (48mph average) New York-Chicago train put in service in 1902 as the *Twentieth Century Limited,* a name destined to become the most widely recognized in the world and considerably more striking than that of the rival PRR's *Pennsylvania Special.*

Why such emphasis on service and speed on a competitive run? During the standard rail-roading era, people made most long-distance journeys for business purposes. For such clients, sleeping-car comfort was easily affordable; and for businessmen each hour clipped off a long overnight trip represented an additional hour at the destination — an hour that could be used to close the deal. After the Interstate Commerce Commission (ICC) took control over passenger fares, no price competition was allowed between any two points, the fare being based upon the mileage of the shortest line. Business could only be won, therefore, by offering a superlatively fast train; and then by persuading potential travelers, through advertising, that your railroad offered the most luxurious, most attentive service.

Between the nation's two largest cities — New York and Chicago — the New York Central and the Pennsylvania competed directly against each other, with the Central advertising itself as 'The Water Level Route — You Can Sleep' — implying that the quality of ride on the rival Pennsy's trains must be rougher as their locomotives were battling their way up and down the Alleghenies. The Pennsy's route was 52 miles shorter and so its trains had no problem catching up after cresting the mountains, but they did have the serious handicap of starting from Jersey City, a ferry ride away from Manhattan and NYC's Grand Central Terminal. (Passing through Philadelphia, however, the Pennsy tapped a considerably bigger population base.)

At about the time the *Century* went into service in 1902 another event in Manhattan was the trigger for events of much broader overall significance to passenger train technology throughout the continent. Smoke from a train in the tunnel leading to Grand Central (an earlier version of that terminal) obscured a signal, causing a collision in which 15 were killed; the city then directed that all trains on the island would have to be electrically propelled, accelerating the process of developing an electric locomotive capable of hauling mainline trains.

The Pennsylvania, which had been debating whether to reach Manhattan by a bridge or

Pennsylvania Railroad K4-class 4-6-2 'Pacific' type, 1914-1928.

The Pennsy K4 was one of the most famous steam locomotives ever, with 425 constructed; CNJ No. 1000 — built by American Locomotive Co., General Electric, and Ingersoll-Rand — began the diesel revolution; the 4-8-4 'Northern' type became a standard passenger and freight engine on many railroads; the NYC 'Hudson' was the pinnacle of purely passenger design.

tunnels under the Hudson, promptly selected the subterranean route, with electrification continuing to Long Island and coach yards through tunnels shared with the commuter railroad. In accordance with standards already governing the equipment on the subways then entering service, no wooden cars would be allowed in the tunnels.

For the Pennsy the result was a crash program to develop designs and manufacturing capacity for steel coaches; the Pullman Company faced a similar deadline. After various false starts in steel car designs (which resulted variously in cars that were either overweight, or freezing cold in winter and frying hot in summer), a 'standard' carbody emerged. Although the Pullman designers at first declared exposed rivet heads aesthetically unacceptable and sheathed their early steel cars with sheetmetal siding imitating the grooved surface of their wooden predecessors, their sleeping-car design of 1915 essentially became the standard for all passenger cars and remained so for the next 15 years.

Frequently referred to as 'battleships,' the sleepers weighed 70 to 80 tons. Their six-wheel, all-steel trucks (at 11 tons each) and heavy underframes (at about 20 tons) represented half

Right: *Steam and speed: Ted Rose's painting* View from the Bridge *captures the sense of what it was like to watch a GN passenger express leaving Seattle, WA, in the late 20s.*

Central Railroad of New Jersey No. 1000, first commercially successful diesel-electric, 1924.

Northern Pacific A-class 4-8-4
'Northern' type, 1927-1943.

of the total; a wooden car of about the same 80ft
length with reinforced end bulkheads of similar
strength would weigh 15 tons less.

To make them fireproof, car interiors in the
new steel fleets were almost entirely constructed
of metal; the ornate Victorian interiors with their
carved wood trim and heavy draperies were out
of style in the new century, although walls and
upper-berth fairings were initially grained to
imitate inlaid wood. In due course reasonably
satisfactory insulating materials were developed,
allowing the steam heat systems to keep the cars
at least as warm in winter as their wooden
predecessors had been.

One thing that changed little during the
wood-to-steel transition was the sleeping-car
interior. The '12-1' was the typical configuration:
each car consisted of 12 open sections (each
with a pair of facing seats which could be 'made
down' into upper and lower curtained berths
for night travel), and one drawing room with its
own enclosed washroom, a standard section by
the windows and a sofa-bed along its corridor
wall. In the interests of a quieter and perhaps
less cigar-scented atmosphere for the more
upscale clientele to be expected in the drawing
room, the latter was always located at the
ladies'-room end of the car. Over 4000 cars
with this '12-1' floor plan were in service in the
1920s.

With only a few minor exceptions in the
United States, sleeping car meant Pullman. In
Canada, the Canadian Pacific and Canadian
National offered service in a fleet of equally
massive sleepers of almost identical design; the
only significant difference was that they were
of a slightly greater overall height, the extra
inches providing a bit more headroom in the
upper berths.

More important than the cars themselves was
the concept of Pullman service, a broadly
identical level of staffing and maintenance

Left: *So high was the Pennsy's reputation that
Campbell's Soup was happy to identify their
quality product with the PRR in this* Saturday
Evening Post *advertisement of January, 1926.*

New York Central J-class 'Hudson' type,
1927-1938.

throughout the country on whatever railroad's train the sleeping (or parlor) cars were operating. The smoothness of the track, the reliability of the timekeeping and the convenience of the scheduling over a route would depend on the individual railroad, of course, but the passenger was assured of familiar facilities and the services of a porter schooled in the identical, detailed rules that governed his 12,000 fellows.

Even taking into account the mergers which had already reduced the number of Class I railroads by this time, more than 50 were offering Pullman services in the late 20s, ranging from the longest (Santa Fe's — 13,000 miles) to such short but scenic lines as the Yosemite Valley Railroad, with its Los Angeles and San Francisco cars enroute to the very gateway of the park. Each line over which a Pullman-owned car was scheduled had to provide a certain daily revenue to Pullman to fulfill the contract; if it was not sufficiently patronized the railroad had to make up the deficit to Pullman. In general, a line averaging eight to ten passengers every night would meet the guarantee, so any car whose lower berths were filled was running in the black. 'Dedicated' sleepers connecting a single community to the Big City might thrive with a population base as small as 5000 to 10,000; over the years many exotic routings such as Globe, Arizona to New Orleans might come and go as the fortunes of their termini waxed or waned, but in the 20s an average of 40,000 passengers per night slept in Pullman cars.

Where could you go by sleeper in this era? From almost anywhere to almost anywhere else.

Above: *Troubadours serenade passengers on the* Los Angeles Limited *at Riverside, CA, in 1927. Any stunt that would get a railroad's crack trains some publicity was worth a try.*

Below: *Santa Fe No. 3286 hauls a fast freight in a scene typical of the standard railroading era. The locomotive was built in 1920, and this photograph was made in the 30s.*

Above: *Great Northern engine No. 2517 with a 19-car silk train at New Rockford, ND. On September 30, 1925, this engine ran 3567 miles in just 99 hours, 55 minutes.*

Cars originating at the end of a branch would be picked up by a main line train at the junction to arrive in a destination city in the morning. Some runs were available one-way only, and then not always on a daily basis; there was usually a good reason for this. Take, for example, a '12-1' sleeper that the Pennsy hauled from New York's Penn Station via Philadelphia and Harrisburg on the Erie-bound *Northern Express* to Emporium, Pa. (population 2800) on Mondays and Thursdays only. Arriving at 4.05a.m., it was set out for occupancy (meaning that sleeping passengers could stay aboard) until 8.00a.m. — but, at least according to the timetable, the car never came back to New York. What about the executives of an electrical firm with headquarters in Manhattan and a number of plants in that northwestern Pennsylvania area who were the reason behind this sleeping car line? They could come back to New York any night on the Erie Railroad train which arrived at a reasonable 11.05p.m.

Medium-sized and larger cities in the hinterlands, however, were likely to have two or more competitive routes to several important destinations. Here, since the fare was the same for all routes and the Pullman cars were also essentially the same, any extra amenities one railroad could advertise, like early boarding, might give it a significant edge.

On runs of 250 or 300 miles, where an overnight train with early boarding for sleeping-car passengers leaving around midnight would represent the best combination of comfortable speed and timely arrival, all competitors would naturally leave at about the same time, splitting the business. Between Chicago and St. Louis, for example, the Wabash, Illinois Central, Alton

and Chicago & Eastern Illinois Pullman trains were all 'Midnight Specials,' at least in timing if not in name.

The network of sleeping-car lines covered the country, but with some major interruptions, of which the Mississippi River and Chicago were the most significant. More railroads (20) went into the Windy City than any other hub. Unfortunately, they went into seven different stations. The largest fleet of eastern trains (the New York Central's) went into La Salle Street station, whose only western line was the Rock Island, a bit of an also-ran with its routes reaching only to the southern end of California. Santa Fe's heavily patronized fleet of *California Limiteds* operated out of the crowded Dearborn station, whose trains to the east (Erie and Grand Trunk) were those least likely to be of interest to through passengers.

As a result, during the golden age passengers passing through Chicago were beholden to the Parmelee Transfer System's network of coach lines to get them between stations in time. Although hair's-breadth escapes from missed connections may have been a hallmark of Parmelee's intrepid coach-loaders and drivers, train schedules were such that most passengers had plenty of time to spend money in Chicago, a situation which seemed to dampen any local enthusiasm for making passing through the city any easier.

St. Louis, with trains from all 18 of its lines backing through interlaced trackage into a train-shed ultimately spanning 32 tracks, afforded an easy transfer for all; Pullmans left for points on both coasts and almost all points from border to border in between. In the standard-railroading era, however, only a few cars on such short runs as Chicago to Kansas City were scheduled actually to run *through* this truly Union Station.

Further south a few Pullman lines crossed the Mississippi — Kansas City to Florida (Frisco-

RACE OF THE SILK TRAINS

In the early years of this century, silk enjoyed its heyday in North America. Before cheaper substitutes were developed, many garments were made of pure silk.

The substance silkworms create is extremely perishable. Seventy years ago, the silk was shipped from the Far East and, when it arrived, it was rushed to the mills via railroad — particularly the Great Northern Railway (GN).

Since GN's Seattle-St. Paul, MN, route to the silk mills was the shortest and had the easiest grades, GN won the lion's share of the silk business. Records show that the first silk trains moved on GN in the 1920s.

Silk trains caused such a stir people would talk about them all over town. When a silk train came through, even the flagship expresses had to give way.

The race with the silk began as soon as the ship docked in Victoria, Canada. Men would swarm over the ship's sides to unload it the instant the liner was motionless. Before even half the ship's passengers had descended the gangway, bales of silk had been transferred from the ship to the dock.

The bales were then wheeled into a warehouse, sorted and piled, inspected by customs officials and trucked into waiting baggage cars. After the cars' doors were sealed, the train roared off. The silk train often left dock before the last of the ship's passengers had passed through customs.

Silk trains usually consisted of a steam locomotive, fuel tender, coach and a string of baggage cars packed with bales of raw silk. The train would often be hauled by powerful P-2s, or 'Mountain Class' locomotives, one of the fastest and heaviest steam locomotives available.

Special agents or detectives guarded the valuable shipments because hijackers were a constant threat. Hoboes who tried to hitch a ride on a silk train had a good chance of being shot.

A retired trainman notes, 'It was an honor to handle silk trains. There was a friendly rivalry between operating divisions. It was a challenge to handle a silk train over your own territory in less than the allotted time. Divisions strove for better performances as a matter of pride.'

When the Cascade Tunnel was completed in 1929, trains had an easier route through the Cascade Mountains. Even without the tunnel, the silk trains' running time between Seattle and St. Paul was comparable to that of modern diesels.

By the 1930s, the advent of synthetic materials, and deteriorating US-Japanese relations, put an end to the magnificent era of silk train expresses.

Note
This piece first appeared in *Burlington Northern Railroad News* (Spring/Summer,1991) p.23. It is reproduced here with permission of the author, Sheila Geene, and of BN.

THE ART OF RAILROAD ADVERTISING

Railroads borrowed many promotional techniques from American political campaigns, which by the middle of the nineteenth century had adopted colorful graphics, snappy slogans, and the wide distribution of souvenirs, gew-gaws, memorabilia, and gimmicks. If it worked for the politicians, it would work for the railroad.

By the 1880s, rapid improvements in printing technologies and the steady fall in price of manufacturing inexpensive 'premiums' resulted in a seemingly endless variety of useful and not-so-useful advertising favors handed out free to railroad shippers, government officials and politicians.

Railroads issued hundreds of timetables each year, with colorful covers and often lavish maps and graphics to attract the passenger's eye. They sold or gave away playing cards and key chains, alligator paperweights and desk sculptures of giant potatoes. Ash trays, ink blotters, calendars, and letter openers graced desks in offices across the United States and Canada, reminding the businessman and clerk of their friends on the XYZ railroad.

As advertising in general became more sophisticated, railroad promotion emphasized the 'safety, speed, and comfort' of train travel, and the scenery to be seen enroute.

These same railroads were some of the first businesses to recognize the power of brand-name association and of bold logos. To this day, railroad emblems are some of the most identifiable items in the history of advertising.

All the items featured in the photograph are from the collection of John Fowler.

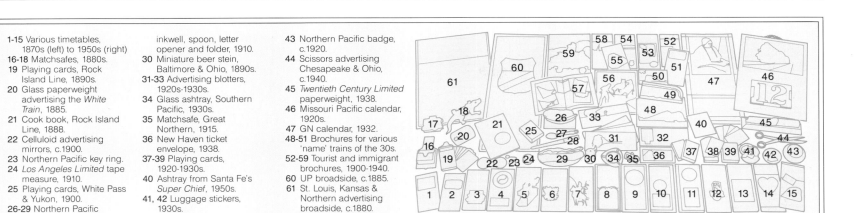

1-15 Various timetables, 1870s (left) to 1950s (right)
16-18 Matchsafes, 1880s.
19 Playing cards, Rock Island Line, 1890s.
20 Glass paperweight advertising the *White Train*, 1885.
21 Cook book, Rock Island Line, 1888.
22 Celluloid advertising mirrors, c.1900.
23 Northern Pacific key ring.
24 *Los Angeles Limited* tape measure, 1910.
25 Playing cards, White Pass & Yukon, 1900.
26-29 Northern Pacific

inkwell, spoon, letter opener and folder, 1910.
30 Miniature beer stein, Baltimore & Ohio, 1890s.
31-33 Advertising blotters, 1920s-1930s.
34 Glass ashtray, Southern Pacific, 1930s.
35 Matchsafe, Great Northern, 1915.
36 New Haven ticket envelope, 1938.
37-39 Playing cards, 1920-1930s.
40 Ashtray from Santa Fe's *Super Chief*, 1950s.
41, 42 Luggage stickers, 1930s.

43 Northern Pacific badge, c.1920.
44 Scissors advertising Chesapeake & Ohio, c.1940.
45 *Twentieth Century Limited* paperweight, 1938.
46 Missouri Pacific calendar, 1920s.
47 GN calendar, 1932.
48-51 Brochures for various 'name' trains of the 30s.
52-59 Tourist and immigrant brochures, 1900-1940.
60 UP broadside, c.1885.
61 St. Louis, Kansas & Northern advertising broadside, c.1880.

Southern), for one — but otherwise the river acted as an effective barrier. Curiously, the only sleeping-car line from New York City continuing for any distance west of the Mississippi was the Shreveport, Louisiana two-night route, which involved four railroad-to-railroad connections (Pennsylvania/Southern/Norfolk & Western/ Southern /Illinois Central).

With these exceptions, the Pullman network was relatively seamless, with even such remote resorts as Boca Grande, Florida; Murray Bay, Quebec; Pacific Grove, California; and French Lick, Indiana rating through service in season from cities as far as 2000 miles away. Some glitches still remained to be eliminated in 1930 — for example, Southern Pacific trains to Oakland (from where passengers could take the ferry to San Francisco) also had to cross the Carquinez Strait. This involved a time-consuming transfer in which the entire consist including the locomotive was transported on one of the two largest ferryboats in the world. New Orleans, meanwhile, had five stations but no bridge connection across the Mississippi. And in Syracuse, NY, the 'Great Steel Fleet' of the New York Central (including the *Century*) steamed down the middle of Washington St. for many blocks.

Making much of this seasonal service possible was the Pullman pool of sleeping and parlor cars. While the more prominent trains had regularly assigned cars, almost half of the fleet of some 9000 cars were available to be shifted from one hot spot to another throughout the country. As the fleet became standardized, the varied and colorful car liveries typical of the late nineteenth century came to be replaced by a sedate, uniform Pullman green. Said to have been selected 'because it looked good with dirt on it,' this was the shade to be found on all the trains of the vast majority of railroads from coast to coast. Exceptions were the Tuscan red cars assigned to Pennsylvania Railroad service, the two-tone green and gold cars used for the Southern Railway's *Crescent Limited* and some orange and maroon cars in service on the Milwaukee Road.

The volume of holiday resort traffic which could be accommodated by the Pullman pool was astounding: one Labor Day night saw the Maine Central bringing 102 cars down to Boston from the various resorts to be forwarded by its Boston & Maine Railroad connection. A lesser traffic bulge twice a week throughout the year and across the country was the result of the preponderance of business travel — Friday and Sunday night traffic was as much as double that of midweek. In New York in particular, station capacity was strained each 'rush hour.' With the vast majority of the 100 or so sleeping-car lines terminating in the morning on Grand Central Terminal's 24 upper-level platform tracks, it was no wonder that arriving consists had to be unloaded immediately; a passenger who somehow overslept was likely to find himself being hauled back to Mott Haven coachyard in the South Bronx.

With fares and sleeping cars the same by any routing, a passenger's choice of railroad was likely to be determined by the other features offered: lounge facilities and dining car service.

At the rear end of any worthwhile train was an open observation platform, with a traditional awning above to moderate the breeze. Inside

THE BROTHERHOOD OF SLEEPING CAR PORTERS

Since the earliest days, African-Americans have played a vital role in building and operating America's railroads — and none more so than the sleeping-car porters.

Well into the twentieth century, more African-Americans worked on railroads than in any other industry, but discrimination confined them largely to jobs such as track laborer, porter, chef, waiter, maid and fireman. The largest single railroad employer of African-Americans was the Pullman Company, and the efforts to provide effective union representation for Pullman porters in the 1920s and 1930s was a heroic labor and civil rights struggle.

George M. Pullman founded a company in 1867 to build and operate a national fleet of comfortable sleeping cars on US railroads. His service would feature the finest equipment, with servants to attend to the passengers' needs. It was early decided to hire only African-American men as porters: it was a symbol of status among white travelers to be waited on by them.

The open-section sleeping car with seating sections convertible to upper and lower sleeping berths was the standard type of overnight accommodations on railroads from the early 1870s through to the 1950s. The porter was the key to its success: he would carry baggage, provide pillows, games and light refreshments, and generally look after the needs of passengers during the day, and

Above: *On dining cars, the steward was always white and male, while African-Americans worked as waiters and chefs (as here, on a dining car in 1924).*

Right: *A page from the Pullman employees' manual. Instructions for everything from the making of beds to serving drinks were included; they were followed to the letter.*

make up the sleeping sections at night. All night he kept watch over the comfort of his passengers, ready to adjust the heat or bring a berth ladder if needed. A businessman could have his suit brushed, shirt ironed and shoes polished, all thanks to the porter.

By 1918, the Pullman Company was the largest single employer of African-Americans, with 12,000 porters on the payroll. Working

PREPARATION AND SERVING OF FOODS

Asparagus. Serve hot or cold. If served hot, place can in boiling water for 20 minutes. Open, drain off liquid and serve on small platter, with one-half ounce butter over the asparagus, taking care to retain the tips in their original form. If served cold, arrange and serve in the same manner (omit butter), olive oil, vinegar, pepper and salt (or mayonnaise) accompanying order.

Asparagus on Toast. Serve hot. Place one piece of toast in center of medium platter. Cut another piece of toast triangular and place a piece at each end. Place asparagus on center piece of toast with one-half ounce butter over asparagus. Garnish with sprig of parsley.

Beans, Baked or Mexican Style. To be served hot or cold, as desired. If hot, place can in boiling water for 20 minutes before opening. Serve Boston Baked Beans on hot medium platter. Serve Mexican Style Beans in hot cereal or soup bowl. If cold, serve in same manner without heating, using cold dishes.

Bread or Rolls and Butter. Serve three slices of bread, 4½ to 5 inches square each slice ½ inch thick, halved and neatly arranged on bread and butter plate. Serve two rolls, either hot or cold, as desired, on bread and butter plate. Rolls furnished in sanitary envelopes must be served in original package.

Bread, Brown. Serve hot or cold, as desired. If hot, place can in boiling water for 20 minutes. Remove from can, slice, and serve on warm tea plate in neatly folded napkin, with butter on chip.

Above: *Publisher A. Philip Randolph, first President of the Brotherhood of Sleeping Car Porters, went on to become one of the key leaders of the Civil Rights Movement.*

Below: *A Santa Fe Sleeping Car Porter Instructor's badge. Although it was tough work (the porter had to work 400 hours per month in the 20s), the job was sought-after.*

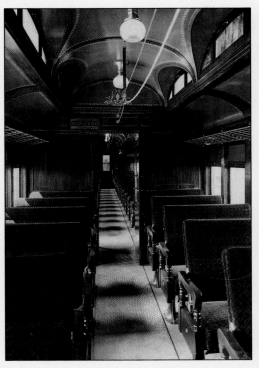

Above: *A 'Jim Crow' car, 1911. In the south, African-Americans were forced to ride in these segregated cars, despite their contribution to the operation of the railroads.*

Above: *A porter makes up berths in an open-section Pullman. As well as completing such tasks, the porter was expected to 'look after' the passengers generally, as below.*

for Pullman was seen as prestigious and fulfilling — but a porter was on duty nearly around the clock, performing demanding and often demeaning work at low wages. In 1926 porters made a monthly base wage of $67.50 plus tips, and were expected to work 400 hours. They had to pay many of their own expenses — even the cost of polish for passengers' shoes! On top of this, as retired Pullman porter Mr. L.C. Richie notes:

> . . . [the Pullman Company] . . . did not have any place for the porter to sleep. And we couldn't go to sleep. That's in '26, 1926. Well, from 1926 until '30, they didn't provide any place for a porter to sleep during those years. And they had inspectors on the train that would do nothing but walk through the train to see if the porter was asleep. And if he caught him asleep, they would bring him up, reprimand him for it, or give him time, or time off, or anything like that.[1]

And in return for their tip, the passenger expected much from the porter, as Leon Long comments:

> We'd carry the top people back and forth and they'd tip you good. You always knew that you were going to have something at the end of the line. Of course, you had to show appreciation even before you got to that. You got to treat the passenger nice, you got to take care of them. You got to be their nurse, doctor. You got to be the maid. You got to be everything.[2]

In 1925 a few porters started to agitate for full bargaining rights in order to secure better working conditions and higher wages. They approached publisher A. Philip Randolph for help, and on August 25 were able proudly to announce the creation of the Brotherhood of Sleeping Car Porters.

Randolph's closest lieutenant was C.L. Dellums. Born in Texas in 1900, Dellums had moved to Oakland and secured a job as a porter in 1924. Joining the Brotherhood when it was organized in 1925, he became a full-time official of the new union in 1927.

For the next decade, through the Depression and in the face of opposition from the Pullman Company, white labor unions and even other African-Americans, the Brotherhood fought for recognition. The union was finally granted jurisdiction over porters and maids, and in 1937 signed an agreement with the Pullman Company. The union, symbolically and in fact, led the transformation of attitudes toward organized labor and the rights of black workers.

Notes

[1] In Jack Santino, *Miles of Smiles, Years of Struggle* (Urbana: University of Illinois Press, 1989), p.23.
[2] In Jack Santino, *Miles of Smiles, Years of Struggle*, p.82.
Contributed by Walt Gray.

was the observation lounge, its comfortable chairs facing inward, unless someone was sufficiently interested in the view to turn one to face the rear windows. Somewhere in the car would be a few camp chairs for any hardy souls who wished to ride outdoors.

In the east the observation car was likely to be a Pullman-owned vehicle with some open-section or room space (or parlor seats on a day train) forward of the lounge. This being the Prohibition era, the buffet would have provided nothing stronger than sodas.

Western routes with their two- and three-night schedules typically featured full-length lounge cars. Owned by the railroad, these provided valet, bath, barber and soda fountain services, all of which meant that it was worth making the trip back from the farthest sleeper ahead. These cars provided the opportunity for the railroad to display some individuality — writing paper proclaiming the Limited's identity, a library, decor appropriate for the country being traversed, and perhaps, once there were a few stations along the route, radio. (Reception was at best likely to consist mostly of static, but it did look good on the timetable's list of features.) A ladies' room (no cigars!) was another essential feature.

On the all-Pullman trains common in the east, the barbershop and bath facilities were likely to be provided in the Pullman-owned baggage-lounge at the head end. A train secretary might also be aboard to keep the traveling executive's office work moving during his journey.

The real opportunity for distinction lay in the dining car service. Once the closed vestibule connection between cars was perfected in 1888 — meaning that getting to the diner from other cars was no longer a hair-raising adventure — a dining car could count on first-class

Left: *Traveling on one of the crack 'Limiteds' of the 20s was an experience. After checking in and boarding (top: at Chicago in the 20s; center: at Los Angeles in 1915), passengers found themselves in catered luxury. Demand was so great that some trains, such as the* California Limited, *occasionally ran in seven separate sections, as below.*

Left: *A chef at work on a B&O train in the 20s. The food served in dining cars was usually of a very high quality, remarkable given the limited space available in the galley.*

Right: *The men's washroom on a Pullman. Some trains boasted barbershops and even seawater baths; hot and cold water for washing, and iced water to drink, were always available.*

passengers' patronage. As his or her satisfaction (or otherwise) with the food and service was the crucial matter most likely to color his or her remarks to fellow passengers, the railroads spared no expense to ensure that a positive recommendation was going to be made.

From its inception the dining car was the heaviest and most expensive car in the train. Steel cars of the standard era weighed 85 to 90 tons (about 10 tons more than the last wooden diners) and cost $50,000 in 1925. The full 80ft of the car was used for kitchen, dining room and locker space; food, crockery, linen, fuel and ice required that every cubic foot not needed for working space be equipped with doors and locks. A kitchen to prepare 100 meals measured, at best, 8ft by 30ft.

Dining car design in the standard era had few variations. Six pairs of tables seating four on the right, two on the left, gave a total of 36 passengers per seating. While some 48-seat cars had been built as early as 1890, the fixed width of the car interior was considered a bit too crowded in a four-by-four arrangement. An impressive 'sideboard' divided the seating area from the pantry/kitchen.

While feeble electric fans were often added to diners soon after electric lighting became standard, there was rarely enough generator and battery capacity for more than two or three per car, including the kitchen. A small fleet of Santa Fe diners boasted a primitive ice-activated cooling system, phased out in 1926 after a few trouble-filled years. Otherwise the temperature in the summer would be similar to that in the best restaurants of the day — hot or perhaps somewhat better, so long as the train was moving fast enough to enable the exhaust ventilators to continue discharging the hot air from inside the car.

To provide the high level of service needed to be competitive (and in keeping with the times, a high level it indeed was — all six waiters would remain on call so long as a single passenger was being served) the diner was highly labor-intensive. A standard crew consisted of 11 people: the waiters, a steward, three cooks and a dishwasher. With all the table cloths and napkins that had to be provided, the laundry bill was impressive (one of the highest single items in the budget) — and this was just one of the factors to be considered if the service was to be distinctive. Cut flowers on each table, an intimidating array of silverware at each place (plus finger bowls) would be considered a minimum standard.

Even with less posh cafe or buffet cars on runs where patronage was too light to support a full diner, the service was never profitable. For the United States railroads at the end of the standard era, serving about 60,000 meals a day brought in $22 million dollars every year; the reported expenses (which probably did not include the cost of switching and hauling the cars) was $30 million. Was the loss worth it? Considering the consequences should the word that 'my dinner last night on the _____ just wasn't up to snuff' get around, most roads concluded that it had to be.

What was a trip on a typical great Limited like in the late 20s? Making a reservation and getting a ticket for the outward trip would be no problem — there were downtown railroad ticket offices in most large cities. Making the return reservation could be more difficult, since the agent would have to wire a request and wait for a return message, probably the next day. You book a lower berth. Your train promises a comfortable ride, averaging 45mph and rarely exceeding 65mph over a good roadbed unless — heaven forbid — something delays it and the engineer has to make up time at 80mph.

Although your train doesn't quite rate the 200ft red carpet rolled out each afternoon alongside the New York Central's *Twentieth Century* at Grand Central, your train's departure from one of the nation's newer and larger

PALACES ON WHEELS

Providing the passenger with a memorable experience in the dining car was a goal rating top management attention — for it was here, in the quality of the food, service, and 'ambiance' provided, that the railroad had its best chance of conveying its uniqueness, to distinguish itself from the opposition. Whatever an attractive menu, a brilliant array of silverware, fresh flowers or an exclusive porcelain pattern could do to complement the fine food on offer was thus in order.

What constituted good taste in each of these elements, of course, changed with the times — compare, for example, the Santa Fe menu of the 1880s, with its somewhat fussy design, and the art-deco-style menu produced for the Illinois Central's Chicago-Iowa *Hawkeye* in the 30s. But whatever the decade, within his budget the manager of the dining car service was expected to create an ambiance neither too *avant garde* nor too *passé* for the comfort of the businessmen who accounted for most of the first-class passenger traffic during the 20s and after.

1-11 Menus, from different railroads, from 1888 (far left) to 1948 (far right).
12 Butter pat, Lehigh Valley, 1900.
13 Ice cream shell, UP, 1925.
14 Butter pat, Lackawanna, 1900.
15 Gravy boat, Pittsburgh & Lake Erie, 1930.
16 Silverware from different railroads, 1890-1920.
17 Dinner plate for the Monon Route's *Hoosier Limited*, 1901.
18 Napkin, B&O, 1930s.
19 Sauce dish, Colorado Midland, 1910.
20 Service plate for the Illinois Central's *Panama Limited*, 1918.
21 Union Pacific and Northern Pacific eggcups, 1930s.
22 Ashtray, Chesapeake & Ohio, 1930s.
23 Platter, Chicago & Alton, 1880s.
24 Teapot, Western Pacific, 1930s.
25 UP eggcup, 1930s.
26 Dinner plate for the New York Central's *Twentieth Century Limited*, 1938.
27 Ashtray, Great Northern, 1930s.

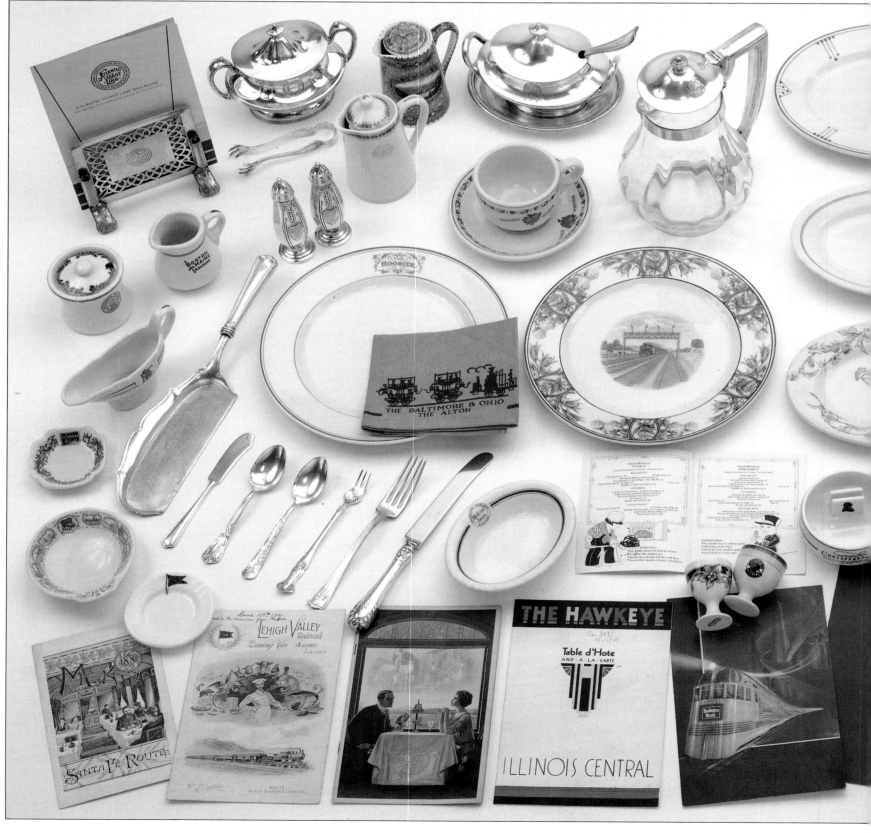

28 Platter and napkin for Milwaukee Road's *Hiawatha*, 1937.

29 Salt and pepper shakers, Missouri Pacific, 1946.

30 Service plate for Chicago & Northwestern's *400*, 1940.

31 Silverware from various railroads, 1920-1950.

32 Southern Pacific napkin, 1940s.

33 Cup and saucer for C&O's *George Washington*, 1932.

34 Teapot, for Santa Fe's *Super Chief*, 1937.

35 Menu and holder,

Richmond, Fredericksburgh & Potomac, 1947.

36 Butter pat, Atlantic Coast Line, 1931.

37 Cocktail shaker, New York Central, 1938.

38 Teapot for NYC's *Twentieth Century Limited*, 1938.

39 Plate, New Haven, 1938.

40 Teapot, Santa Fe, 1920s.

41 Cup and saucer, Burlington Route, 1928.

42 UP water pitcher, 1937.

43 Glass, Northern Pacific, 1930s.

44 Platter, Maine Central, 1910.

45 Platter, Texas & Pacific, 1925.

46 UP water pitcher, 1925.

47 *Golden State Limited* cup and saucer, 1920s.

48 Tureen, Denver & Rio Grande, 1915.

49 Chocolate pots, B&O, 1920s.

50 NP sugar bowl and tongs, 1920.

51 Salt and pepper shakers, Burlington Route, 1920s.

52 Cream pitcher, Boston & Maine, 1910.

53 SP mustard pot, 1910.

54 Menu and holder, Atlantic Coast Line, 1925.

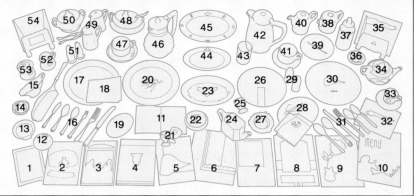

Below: *There was nothing like the bustle at one of the great city terminals in the evening, when most of the 'Limiteds' were preparing to leave. The grandeur of New York City's Pennsylvania Station (below) set the scene for passengers arriving to board the* Broadway Limited *.*

Above: *Chicago's Union Station was constructed between 1916 and 1925; this was only one of four or five major stations in the Windy City.*

Above: *Washington, DC's Union Station — depicted in a postcard of 1928 — was opened for service in 1907, while work began on Cincinnati Union Terminal (below) in 1929. As built, the huge station complex could handle 108 trains daily, inbound and outbound.*

Below: *The Grand Concourse of Pennsylvania Station (the Central Waiting Room is seen in the photograph above). The building was completed in 1910, and demolished in 1966.*

Right: *The Lackawanna Railroad dreamed up the glamorous (but thoroughly pure) 'Phoebe Snow' to tout its 'smoke-free' trains, which burned anthracite coal.*

terminals is still somewhat of a thrill. The Union Station's clock tower dominates the local skyline, the waiting room is squeaky clean (even if its benches are oak-hard), and train announcements echo to the point of complete unintelligibility; 'red caps' are on hand to handle your luggage.

Your porter welcomes you to Lower 6, near the quiet center of the car; latecomers get the berths over the wheels. Thinking back to your nights upstairs on a Pullman, you reflect on life in an upper. Getting up there is a matter of ringing for the porter to bring the ladder, but considerable pre-planning is called for since once you are up there, that's it. Items too heavy or bulky to stash in the hammock-like shelf upstairs will spend the night on your ankles.

After the preliminaries the upper is great for sleeping, since there is nothing else to do. In the morning comes a final decision. Ring for the ladder (as the sign directs) or rappel down on your own with the aid of the stout curtain rod overhead and assorted other handholds? Not really hazardous, except perhaps to the Pullman conductor or other passengers on the move below. All in all, the 20 percent lower Pullman fare for the upper berth (a 50- to 75-cent break on an overnight trip) isn't quite enough to compensate for all the awkwardness involved.

In due course the railroad and Pullman conductors come to 'lift' their respective tickets. On portions of a run where there is only one Pullman on the train, the porter performs the conductor's functions.

At $1.75 (these are 1929 dollars), your four-course steak dinner seems a bit pricey in comparison to restaurant meals or those on less prestigious trains. But it is a fine meal, selected from an extensive menu and served with panache, although you have to write your choices on the check yourself.

A long-standing remark was that the only improvement made to the sleeping car since 1865 was the installation of a slot in the men's washroom for the disposal of the new-fangled safety-razor blades. There were, however, many, mostly subtle, improvements in this last series of heavyweight '12-1' cars compared to *Carnegie*, the very first production steel Pullman of 1910.

Most noticeable, perhaps, are the permanent headboards between the sections which provide a far more private feeling during the day; earlier cars had featured folding partitions, stored in the uppers until the beds were made down. Wash-basins would now be made of porcelain rather than nickel, but the hook for the razor strop has been retained in case some patrons continue to amaze their fellow travelers by shaving themselves with a straight razor at speed. Reading lights in the lowers now sport attractive lampshades; gone are the mahogany-grained interiors, which have been repainted in quiet tones.

As your train gains speed after picking its way through the maze of trackage leaving the terminal, the heat of the day trapped in your car begins to dissipate; the Garland ventilators along its clerestory are using the outside air flow to

RY & LOCO HIST. SOC.

Along the Lackawanna

Lackawanna Railroad

*It's time to go
With Phoebe Snow
And view the scenes
She loves to show
Each mile is quite
A new delight
Upon the Road
Of Anthracite*

**NEW YORK
BUFFALO   CHICAGO**

suck out the stale atmosphere inside. The *McNair*, another '12-1', has just become the first successfully air-conditioned Pullman, using an ice-activated system worked out by refrigeration inventor Willis Carrier, but it will be another four years before your train can be advertised as an air-conditioned train.

Life on your train and its all-Pullman peers such as the Illinois Central's *Panama Limited* to New Orleans, the Chicago & North Western/Union Pacific/Southern Pacific *Overland Limited* to San Francisco, the Santa Fe *Chief* et al to Los Angeles, the seasonal Atlantic Coast Line *Florida Special* and its Seaboard Air Line *Orange Blossom Special* rival, and other flagships too numerous to mention is pampered, even if subject to the limitations of the open sections. How did the less-than-first-class passengers fare?

In the west, many trains carried Tourist Sleepers, mostly elderly, downgraded, 16-section Pullmans with only a thin strip of carpeting down the aisle and somewhat harsh rattan or plush upholstery. For a price intermediate between coach and first class these cars provided much of the nighttime comfort of the regular sleeper. Usually Pullman-operated, they often filled up from the top down — the difference in price was sufficient to cause the upper berths to sell better than the lowers.

ANTHRACITE AND 'CAMELBACKS'

The fortunes of a railroad, however well managed, must rise and fall with the fortunes of the areas and industries it serves, as is illustrated most vividly by the story of the 'Anthracite Roads' during the standard era.

'Hard' coal abounds only in a relatively small area in the mountains of eastern Pennsylvania. Only by the middle of the nineteenth century was it realized that this mineral could in fact be burned; once ignited, its flame was hot and almost smokeless. As a result it rapidly displaced wood and smoky bituminous coal as the preferred home heating fuel.

The 'Anthracite Roads' transported millions of tons of this coal to cities and ports — the Lehigh Valley and the Delaware, Lackawanna & Western were among the longer lines (both extended as far west as Buffalo), while the more regional Reading, Jersey Central, Delaware & Hudson and Lehigh & New England catered to localized markets.

Millions more tons of anthracite screenings — too small to sell and, as 'culm', considered waste — accumulated around the 'breakers' where coal was readied for shipment. Could this stuff be used for locomotive fuel? If a large grate could be provided on which a fire could burn enough culm to power a locomotive of gay nineties proportions, the answer was 'yes'. The Wooton firebox, shallow enough to fit above the rear drivers, could spread out to the full width of the locomotive and provide the grate area needed for 2-8-0, 4-4-2 and 4-6-0 engines.

The cab could not fit over such a wide firebox, however, so it was moved forward over the boiler barrel, which of course separated the engineer and fireman. Most of the time the fireman would be back by the tender shoveling; a second cab (really just an open-sided shelter) was added for him, resulting in an engine variously referred to as a 'Camelback', 'Double-cab' or 'Mother Hubbard'. The hundreds of these startlingly different locomotives became hallmarks of the Anthracite Roads.

Another of the Anthracite Roads' hallmarks was the promotional use they made of the fact that the fuel was 'cleaner'. For example the Lehigh Valley called its premier train *The Black Diamond*, and the Lackawanna's admen came up with 'Miss Phoebe Snow,'

*Whose dress stays white
From morn to night
Because she rides
Upon the Road of Anthracite.*

By 1920 construction of additional 'Camelbacks' had been banned for safety reasons, though many remained in service until the end of steam. The anthracite roads, by now mostly burning bituminous, remained among the most progressive and prosperous in the nation as they handled increasing volumes of merchandise freight throughout the 20s.

Although chair car seats allowing various degrees of nighttime reclining and comfort were in use in the nineteenth century, the 1920s coach featured walk-over plush seats, 76 to 84 per car. On some competitive trains on daylight runs 'individual' seating that looked considerably more comfortable would be advertised; at night, their fixed armrests meant that the old walk-overs were preferable.

If the flagship Limiteds represented a railroad's quality and prosperity during the standard era, what about the less publicly-apparent goings-on that had more to do with a railroad's profitability?

Local, commuter, branchline and secondary mainline trains first began to feel the effect of better highways and the proliferation of automobiles in this period; the number of passengers carried peaked by 1921. Since the elimination of such services was made virtually impossible by state service commissions, the emphasis for the railroads operating them turned toward cost reduction. The most obvious manifestation of this was the switch to 'doodlebugs' as substitutes for steam passenger trains. These gasoline-electric cars, developing 250 to 600 horsepower and providing various combinations of express, railway post office and passenger hauling capacity in the power car and in a trailer car or two, became fairly reliable by the late 20s, to the extent that perhaps 1000 of them were rambling along the rails in the United States and Canada by the end of the decade.

The standard era in motive power is less easy to date — perhaps a starting point can be the large-scale production of heavy 2-8-0 locomotives whose boilers had become as fat and heavy as roadway clearances and axle loads could stand. They could haul the mainline freights of the era, but only slowly.

The most common heavy passenger locomotives of the day were fleet 'Atlantic' 4-4-2s and lower-wheeled but stouter 4-6-0 'Ten Wheelers'. In a search for greater efficiency various improvements to locomotives appeared, such as compound cylinders, and superheating.

Placing a wide firebox behind the driving wheels over a two-wheel trailing truck brought both freight and passenger power into what we might call the 'modern' steam standard era. The 2-8-0 developed into the 2-8-2 'Mikado' (named for a number of small examples exported to Japan) and the 4-6-0 into the 4-6-2 'Pacific' (named for the Missouri Pacific, its first user).

Throughout railroading's history nothing has remained big enough for long. Adding another driver to the 'Pacific' and 'Mikado' created the 4-8-2 and 2-10-2 types. Both were slower than their predecessors. Largest of all freight locomotives were the 'Mallets' with their two sets of cylinders and drivers under a single boiler. With the front 'engine' pivoted to swing laterally under the boiler they were able to negotiate curves freely. The 2-6-6-2 and 2-8-8-2 types were the most common, used in hump, drag freight and pusher service.

During World War I the Federal government took over management of the United States' railroads, with results in general considered to be somewhere between unfortunate and disastrous. However, as part of the United States Railroad Administration's (USRA's) program, a committee of engineers from several railroads and the three locomotive builders (American, Baldwin, and Lima) developed plans for 12 classes of standardized engines (0-6-0 and 0-8-0 switchers, 2-6-6-2 and 2-8-8-2 'Mallets', and light and heavy versions of 4-6-2, 4-8-2, 2-8-2 and 2-10-2 wheel arrangements) which were built in quantity to be assigned where most needed.

Although many railroad master mechanics argued that machines built to such a common standard could not possibly meet the requirements of their particular division, the 'McAdoo' locomotives (so called for the USRA's chief, often for many years after he and his organization were long gone) generally performed well and lasted until the end of the steam era.

As track continued to become heavier (mileage of rail weighing 100 pounds per yard or more increased from 33,000 to 83,000

Below: *Canadian National Railway's sleeping car* St Hyancinthe, *delivered in 1929, was of a standard Pullman design of 10 open sections, one drawing room, and one compartment.*

expected to desire full meals. While four could be seated at each of the three tables in this miniature diner, the waiter would find laying out the extensive silverware and china service called for in the Pullman service manual much more pleasant with just two people seated at each table.

Six more lounge seats completed an 'observation room' section, with rear-facing windows affording a fine view (whenever the car could be located at the rear of the train, that is). Also a hallmark of any Pullman lounge ('bar-lounge' in the post-Prohibition years) was that massive beverage table-ashtray, heavily weighted to prevent jolting as the train raced along.

Originally built in 1913, *El Quivira* and her nine sister cars were given Spanish-flavored '*El*'-prefixed names for mid-train service on the Santa Fe's Chicago-Los Angeles *California Limited*, the flagship train on that popular run through the Southwest, to augment the lounge capacity of its baggage-library and open-platform observation cars. In 1936, *El Quivira* was equipped with ice-activated air conditioning and reconfigured into the 'Club Series' 8-section, dining-lounge *Lotos Club* seen here, for general assignments warranting full meal service.

Identified only by their names — preferably fancy, flowery, poetic, romantic, historical or exotic — Pullman sleeping and parlor cars were classified by their 'Diagram' numbers; *Lotos Club* as rebuilt has the eight open sections and dining-lounge configuration designated as 'Diagram 91'.

Today, the *Lotos Club* is on display at the Railroad Museum of Pennsylvania, Strasburg, where it can be viewed in the main hall.

Left: *The Lima works' Shay shops in the 20s. Shays were specialized engines for use in logging. Presaging the coming Depression, orders for Shays fell through the decade.*

railroads realized that shorter schedules could also reduce the number of freight cars that had to be maintained.

In 1925, the Lima Locomotive Works built a new 2-8-4 demonstrator with the same axle load as the large 'Mikados' of the time, but with several new features. The 'A-1' showed what a vastly enlarged fire-box could mean in terms of moving the same tonnage considerably faster on a good deal less coal. This 'Super Power' principle (as Lima called it) did catch on; within two years all three builders were turning out new 2-10-4, 4-6-4 and 4-8-4 super power locomotives in profusion alongside the 2-8-4s.

The New York Central designed the first 4-6-4, proudly named it the 'Hudson' type and found that it could not only handle longer sections of the *Century*, but also eliminate many engine changes by running over several divisions at a stretch. Most popular of the super power wheel arrangements was the 4-8-4, first built for the Northern Pacific. On many roads, the 4-8-4 revived the 'dual-service' idea that had last been in vogue 80 years earlier, when 4-4-0s were expected to haul the freights of the time as well as passenger trains. With 70- to 80-in. drivers and 60,000 to 75,000 pounds of tractive force, the 4-8-4 'Northerns' could make time with the passenger Limiteds, and also raise tonnage ratings in fast freight service.

Another of the advances of the standard era was better signaling. An example was Absolute Permissive Block (APB) signaling. The semaphores might not look any different than for the Automatic Block Signal (ABS) systems which had come into being by the turn of the century, but some very clever relay circuitry caused all the signals for opposing traffic all the way to the next siding to go to stop once a train moved into a 'block' section of single track. This provided complete protection against a head-

Below: *These models from the Smithsonian Institution show how the passenger car evolved (from left to right, bottom to top): coaches made by James Goold, 1831; an 'American-type' eight-wheel coach, 1856; a clerestory-roof coach, 1868; a semi-vestibule coach, 1894; an all-steel coach, 1907; and a stainless-steel coach built by the Budd Co. in 1939.*

between 1920 and 1930), axle loads increased and locomotives of the same wheel arrangement grew larger. The most significant change, however, was a shift toward higher horsepower. Fast freight was becoming a more important part of the traffic mix: companies realized that speedier transit could mean smaller carrying charges for enroute inventories, and

Above: *Granville Woods patented over 60 inventions, most electrical. In 1887, he discovered a way for trains to receive signals inductively, from the track itself. Later on, this permitted the development of in-cab signal systems, and automatic train-stop.*

on collision, since there was now no way two trains approaching each other could by chance both receive approach indications at the ends of the same block. The circuitry did, however, allow a following train in the same direction to enter the single track and move along two blocks behind. APB greatly increased traffic capacity at little cost — compared with the expense of building more sidings or doubling track — and many thousands of miles were put in service.

Signal lamps strong enough to be seen in daylight were another noticeable advance of the standard era. From 1915 on, various position-light, color-light, searchlight and, finally, color-position-light signal systems became standard for all new installations, eliminating the need to maintain semaphore arms and mechanisms.

Another innovation was Automatic Train Control (ATC), an overlay on the signal system which would stop the train should the engineer fail to observe a restrictive signal. ATC systems relied on the inductive pickup of signals carried in the track itself, an early form of which had been pioneered in the 1880s by inventor Granville Woods. In 1922 the ICC ordered each of the 49 railroads with passenger service to equip at least one division with ATC. The inductive cab-signal and train control system on the Pennsylvania Railroad was the very first application of vacuum-tube electronics outside of the communications industry.

The standard railroading era of 1900-1930 created most of the imagery that we today associate with railroads — the huge locomotives heading grand passenger trains or mile-long freights, the imperial big-city station, the sprawling rail yards, the railroad as part of heavy industry. More than imagery, however, was a rich legacy of change that still helps to shape the railroad story.

Top and above: *With increasing competition from automobiles and electric interurbans in the new century, vehicles such as these SP McKeen cars were introduced on local lines.*

Below: *In the 20s and 30s the Pacific Electric System in Los Angeles was the world's largest interurban electric railroad system. It was closed down by the 1950s.*

HARD TIMES

DISASTER STRUCK THE AMERICAN ECONOMY in the fall of 1929. On the blackest day in the history of Wall Street — Tuesday, October 29 — stock market share prices crashed dramatically and investor confidence vanished overnight: the Great Depression had commenced. By 1932 the ranks of the unemployed had swelled and relief organizations were struggling to cope; by the spring of the following year nearly 15 million people were out of work. Failed businesses and 'No Work' signs were seen everywhere. Canada, too, experienced terrible economic problems: one out of every two Canadian adult males was unemployed at the depth of the depression.

The railroad industry, always sensitive to economic cycles, reflected the deepening financial crisis. Freight tonnage in the United States dropped markedly: it stood at 2.45 billion tons in 1929 but plummeted to 1.1 billion tons in 1932. Similarly, passenger traffic sank: carriers transported 780 million riders in 1929, but only 478 million in 1932. Hard times cut savagely into operating revenues: overall, the railroads generated $6.2 billion in 1929, but only $3.1 billion in 1932. Canadian railway traffic also reached its lowest ebb in decades. Grain shipments in 1935, for example, stood at only one-eighth of what they had been in 1928. With widespread and prolonged drought in large sections of the continent, the adage 'No rain on the plains means no grain in the trains' rang horribly true. Economic conditions did not improve significantly in either the US or Canada until after the outbreak of World War II. Indeed, a sharp downswing in 1937 and 1938 shocked Americans; it was the worst economic decline since 1933. Freight traffic in the country for 1938 was a disappointing 1.6 billion tons, far below the levels of the late 1920s.[1]

Not surprisingly, many railroad companies failed during the Great Depression. In 1933 the giant Missouri Pacific became the first major American carrier to file for legal protection, and then scores of firms joined it in bankruptcy.

Mileage in receivership peaked at a record 77,013 route miles in 1939, or nearly one third of American trackage.

Had railroads been in robust health during the 'Roaring 20s,' they might have weathered the Great Depression more effectively. But many companies had not yet recovered fully from the negative consequences of being under government control during World War I; they also confronted increased competition from automobiles, buses, and trucks. The expanding ownership of motor vehicles particularly hammered passenger train earnings, especially on branch lines and short-distance runs. Carriers also remained victimized by what historian Albro Martin has called 'enterprise denied'. Progressive-era reforms, most notably the Hepburn Act of 1906 and the Mann Elkins Act of 1910, hurt the railroad companies' ability to price their services and to generate funds for modern-

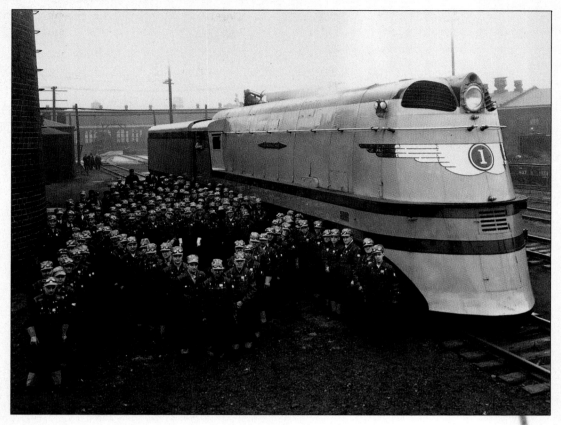

During the Depression the C,M,St.P.&P responded to intensive competition on the Chicago-Twin Cities route by ordering the first locomotives designed for daily operation at 100mph. The first of these (Class A No. 1) leaves the builder's yard (above) in 1935, while a later type (F7, ordered in 1937) pulls the afternoon Hiawatha *out of Milwaukee's C,M,St.P&P depot in 1938 (below).*

ization and debt reduction. So, although the passengers may have benefited from those reforms (at least in the short term), the railroads did not. The business climate of the post-war years further weakened the industry. The frenzied financial activity that characterized the period led to an assortment of vulnerable enterprises, and this speculative zeal hardly created depression-proof corporations. Some leading railroads built corporate structures that resembled a house of cards.

The premier steam railroad empire to falter during the Great Depression belonged to two bachelor brothers from Cleveland, Ohio: Oris Paxton Van Sweringen and Mantis James Van Sweringen. These brothers, known as the 'Vans,' had initially concentrated on Cleveland area real estate ventures, only entering into railroading shortly before World War I. They then took control of the woebegone Nickel Plate Road — linking Buffalo, Cleveland and Chicago — and under their direction it flourished.

The success of the Nickel Plate whetted the appetite of the Van Sweringens for more railroads; it also enabled them to make more acquisitions. Initially, they utilized the traditional corporate merger. They won approval from the Interstate Commerce Commission (ICC) in 1923 to combine the Nickel Plate with two adjoining roads, the Toledo, St. Louis & Western and the smaller Lake Erie & Western, creating a 1700-mile system. The brothers subsequently purchased a controlling interest in the Chesapeake & Ohio, a thriving coal carrier, and also a major position in the Pere Marquette, a mostly Michigan road with a prime Chicago connection. The Erie, a fast-freight road, entered their orbit as well. By the mid-1920s the Vans controlled more than 9000 route miles of rail line from the Atlantic seaboard to the nation's mid-section, and had assembled the fourth-largest eastern trunk network. But the Vans did not stop at Chicago; they not only took over the 12,000-mile Missouri Pacific system (which extended from St. Louis into the southwest and west), they also acquired the Chicago & Eastern Illinois, which tied their eastern holdings with the Missouri Pacific.

The transactions of the Van Sweringens became progressively more complex as they assembled this unwieldy, far-flung empire. Following the economic fashion of the 20s, they opted to control their railroads mostly through

Below: *A PRSL train and the CNJ's Blue Comet in the terminal at Atlantic City, circa 1935. The depot is virtually bereft of passengers on this freezing and gloomy winter's day.*

holding companies. The Vans employed this strategy for good reason. Holding companies gave them control in a highly leveraged fashion, yet they could attract investors through financial inducements. While the Vans held the majority of the voting common stock, other investors owned non-voting preferred shares with attractive, fixed dividends. Hard times, however, revealed that the holding company was far from being a depression-proof entity.

In the early 1930s the Van Sweringens' railroad combine encountered extreme difficulties. The combination of high fixed costs and low business levels led to red ink on the bottom line for their several holding companies, including the cornerstone of their business domain, the mighty Alleghany Corporation. But the brothers retained most of their rail and real estate empire, except for the bankruptcies of the Missouri Pacific and Chicago & Eastern Illinois. They juggled money from company to company, refinanced loans, and won delays on debt repayment. Still, the pressure of creditors and worsening economic conditions led to a desperate reorganization in 1935, which may have contributed to the Vans' premature deaths; 'M.J.' died in December 1935, followed by 'O.P.' 11 months later. Nevertheless, the Alleghany Corporation remained afloat, albeit badly battered.

While the troubles of the Van Sweringens captured headlines in the press and the public sensed that the halcyon years of the previous decade had ended, the nation's ailing railroads actually profited from an overhaul of the bankruptcy code in 1932. Worsening economic conditions prompted President Hoover to sign a much-needed business reform, the Federal Bankruptcy Act, during the final days of his administration. Prior to this, if a railroad had gone into bankruptcy a receiver would have been appointed by the court to sell the railroad's property, usually to a group of bondholders. Under Section 77 of the replacement statute, however, a bankrupt carrier was allowed to continue operating under the aegis of one or more trustees whom the court and the federal Interstate Commerce Commission supervised. The latter for the first time played an active and positive role in the restructuring process. 'In the entire history of the ICC,' commented George W. Hilton, 'probably nothing that the Commission undertook has met with such general approval as its behavior in reorganization of the bankrupt carriers of the 1930s.' Argued Hilton: 'The Commission helped bring about the reorganizations quickly and typically with conservatism concerning the railroads' future prospects.'

Above: *An NP apple refrigerator car being reconditioned at shops in Washington State, August, 1931. To repair and make do was the rule in the Depression.*

Below: *Canadian families being resettled from Montreal to Lois, Quebec. In Canada, a drought on the Prairies exacerbated the nation's — and the railroads' — difficulties.*

Even though the bankruptcy legislation became less draconian after 1932, railroad leaders hardly welcomed the opportunity to take their companies 'through the wringer.' Rather, they sought to avoid the federal courts by remaining solvent — and this usually involved reducing costs as far as possible. Like other business executives, they slashed expenditures to the bone: they curtailed purchases, cut services, limited salaries and reduced employment.

Cutbacks in labor were heavy. The carriers needed to pare payrolls, and this they did throughout the 1930s: the industry employed approximately 1.7 million workers in 1928, yet only 939,000 a decade later. Thousands, too, were furloughed. It was not unusual for personnel to labor only a few days a month during the slowest periods. Some employees only clung onto their jobs because of family ties, although they likely worked fewer hours and earned less than before the onset of hard times. Nepotism, even during the Great Depression, remained a powerful tradition.

Railroads also attempted to bolster revenues, but they found this altogether more difficult than making cutbacks, although the Baltimore & Ohio Railroad came up with an imaginative

Above: *Railroads attempted to boost passenger revenue by putting on connecting bus services. This SP bus waits for the passengers off the train at a depot in California in the 30s.*

Below: *A PRR prototype GG-1 and train pause at platform for 30th. Street, Philadelphia, in 1934. Well-designed locomotives ensured success for PRR's electrification.*

Above: *Two Erie Railroad freights — 4-6-2 No. 2526 and 2-8-4 No. 3352 — in the early 40s. By competing for freight, the Erie managed to remain viable during most of the 30s.*

Above: *The grand opening of the Great Northern's Cascade tunnel in 1929.*

By 1910 the New York Central, New Haven, Pennsylvania and Long Island lines had met a mandate that all services into Manhattan had to be electrified. Furthermore, these railroads inadvertently demonstrated that no less than four different ways of doing it would work: over-running or under-running third rail, 660-volt direct current, locomotive-hauled or multiple-unit trains and 11,000-volt alternating current via overhead catenary.

By 1916 the Chicago, Milwaukee, & St. Paul was hauling freight and passenger trains over the first of four major mountain ranges on its recently-built Puget Sound extension to Seattle that would ultimately be electrified with 3000-volt DC catenary. Seven years earlier the Great Northern had opted for an electrically simple, catenary-complex three-phase AC system (twin contact wires required) to haul steam locomotives and their trains through its Cascade tunnel.

All of these electrifications, after some growing pains, met or exceeded expectations; locomotives seemed to last practically forever. At 656 miles (in two disconnected segments) the Milwaukee Road had the longest electrified line in the world. Thus during much of the 'standard era' electrification clearly seemed to have a great future — but it was a great future that was never actually to become reality.

As private enterprises, railroads in the United States simply had to figure the return on electrification's investment, and the numbers just didn't add up. The high capital cost could never be earned back, even though electrification enabled more traffic to be handled.

The thin traffic on the Milwaukee main line didn't increase just because the line had been electrified, and the company entered bankruptcy. By the end of the 20s there was one other major electrification project under way, but this was not to see service until 1932 — the Pennsy's consolidation of through electrification from New York to Wilmington, Delaware. Described by the railroad itself as a leap of faith toward better service rather than as a cost-saver, even this scheme had to wait some time — and the introduction of the phenomenal GG-1 locomotive — before it was to achieve unqualified success.

response to the depressed conditions. The firm's resourceful and hard-driving president, Daniel Willard, who had earlier gained recognition for a program of employee involvement in workplace decision making, endorsed creation of the 'Cooperative Traffic Program,' or CTP. Inaugurated in December 1933, the plan sought to involve employees in generating revenues. Operating through a network of grass-roots groups, the CTP urged the 'B&O family' to solicit business for the railroad. And this the members did, whether it was by convincing home-town merchants to use the firm's Less-Than-Carload (LCL) service, or by persuading clubs to travel on B&O passenger trains. Their efforts meant much. The CTP increased the road's revenues during the 1930s by more than one percent annually. Although this was a modest figure, it was significant; the CTP likely saved the company from bankruptcy.

While the B&O boasted the sole CTP, other carriers took to urging their employees, often through the pages of in-house magazines and newsletters, to drum up business, both freight and passenger. Railroads, moreover, frequently ballyhooed special transportation plans, nearly always conveniently arranged and at very attractive prices.

The activities of the Erie Railroad during the 30s provide a good example of such aggressive self-help schemes. While the company succumbed to bankruptcy in 1938, in part because of the financial woes of its parent Alleghany Corporation, it made mighty attempts to remain viable. First, the Erie provided a much more competitive freight service, particularly for LCL shipments. Following the lead of the Chicago Great Western Railroad and several other hard-pressed carriers, the Erie inaugurated an expanded freight collection and delivery program on December 1, 1933, advertised with the jingle: 'Today a phone call to your Erie agent solves *all* your problems on less-than-carload shipments.' A few years later this service was provided at 'no extra charge.' Customers liked the Erie plan, and income from LCL traffic rose most years during the remainder of the depression.

The Erie did not ignore the passenger sector, though. Already smarting from the sting of increased automobile usage and bus competition because of new bridge and tunnel construction in the New York City area and better roads generally, the company worked to attract riders, most of all on the more profitable long-distance runs. Sensible scheduling of trains helped to mitigate losses. 'The Erie did a good job servicing its on-line towns with good passenger service in the 1930s', remembered a former employee, 'so that there was always convenient service between any two local points at decent hours'. But the company needed to do more than fix its timetables in an attractive fashion. While the road's flagship passenger train, *The Erie Limited*, continued to race through the night between New York (Jersey City) and Chicago, enjoying a loyal and steady clientele of sleeping-car patrons, coach traffic dropped noticeably on the *Limited* and on companion trains. Management tried various incentives to regain coach business. It reduced rates to special events, including the popular Century of Progress Exposition in Chicago during the summer of 1933, and promoted budget 'coach luncheons' where attendants 'carrying baskets containing various kinds of tasty sandwiches, pies, fruit, etc., also hot coffee, pass through the coaches at frequent intervals.'

And like other major railroads, the Erie's passenger department vigorously promoted special trips. The company's '4-Way Tours' (airway, highway, railway and waterway), for instance, offered opportunities for a pleasant, moderately priced six-day outing via *The Chicago Express* from New York to Cleveland, sightseeing in the Ohio metropolis, an airplane ride to Detroit and more sightseeing, an overnight lake steamer to Buffalo and side trip by bus to Niagara Falls, and then return to Gotham on *The Erie Limited*. As a descriptive folder proclaimed, 'The Erie Railroad has succeeded in creating a spirit of camaraderie in its personally conducted parties that permits of no wall flowers.' It added that 'No one travels "alone" on an Erie tour. Whether you are a youngster,

oldster or an in-betweener, you are with friends.' Management's response to the decline in passenger travel helped to halt the slide. While passenger revenues dropped 50.5 percent between 1929 and 1932, they slipped a mere 2.9 percent between 1933 and 1936. Such aggressive promotion surely prevented further losses of passenger revenue.

Not all Americans could afford rail travel bargains and incentives during the 1930s. With high unemployment and jobs still difficult to find (even after the launching of the New Deal with its variety of relief and recovery programs), hundreds of thousands of predominantly white males, some only teenagers, took to the steel highways of North America in search of work. One notable woman traveler, 'Boxcar Bertha,' estimated that at least 1½ million hoboes roamed the United States and Canada at this time. Many hopped freights for the wheat fields of the Great Plains, the orchards of the Pacific Northwest, the sugar cane fields of the South, or wherever chances of employment looked promising. Others rode these 'side-door Pullmans' for different reasons, perhaps to visit family members, to attend school or merely for adventure or escape.

Graydon Horath, a youngster from Chester, Illinois, who had little money but a strong desire to work while seeing the country, journeyed with harvesters through the wheat belt of the Central Plains during the summer of 1937. His

Above: *Hoboes relax for the camera during a stop, about 1917. As unemployment grew in the 30s, huge numbers of people jumped freights to look for work in other areas.*

Below: *Ted Rose's painting* Underpass *depicts a hobo outside Columbus, OH, in the 30s. The graffiti voices resentment at President Hoover's failure to halt the Depression.*

Above: *A Chicago & North Western publicity shot of passengers aboard the new, deluxe* City of San Francisco, *circa 1937. It ran between Chicago and San Francisco.*

reminiscences provide a glimpse into a mostly forgotten dimension of railroad travel.

Days, nights, it made little difference, we chugged on through Miltonvale, Concordia [Kansas], ever increasing the number of men on the train, as the rail-road men worked around them now without a seeming care. One day I was in a boxcar and by afternoon there must have been a hundred men in the same car, maybe due to it being the only boxcar with an opened door, I don't know. Regardless of what I did or didn't know was of little importance. They were a rowdy carefree lot with a poker game going on in one end of the car and a dice game of nickels and dimes in full swing in the other. Now I figured that I wasn't smart enough to play poker and I'd had my share of dice playing in Chester, for it was, in the 30's, a wide open town . . . So I was educated enough not to get suckered into a palmed dice, loaded dice or slid dice game. Besides, if these sharpies wanted money — let them bend their backs for it as I had mine.

The train was slowing down and suddenly halted and so did the games. I'd been in one end of the boxcar watching the poker game; suddenly I realized everyone was getting out at this little [Kansas] town. But this little town proved to be different — the crowd demounting was now quiet, although by the time I got to the open door, the men were all standing, elbow to elbow, in a line. The Engineer had conveniently stopped the train with the door of our car exactly in the center of the hi-way. When I looked out, the first thing I saw was a well armed Sheriff with an extra large, shiny star; and he wasn't alone! Four armed Deputies stood nearby. When the train man assured him we were all off the train,

he began. "Gentlemen! I am the sheriff of the county and we profess to have a quiet, clean little county seat town. But recently we have had rumors of some towns having a few nuisance happenings and we just don't cater to problems of this kind. Now I didn't say you were unwelcome on our streets and in our stores — but believe me I'll not allow pandering or pilfering; understand? However, if you're just passing through and should need directions — me or any of my boys will help you. We know all the hi-ways and where they go; even rail-road schedules are no trouble for us. In fact — the train you came in on will be leaving town right after dusk." After staring at us for a long moment, they all got in the one car and drove back up town, possibly satisfied that there [sic] message had been clearly received.

Horath and his fellow travelers — the hoboes, tramps and bums,[2] — must have realized that this local constabulary had treated them well. For a risk that all hoboes ran was meeting unsympathetic law-enforcement personnel. Railroad police — 'bulls' or 'dicks,' especially gained a reputation for cruelty. And, too, a migratory worker such as Horath might meet unsavory 'yeggs,' various types of crooks who also frequented the 'hobo jungles.' Of course, the other dangers of such unauthorized travel were also legendary, and included train derailments, falls from moving rolling stock and accidental entrapment in boxcars and refrigerator ('reefers') cars. But everyone expected these hazards and believed that trips of this nature were their only practical option. Recalled another teenager, who rode with an older brother from Idaho to North Dakota to attend college in September 1936:

> If I wanted to enroll for the fall semester I must go with him: I had no other choice. [And, he added,] Looking back to the day we left home, I know Mother and Dad felt diminished and shamed by our arrangement. They simply did not have enough money to send us off in style, but they were flexible and adapted to the tough economic times. They trusted that I, their youngest child, would be safe, protected by Huck [the older brother] on this adventure. They knew he was thoroughly experienced in riding the freights.

While corporations and individuals suffered during the 30s, there were still a few bright spots. The public relished reports of futuristic passenger trains that debuted one after another and repeatedly set speed records. The Union Pacific and the Chicago, Burlington & Quincy railroads deserve credit for developing 'tomorrow's train.' The UP, the railroad giant which had long spent heavily on technological improvements, saw its articulated three-car, aluminum-alloy streamliner, *M-10000,* attract enormous attention when it toured the country in February 1934 and after. Powered by a 600-horsepower distillate engine, it could speed at 90mph with a full complement of 116 passengers and crew and 25,000 pounds of baggage and mail. After a period on display at the Century of Progress Exposition, the train entered revenue-earning service between Kansas City and Salina, Kansas, as *The City of Salina.*

HOBO ON THE CP

Above: *Waiting for the next ride.*

Unable to find work during the Depression, Jack Friedlein set off to explore Canada the low-cost way; here, he jumps his first Canadian Pacific freight.

[The train] was a truly magnificent sight, one that I would never forget. There were about 120 box cars and a caboose on the seaboard manifest making it about a mile and a quarter long. Almost mesmerised, I watched the box cars going past. Then I pulled myself together — this was it! I made a grab at the rung and jumped, knee on the bottom rung — pull up — another leg on, pull up to the ladder, climb up, and I was there. I had done it! I groped around and found three boards which ran from end to end of the box car, which was about 50ft long and which was called the 'catwalk' or 'deck' . . . Breathing a sigh of relief that I was safe, I made a pillow with my pack and lay down on my back holding myself with my hands on either side of the catwalk. I . . . was 'riding high' while I rocked along the track. I heard the whistle going . . . and the cinders were falling on top of the metal-topped box cars.

I could see no one else since everybody had become separated when jumping the train. It was still a pitch black night and so I lay there, hanging on, rocking with the rhythm of the train. I was utterly exhausted, physically and mentally, and although I did not mean to do so, I fell asleep. When I awoke and realised that I had fallen asleep, I was amazed that I should have done so in such danger. It is really wonderful how one's subconscious works for self-survival. If I had let go of the catwalk, I would have fallen to my death. It was dawn and I reckoned I had been asleep for about three hours. I sat up [and] stretched . . . I could hardly move I was so cold.

Note

From *Hobo over the Hump*; ed. E. Wilde, p.13 Reproduced with permission of Elizabeth Wilde and Dorrance Publishing.

RAILROAD POLICE

'Cinder Dicks', 'Yard Bulls', 'Gumshoes' — railroad police have endured many nicknames, most of them uncomplimentary. The stereotype of a thick-necked tough rousting unoffending hoboes has long been a part of railroad folklore. From the point of view of the railroads, however, their officers, detectives or special agents perform a much needed service which emphasizes public safety as much as law enforcement.

The tradition of protecting railroad property and passengers is almost as old as the industry itself. Beginning in the 1850s, companies utilized private detectives, including those of Allan Pinkerton's famous agency, to investigate thievery of freight, keep transients from hitching free rides on trains, and curb the activities of pickpockets, card sharps and other petty criminals plying their professions in the stations or aboard the cars.

Railroads started hiring their own police after the Civil War. They worked closely with local marshals and sheriffs, express companies and detective bureaus in combatting the rising problem of train robberies. In addition, railroad police forces occasionally served as virtual private armies in contests between companies over rights of way, and in the often violent labor disputes of the late nineteenth and early twentieth centuries.

Today, railroad police are highly professional peace officers. Although many of their duties remain similar to those of 100 years ago, vandalism has become a serious problem, and the ubiquitous urban graffiti artist has replaced the hobo as one of the railroad policeman's chief headaches.

1-5 SP policeman's hat, on strong box with D&RG police badge, handgun and H.S. Dewhurst's 1955 book on the railroad police.

6, 7 REA wood lock box with American Railway Express padlock and chain.

8, 9 News clipping about the arrest of John Bostick for robbery and murder aboard an SP train in 1913 with (9) his California State Prison record card. This states that he was executed in 1915.

10-14 Gunpowder box, oil can, and dynamite plungers, with the kind of implements that would have been used for breaking into property.

15-18 Reward posters.

19 Note detailing how a hold-up of an SP train would be carried out. Dates from the early 20th.C.

20 Central California Traction Company sign.

21-23 Storybooks and comics about the railroad police.

24, 25 1914 mug shot of James Singleton Hogue, train robber, with a telegram announcing that

Hogue can be identified by a brakeman who worked with him on the Grand Canyon Railroad.

26-35 Railroad police and other badges, including Wells Fargo post office and express agents' badges. Various periods.

36, 37 1897 Winchester shotgun and 38-caliber Colt handgun.

38, 39 Freight car seals, with the sealing device. If the seal was broken on arrival, the railroad knew the contents had been interfered with.

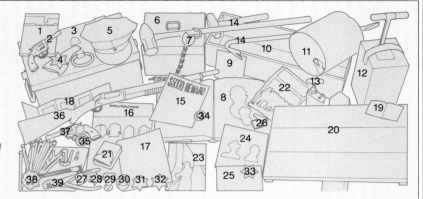

The Burlington was engulfed by an even greater avalanche of public enthusiasm when it cleverly showed off its innovative, three-car articulated diesel-electric train, the *Zephyr*. This stainless-steel streamliner, propelled by a 600-horsepower diesel engine, dashed from Denver to the stage of the Century of Progress in Chicago on May 27, 1934. Passengers lauded the smooth ride and marveled at the speeds achieved by the train, which reached 112mph. The Burlington's president, Ralph Budd, who had recently reread Geoffrey Chaucer's *Canterbury Tales*, wished to honor Zephyrus, the god of the west wind. Like Zephyrus, this special train typified renaissance.

The Burlington placed the *Zephyr*, appropriately renamed the *Pioneer Zephyr*, on regular runs between Lincoln, Nebraska, and Kansas City, Missouri, on November 11, 1934. Three railroads — the Chicago & North Western, Union Pacific and Southern Pacific — which jointly operated passenger service on the 'Overland Route' between Chicago and San Francisco, beat the Burlington between the Windy City and principal western points with their own diesel-powered streamliners. Intercity passenger travel recorded a major event on June 6, 1935, when the *M-10001*, better known as *The City of Portland*, (Chicago & North Western and Union Pacific) made its maiden trip between Chicago and Portland. This first diesel streamliner with sleepers averaged nearly 60mph, and slashed 18 hours from the best regularly scheduled steam-powered runs. Then, a year later, the Overland Route roads introduced *The City of Los Angeles*, *The City of San Francisco* and *The City of Denver*. The latter sped over the 1048-mile North Western-Union Pacific route at an impressive 65mph. But in November 1936, the Burlington introduced its *Denver Zephyrs*, and three years later the Chicago, Rock Island & Pacific attempted to meet this fierce new

Above: *The* City of San Francisco, *circa 1937 — one of the streamlined diesels that revolutionized train travel in the 30s and set new standards for speed and comfort.*

competition between Chicago and Colorado with its *Rocky Mountain Rockets*.

By the end of the 1930s, the diesel-powered streamliner knew no geographical bounds. Southerners, for example, first encountered this equipment in 1935, when the struggling Gulf, Mobile & Northern upgraded its through passenger service between Jackson, Tennessee and New Orleans with its *Rebel* trains. These were the first diesel streamliners made up of separate (that is, nonarticulated) cars. New

Below: *Twin Burlington Route* Zephyrs. *On May 27, 1934, the first Zephyr dashed from Denver to Chicago in just over 13 hours — at an unheard-of average speed of 78mph.*

Englanders, too, greeted the diesel streamliner about the same time. *The Flying Yankee*, which sped over the rails of the Boston & Maine and Maine Central railroads, whisked riders between Boston and Bangor, Maine. These trains, as a group, brought passengers back to the railroads by the tens of thousands — as had been hoped and intended by the railroads concerned.

Yet, not every railroad could afford this exciting form of passenger service for its flagship trains. Some railroads embraced high-speed steam-powered service, largely because of limited financial resources and the relatively small number of trainsets in production. A good example of innovation with modest expenditure came from the Chicago & North Western. Although the company would shortly be an operating partner with the wealthier Union Pacific and Southern Pacific with the *City* streamliners, it ran the competitive Chicago to St. Paul-Minneapolis (Twin Cities) route on its own. The railroad won extensive media coverage with the inauguration of its *400* service between Chicago and the Twin Cities on January 2, 1935. While the trains were conventional — standard heavyweight, albeit newly air-conditioned cars, pulled by an E-2 class 'Pacific' steam locomotive — they made a positive impression. 'Traveling America soon took this flashing train to its heart.' Averaging nearly one mile per minute ('400 miles in 400 minutes' boasted the promotional literature), train set numbers *400* and *401* operated on the world's fastest schedule for a major inter-city run. '[They] embodied the triple features of *speed*, *comfort*, and *beauty* as never before,' the railroad's copywriters continued.

The new *400s* symbolized the limited abilities of the North Western to meet its competition. Gone were the glory years when bankers deemed the road's securities appropriate to protect the assets of 'widows and orphans.' Hard

times battered the company, so much so that it
could not redeem $1.8 million in bonds due in
June 1935, and bankruptcy followed. With
limited financial resources, the North Western
had to make 'a silk purse out of a sow's ear.' It
badly needed greater income from its passenger
operations and a way to cope with forthcoming
streamliner competition from its arch-rival
Milwaukee Road, the upstart Burlington
between Chicago and the Twin Cities, and ever-
increasing automobile travel.

As popular as the *400s* were (the trains carried
more than 30,000 passengers during the four
months ending April 30, 1935), the North
Western recognized correctly that streamlining
and the costs associated with it were inevitable.
The company finally marshaled resources to
order delivery of 20 smart yellow-and-green cars
from Pullman-Standard and four diesel-electric
locomotives from Electro Motive Corporation.
'A new "400" — Diesel-powered, light weight,
streamlined!' heralded the road's publicity arm
in 1939. 'Acclaimed the most beautiful train in
America — and rightfully so!' As with other
objects of industrial design during the 30s, the
replacement *400s* sported flowing lines and
graceful contours.

While the public rightly associated diesels
with state-of-the-art passenger service, some
scattered freight operations had become
dieselized even before the stunning triumphs of
the *M-10000* and the *Zephyr*. Although railroads

Right: *A Gulf, Mobile and Ohio Railroad 'Rebel
Route' timetable of 1941. It did not take long for
railroads to recognize the publicity value of
modern, clean diesels.*

Below: *The original* City of Portland
*streamliner — the M10001 — in 1936. The
articulated consist included three air-
conditioned Pullman sleepers and a day coach.*

commonly lacked access to financing, a few diesels were already shunting freight cars in switching yards by 1930 and more appeared during the decade. The first successful diesel-electric locomotive worked in a small and physically constricted yard owned by the Central Railroad of New Jersey in 1925. By 1936 nearly 200 diesel switchers toiled in American and Canadian yards. Railroad officials began to recognize that such motive power was ideally suited for switching and transfer chores; diesels were most powerful at low speeds. These internal combustion locomotives also could run nearly continuously and be operated economically, the correct prescription for a sickly industry. Moreover, they complied fully with local smoke-abatement ordinances.

Road diesels likewise began to join locomotive rosters. The first was a two-unit passenger engine built by the Canadian National in 1928. Then, a year later, a road diesel entered service on the New York Central. Yet neither of these locomotives performed well. The first truly successful single-unit passenger diesel was probably the 1800-horsepower unit built by Electro Motive (later Electro-Motive Division of General Motors) for the B&O. This engine — No. 50 — replaced the *Lord Baltimore*, a modern 4-6-4 steam engine, on *The Royal Blue*, a crack passenger train which linked New York City (Jersey City) with Washington, DC. More units for the industry came from Electro Motive and other manufacturers.

As larger diesels were used to pull passenger trains during the 30s, attention turned to the development of freight units for long-distance runs. This was understandable: diesel locomotives had already shown that they could accelerate faster than steam locomotives, take curves at higher speeds (because of their lower center of gravity), and travel farther without service stops. In 1939 Electro Motive built the first diesel freight locomotive and, in 1939-40, took it on a national tour, including Santa Fe, for testing. It was a giant when compared to contemporary diesels: the 5400-horsepower locomotive consisted of four units, which contained 64 cylinders, 4 generators and 16 motors. On its maiden run this experimental locomotive hauled 66 cars from Kansas City to Los Angeles in an economical and efficient fashion. Not surprisingly, the Santa Fe put in the first order for such engines, and they entered revenue service in early 1941. The coming of World War II limited the number of these 'FT'-model locomotives, but some additional railroads — the Erie, for example — put them into operation by 1945.

Even though the Age of the Diesel first began to take shape during the 30s and later resulted in spectacular gains for the industry, other improvements in motive power occurred without the fanfare streamliners had created. The Pennsylvania Railroad, the self-proclaimed 'Standard Railway of the World,' pushed forward with its program of 'heavy traction.' In the 20s several carriers, including the 'Pennsy,' had opted for heavy-duty electrification of sections of their busiest routes. The onset of the depression, however, forced the Pennsy to delay expansion of electrification. But the federal government, which had already granted loans to carriers from the Hoover Administration's Reconstruction Finance Corporation, added

John Grover wrote the following report for the October, 1942, issue of the *Erie Railroad Magazine*.

Eastbound caboose, USA — It can't be done, so they're doing it. That's the nutshell story of the way tough, trained US railroad men are highballing petroleum products to the oil-starved East coast.

I have had a box-seat for this mightiest movement of hot-shot freight in rail history — the bouncing caboose of a 60-car tanker train that's just winding up a record 109-hour trip from the Texas Gulf Coast. (It was one of 550 oil trains in transit that day.) On the way I met the men who make the wheels go 'round, the hogheads [engineers] and monkeys [maintenance workers] and dispatchers and section hands who hitched up their britches and calmly tackled the job

of moving oil after U-boats crippled the seagoing tanker fleet.

Thank your lucky stars for these lean, all-hours guys. If they weren't jockeying the long trains of tankers east, hundreds of oil-fired war factories would be idle now. Millions of oil-heated homes would be stone cold this winter, with grave consequences to civilian health and morale.

From the time Conductor Fred Glines of the Kansas City Southern gave the highball signal that sent our squat, ugly tanker train out of the Port Arthur yards until Engineer Frank Teator of the New Haven [Railroad] slapped on the air in Providence, R.I., nearly one million railway employees coordinated their efforts to save minutes and build the total saving in hours.

The KCS turned the tankers over to the Frisco system in Neosho, Mo., two hours

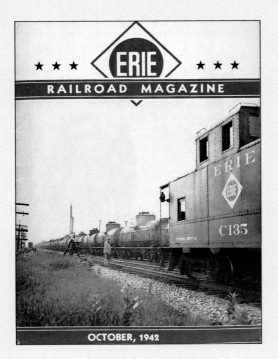

OCTOBER, 1942

Above: *Like the Erie Railroad (John Grover's article was featured in this 1942 issue), most large railroads published magazines to keep employees up to date with developments.*

Left: *A UP poster encourages employees to do their utmost to keep the traffic flowing.*

ahead of schedule after a 612-mile run. The Frisco gunned us to St. Louis more than three hours to the good. The Terminal Railroad Association [of St. Louis] shunted us through the yards in 40 minutes. The Wabash line picked us up for the run to Huntington, Ind., taking us over the road at passenger-train speed. The Erie kept up the hot-shot job into Maybrook, N.Y., where the New Haven took over for the last leg into Providence.

The oil's going through. It's a gigantic effort that compares with the great sagas of our pioneer days.

It's the toughest kind of work, because railroads are shorthanded, like every other big outfit. That means hours up to the limit of Interstate Commerce Commission rules, a quick flop and bath, and back again for a new assignment.

This applies all along the line. Paperwork was multiplied as freight piles up and must be moved. The pressure on yard and roundhouse repair crews increases as equipment is speeded up and wears out. From the Big Guy worrying his brains out in the main office to the last gandy-dancer on the end of a pick on a branch-line right-of-way, railroaders are working the hours it takes to move the freight that's got to move.

This conversation, in the Marion, O., yards of the Erie is typical.

'Yay, Smitty. How y' doing? Playing the horses lately?'

'Playin 'em hell. I'm the horse. I've had only one day off since April.'

'Ya big sissy. What's a day off? I don't remember.'

The railroad men who move the goods that

Right: *Two-thirds of all servicemen were carried in Pullmans; in 1944, the company loaded a sleeper every three minutes or so.*

make the war effort possible are keyed to battle pitch to do the job right. Little incidents I saw from the caboose prove it.

At one station the agent wasn't on deck to pass up orders on the fly. The train had to stop. It cost us eight minutes, and those eight minutes cost a 45-minute lay-over up the line because we missed a block and had to go into a siding. The conductor gave the agent a cussing that would have done a cavalry sergeant proud. It was the only incident of man failure I saw on the whole trip.

Everywhere, among the nation's railroad men, the clock is the enemy. They're always fighting time. They hauled a crippled tank car out of the line at Marion, O. [Erie Yard], slapped a new set of wheels on it and had it ready to go along with us by the time our engine was serviced.

That wasn't extraordinary, just routine. Tank car movement of oil makes a terrific job for railway shopmen. Every rusted, busted tanker that will hold oil has been rounded up and sent flying East.

By reconditioning these old tankers 'on the fly,' the railroads save new steel. Already the railroads are hauling three times as much oil east as that proposed 300,000-barrel pipeline, which would have taken steel enough to build 200 freight ships for overseas duty.

This speed-up movement of oil hasn't meant relaxation of safety standards. Inspectors swarmed over our train at every division stop, at least three times daily. Even

Below: *Serving the Nation, by Dean Cornwell, was used on the front of a map of the PRR system published for servicemen. The PRR and Uncle Sam, it implies, are one.*

minor defects mean a 'bad order' and repairs before that car can proceed.

This teamwork is paying off in new records all the time. Our oil train gunned 2500 miles at three times the normal, pre-war speed of freight. That sort of thing is being done every day. We couldn't fight a war without it.

Don't worry about the railroads. Just tell 'em what you want, where it is and where you want it, and they'll set it down there. We Easterners would be burning furniture in a bathtub bonfire this winter if it weren't for a million guys pushing oil trains across this country every day.

Note
John Grover, 'Highballing Oil to the East,' published in *Erie Railroad Magazine* (October, 1942), pp. 8, 29.

THE BUSINESS CAR

'Private' railroad cars actually came in at least three species. At one extreme were cars owned by a corporation or individual. Next came the equivalent of today's chartered jet — the car rented from the Pullman Company. Most numerous, however, were the railroad-owned 'business' cars assigned to company officials, such as the Western Maryland Railway car No. 203 featured here. Their main function was to provide a mobile office for senior railroad executives when making official visits to different parts of the line.

Business cars assigned to operating vice presidents and general managers would provide facilities for a large staff. At the rear of a typical car was the lounge (as seen below), overlooking the open platform. There was always a speedometer, plus powerful track lights below the platform making inspection of every mile of roadbed a day and night possibility.

Next came the secretary's office, complete with bunks and desk. Further along the corridor — which was almost invariably on the left so that the sleeping rooms would be on the quiet side as trains rushed past on the other track — would be the sleeping accommodation: the master bedroom with its bath, shower and double bed; then two or three further bedrooms with upper and lower berths. Further along the corridor, there would be a bath and shower. The full-width dining room (seating from eight to ten people) was situated toward the center of the car. The showiest feature of even a plain car was likely to be a capacious, mirrored sideboard, perhaps with a pass-through from

the tiny kitchen-pantry ahead. The kitchen was equipped with a stove, iceboxes, and lockers. Another corridor would lead past the crew's bedroom and shower to the front vestibule.

Western Maryland business car No. 203 was built by the Pullman Company in 1914. It displays most of the features described above, but was modernized and remodelled in 1954. The car was retired from service in the early 1960s and, since 1974, has been on display at the Railroad Museum of Pennsylvania, Strasburg.

nearly $80 million from the New Deal's Public Works Administration for completion of this work. Federal officials, of course, knew that these extensions of electric lines would generate badly needed jobs. By 1937 the Pennsy's powerful electric passenger and freight locomotives operated between New York City and Washington, DC and Philadelphia (Paoli) and Harrisburg, Pennsylvania.

Unlike heavy traction, the steam locomotive struck some as a technological dinosaur by the late 30s. But for most, however, it was not considered passé. The Union Pacific, for one, not only embraced diesel streamliners, but acquired a fleet of 4-6-6-4 or 'Challenger' steam locomotives. The first of this powerful high-speed design arrived on the property in 1936. The Challenger's stability at high speeds made it one of the most popular simple articulated locomotives; eastern and western carriers purchased more than 200 4-6-6-4s during the next eight years. Then the greatest steam beasts of all debuted in September 1941. Again, Union Pacific took the lead. Between 1941 and 1944 that company added 25 of the behemoth 4-8-8-4's, called 'Big Boys', to its fleet of locomotives. The only engines of their type, they weighed 600 tons and their 7000-horse-power could pull a loaded 5½-mile-long train at speeds of 66mph on level track.

That the UP could afford to invest in new motive power was understandable. Unlike most carriers, the company enjoyed impeccable credit in the capital markets throughout the depression and so could afford a *M-10000* or a 4-8-8-4. But the outbreak of World War II turned famine into feast for nearly every carrier in terms of both traffic and income.

War shook the United States and Canada. As the nations battled Japan, Germany and Italy, they participated in a global conflict in the truest sense of the word. Residents of both countries united as never before: eligible men and women rallied to the colors, civilians labored in unprecedented numbers on the homefront, and the governments marshaled resources to insure victory for the Allies.

America's railroads responded magnificently

to the enormous demands made of them. Because of the rationing of gasoline, tires (rubber was in especially short supply) and replacement parts, motor carriers were unable to maintain their previous levels of transport, let alone cope with the increase. Moreover, the presence of German submarines in the waters of the Atlantic and Caribbean disrupted the flow of goods through the Panama Canal and along coastal shipping lanes between Texas and New England. As a result, the railroads handled 83 percent of *all* traffic between 1941 and 1944, and they moved 91 percent of all military freight within the country and 98 percent of all military personnel. Revenue freight tonnage soared from 1.8 billion tons in 1940 to 3 billion tons in 1943, and would not pass the latter record figure until 1966. Passenger traffic skyrocketed from 452,921,000 riders in 1940 to 910,295,000 in 1944, and that peak figure would never again be equalled.

To keep all these trains running, the railroads tapped into the available pools of non-traditional and frequently unskilled workers. They had no other option: thousands of their regular employees were serving in the military, yet business was booming. Most notably, women performed many of the duties normally undertaken by men, except for some very physically demanding tasks. 'We had women in the round-houses, in the yards and in the offices,' recalled a Lackawanna Road offical; 'They did damn good work.' Companies also begged employees not to retire, and many agreed to remain, often in the most demanding posts. Some roads recruited workers from Mexico, usually for track maintenance. Even with a shortage of experienced personnel, American carriers were able to expand their workforce, which rose from 1,140,000 in 1941 to a total of 1,420,000 in 1945.

The challenges for the railroad industry were immense at this time. The shortage of skilled workers persisted, most commonly in repair

Below: *The B&O's streamlined 4-6-2 No. 5304 hauls the* Royal Blue, *about 1940. Despite the success of the new diesels, few railroad managers thought that steam was finished.*

facilities. Life was hectic, even dangerous, for personnel. Remembered a boilermaker at the Chicago Great Western shops in Oelwein, Iowa, 'We just didn't have any help. We couldn't get any, so we worked day and night. Every engine that we had was junk . . . War freight sitting in the yards, telegrams coming in continually, "Send that (locomotive) over! We've got to have it! The boys need it!"'

Fortunately, the federal government provided some effective coordination, largely through the Office of Defense Transportation (ODT). But Washington did not attempt federalization as it had in World War I, and surely a less cumbersome bureaucracy helped. Directives and guidelines and even moral persuasion aimed at keeping civilians from over-taxing railroad services generally worked well. For example, on October 15, 1942, the ODT prohibited railroads from accepting for shipment, with some exceptions, any freight cars not loaded to their marked limits or to their visible capacity. The logistics of the war also made a difference. Since between 1941 and 1945, goods and personnel were not bound solely for Atlantic ports in this two-ocean conflict, eastern yards were not overwhelmed as they had been in 1917 and 1918.

Train travel during the war frequently lacked the glamor of peacetime. Coaches, diners and Pullman cars were usually crowded, and some obsolete equipment, which should have been scrapped, remained in service. The Chicago & North Western, for one, had expected to retire its last wooden chaircars by 1941, but wartime postponed that plan until after 1945.

Wartime travel for many meant the ubiquitous troop train. These may not have been pleasant experiences — meals of franks and canned peas hardly ranked as an epicurean delight, and a relaxing night's sleep was not likely with two soldiers squeezed into each lower berth. 'I

Above: *In 1941-44, UP added 25 unique 'Big Boys' to its fleet. The heaviest steam locomotives ever, they were built for the steep Ogden, UT — Green River, WY grade.*

Below: *Wartime finally ended the hard times of the Depression, providing jobs, and plenty of overtime, for all who wanted it: the workforce expanded greatly during the War.*

believe for many GIs that being herded onboard troop trains during World War II convinced them that they never again would travel by rail,' observed one railroad official. 'Likely with the troop trains the industry planted some seeds that grew eventually into the demise of intercity passenger service.' Nevertheless, the government sought to send its fighting men and women to war in sleeping cars rather than coaches. Organized troop movements, which took longer than 12 hours to complete, were given Pullman sleeping car space, if available. What permitted the Pullman Company to carry 66 percent of all troops was a prewar surplus of about 2000 cars, mostly tourist sleepers, which the firm had stored. Pullman would later boast that it loaded a sleeper approximately every three minutes in 1944, and slept an average of 30,000 service personnel every night.

There is nearly universal consensus that the railroads of the United States and Canada did yeoman service for the cause of democracy against fascism. In October 1945, Canadian politician Lionel Chevrier succinctly summarized the industry's accomplishments: 'The railways have been the backbone of this country's war effort. They have nobly upheld the best tradition of railroading. For five and a half years they have proven themselves to be one of the most important lines of defense and offense in a global war . . . Our railwaymen, whether executive, engineer or section hand, have played marvelous roles in keeping supplies moving to factories and to seaboard.'

Toward the end of the conflict the Association of American Railraods (AAR), echoing the sentiments of industry officials, anticipated a promising post-war period; they expected the hardships of the 30s and the dislocations of wartime to be mostly bad memories. In a widely distributed advertisement, 'There's a Great Day

Coming!' the trade group said in part, 'Yes, the war will be over. But our work won't. We will have many things to do — for him, for you, for the finer future we're fighting for — and it is our aim to do them. You want, and we want to give you, finer cars, better roadbeds, faster, more modern motive power to replace the hard-working equipment now rapidly wearing out under war's double load.' The AAR statement concluded: 'The big thing is that the great day that's coming can be more than a day of victorious reunion. It can also be a day of fresh starting in the shaping of a finer America. For him you are waiting to welcome home — for you who have been so patient with war-imposed travel limitation — we intend to do our share in making it just such a day.'

With the surrender of the Empire of Japan in August 1945, the railroads and the citizenry of both the United States and Canada believed that a better world was at hand. Actually, it would be a kind of Indian summer for the railroads. For a winter would truly set in by the late 50s, and would not change into a spring of sorts until the early 80s. Luckily, the nearly universal suffering of the 30s never returned; that decade had truly been the long, hard winter.

Note

[1]Statistics from Association of American Railroads data.
[2]Ben Reitman noted that a hobo works and wanders; a tramp dreams and wanders; a bum drinks and wanders.

Above: *Women track workers, 1944. Women tackled most railroad tasks during the War, proving once and for all that there were very few they could not handle as well as men.*

Below: *The Servicemen's Lounge at New York City's Penn Station, 1944. The railroads had done a superb job, but one thing the returning troops wanted was their own automobile.*

YEARS OF REVOLUTION

VICTORY IN WORLD WAR II came in the summer of 1945. Railroad people celebrated in joy and relief. The railroads had done a massive job, moving all the munitions and supplies that rolled from the factories to ports, moving the soldiers and sailors, and all the while handling domestic transport of freight and passengers on the 'home front.' Railroad people were proud of what they had accomplished. They had been tested, and they had carried the burden well.

In the public eye, the war reinforced the long-standing role of railroads as the backbone of transportation. Certainly, automobiles, trucks, and planes would compete with railroads in the post-war era, but railroads would remain the nation's basic method of overland transportation — or so most people assumed, including railroaders. The nation's highway system at the end of 1945 was pretty much the same as it had been five years earlier; in the press of war, domestic priorities had taken a back seat. Air travel was negligible and not a serious competitor. Railroaders anticipated a prosperous peace,

Time itself seems frozen in this winter scene of Long Island Rail Road barges at Long Island City, February, 1945. But a new era was dawning for the railroads — an era of new technology, perfectly represented by GM's pre-war FT-103 demonstrator (inset).

the 15-year struggle of depression and war now behind them.

But is was a new world. Every GI came home dreaming of a civilian job, a home, a family — and an automobile. Auto sales soared. The motoring public, in turn, clamored for better roads, so their legislators responded by underwriting a boom in highway construction. In the shift from war to a peacetime economy, tax funds to build the new roads came plentifully.

Truckers took to the improved highways, carrying more freight particularly on hauls of short and medium distances where delivery by rail was usually slow. Relishing their success, truckers began to encroach seriously on long

hauls, especially for the carriage of light manufactured goods. The age of the true long-distance, semi-tractor-trailer was dawning.

At the same time, air traffic began to increase. Before the war, flying had been strictly for the few, the rich, and the somewhat daring. The war transformed the technology of aircraft design and production. With the lessons thus learned, builders such as Douglas and Lockheed unveiled planes like the DC-7 and the 'Super Constellation', which were more commodious, more reliable, and cheaper to operate per seat-mile. Air travel began to lose its rakish image.

Cheap gasoline fueled and accelerated these changes on the highways and in the air. With vast supplies flowing from the oil-fields of Texas, Oklahoma, Louisiana, California, and from the freshly tapped reserves of the Middle East, the low price of gasoline helped both truckers and airlines to post more competitive freight rates and air fares. Motorists, too, relished the freedom engendered by bargain gasoline.

A crisis loomed for the railroads. Compared to other commercial carriers, railroads had handled over three-quarters of all passenger-miles between cities in 1944. Six years later, the proportion dropped to 47 percent; by 1960 it would plummet to 29 percent. Travelers voted with their gas pedals and increasingly abandoned trains. The story was similar, but not as stark, for freight: from 69 percent of all freight ton-miles moved intercity in 1944, down to 56 percent in 1950, and eroding to 44 percent by

Above: *A B&M Railroad bulletin board in North Station, Boston, in October 1946. For the majority, however, the automobile, not the train, was the 'magical' way of traveling.*

Below: *Ted Rose's aptly named painting,* Evolution, *depicts a new Santa Fe diesel powering through Cajon Pass, CA, in the late 40s — leaving the steam engine far behind.*

1960. Trucks, rivercraft, and pipelines all increased market share in this period. Freight shippers made their analyses based on costs, delivery time, and reliable schedules — and railroads increasingly came up short.

Simultaneously, the railroads faced a painful situation regarding their physical plant. The depression of the 1930s had curtailed track maintenance, and few new locomotives had been ordered. Although World War II had seen the introduction of some new locomotives, both steam and diesel, and although track work picked up, most of the physical plant — locomotives, cars, rails, communication systems, maintenance facilities, shops — coped with the avalanche of war traffic with only limited renewals. By 1945 and the war's end, the locomotive fleet was, in the main, old and worn out.

Other problems hit in the wake of peace. Strikes in the Appalachian coal fields, the result of long-simmering labor problems which the war had only temporarily preempted, caused coal prices to rise. More-expensive coal helped push rail transport costs up, especially for eastern and midwestern roads dependent on coal for fuel. Railroad workers, too, demanded higher wages. Workers in various crafts walked out on strike and every railroad union bargained

hard for higher pay. For railroad costs, this meant real trouble: the payroll represented over half of all expenses, and there were a lot of people to pay. In the war year of 1944, over 1.4 million people had been employed on American railroads. Yet by 1951, even though rail traffic was way down, employment still held at almost 1.3 million, and wages per employee had increased by a massive 53 percent.

Railroad managers felt themselves to be under intense pressure. The smug assumptions about business continuing more-or-less as usual once the war ended were turning to ashes.

On every railroad, the locomotive fleet stood out as a major sinkhole of cost. The aging fleet was clearly jeopardizing the chances for economic survival. And the question was not just a simple one of steam *versus* diesel.

Diesel locomotives had been around since the 1920s, as small transfer engines and switchers, and since the 1930s in such glamorous form as the Union Pacific's *M-10000* and the Burlington's *Pioneer Zephyr* for passengers

Below: *Sunrise over the B&O's Brunswick Yards, 1953. If steam was still the ruler in this yard, it was not for long: such scenes were to become increasingly rare in the US.*

(see Chapter 7). General Motors' young locomotive organization, Electro-Motive Corporation, began limited production of larger passenger diesels in the mid-1930s. The preferred designs incorporated a diesel prime-mover with an electric transmission: under the hood, a big diesel engine turned an electric generator, which in turn supplied high current to several electric motors mounted directly on the locomotive's axles. Watching these developments, two of the traditional steam locomotive manufacturers hedged their bets. The American Locomotive Co. (Alco) in cooperation with General Electric Co., and the Baldwin Locomotive Works in league with Westinghouse, introduced diesel-electric locomotive designs of their own.

In 1939, when General Motors' new four-unit demonstrator diesel locomotive, built specifically for heavy freight duty, made its 83,000-mile tour of the nation's railroads, it pulled fast freights and drags with equal facility. The No. 103 showed for the first time that a diesel freighter could stand the gaff of rough, mainline service.

More than any demonstration, though, it was the war that had shown what diesels could do. Many railroads acquired some diesels just before and during the war. In particular, the Atchison, Topeka & Santa Fe Railway — connecting Chicago and Los Angeles via the deserts of New Mexico, Arizona, and Southern California — became the first major railroad to 'go diesel' on its freight in a significant way. The Santa Fe had always had chronic problems with water in the desert for its steamers — not only with supply but far more seriously with 'bad' water which deposited scale inside locomotive boilers, thus enormously increasing maintenance. With no timidity, Santa Fe had ordered 68 of GM's new FT-models for delivery beginning in 1940. The diesels shone.

Santa Fe president Fred Gurley became a true believer. 'Time does not permit a discussion of all [the diesel's] virtues,' he declared in a speech in 1946. 'Sufficient to say it is the best which man's ingenuity has produced for our service.' The public, too, took a lively interest: *Life* magazine ran a big photo spread on the Santa Fe's diesels in 1947 and correctly observed: 'Last year 90 percent of the locomotives ordered by railroads were diesels.'

Against this public relations onslaught, the steam locomotive manufacturers spoke up bravely; they meant to compete in the postwar market. At war's end, the United States' big railroads had a fleet of almost 40,000 steamers and just 3000 diesels. Railroads were heavily invested in steam maintenance facilities and backshops. Hundreds of thousands of employees worked as boilermakers, steamfitters, foundry workers, machinists, and other trades tied to steam technology; other thousands worked handling the coal fueling, watering, lubrication, running repairs, and ash of the steam fleet. Roundhouses, coal tipples, and water towers stood as prominent landmarks in American and Canadian cities large and small. A few railroads, such as the Pennsylvania, the Norfolk & Western, and the Canadian Pacific owned shop facilities so extensive that they could design and produce their own steam locomotives, as well as maintain them. If railroads were the very core of overland transportation,

steam was the core of railroad operations.

The real issue was the old age and limited capacity of most steam locomotives in use at the time. Despite the improved steam designs introduced in the 30s and early 40s, newer steamers constituted a small proportion of the total steam roster. The average steamer had been built in the 20s, before the Depression, and had undergone major repairs many times. As any railroad officer could attest, the repair cost per mile to run a locomotive rose sharply as its age increased. Even though the robust construction of steam locomotives allowed them to provide useful service for three or four decades, there was no getting around the maintenance/age cost curve. The answer was obvious: new locomotives were needed.

The 'Big Three' of the commercial steam locomotive builders — Baldwin, Alco, and the Lima Locomotive Works of Lima, Ohio — fully intended to provide these new engines. A few diesels might enter the mix, they thought, but the bulk of the new business should be steam: 'Whenever you hear that the steam locomotive is all done, washed up, and ready to be put away, just remember the old story of the hammer and the anvil,' observed Lima Locomotive Works chief designer Bert Townsend in a speech to the Master Boiler Makers' Association; 'It was the anvil that wore out.'

Improved technology developed for steam since the 20s promised big increases in fuel efficiency and reductions in operating cost. And steam still possessed a significant inherent advantage: purchase price. Compared to new diesels, new steamers built commercially cost about half as much per installed horsepower, and in many applications much less than half.

The marketing blitz had begun even before the war started. General Motors had polished its trade-ad campaigns in the 1930s, touting the fuel and operating cost savings possible with diesels. High purchase price compared to steam was a definite problem, but GM claimed that operating savings could offset the price difference in relatively short order. GM gained an early foothold with diesel switching locomotives. Since steam switchers were often among the oldest locomotives on a railroad's roster, they became an easy target. Steam switchers also were notorious for consuming great quantities of fuel while standing idle for long periods between switching moves in the yard, and so the operating savings of diesel switchers could be easily demonstrated. (A steamer has to burn fuel when standing just to keep the boiler hot; a diesel consumes a relatively small amount of fuel at idle.) For mainline passenger service, GM catered to the railroads' worry about chronic passenger losses. In colorful trade ads — and in ads for the traveling public, too — GM capitalized on the fresh, modern look of brashly painted, streamlined diesels. Fast, smooth-pulling, and clean (no more rain of cinders down the back of the neck!), diesels promised to attract travelers back out of their automobiles.

The steam builders had responded to the diesel-manufacturers' campaign in kind: their own trade ads pointed up the reliability and dependability of modern steam. To catch the public's eye, railroads and builders had installed streamlined, Art Deco casings on passenger steamers in the 30s, in an effort to address steam's image problem. Industrial designers

Above: *By placing ads like this, which appeared in a* Saturday Evening Post *of January, 1949, GM aimed to persuade the traveling public that a new age had dawned.*

Henry Dreyfuss, Raymond Loewy, and Otto Kuhler, respectively, restyled the *Twentieth Century Limited* of the New York Central, the *Broadway Limited* of the Pennsylvania, the 100-mph *Hiawatha* of the Milwaukee Road, and other steam-hauled trains. The public enjoyed the show, but while the new steam streamliners often ran sold-out (or nearly so), overall passenger statistics continued to erode. Railroaders winced when passengers sometimes referred to streamlined steamers as 'diesels' anyway. In the public mind, modernity was more associated with internal combustion than with steam.

A streamlined covering, of course, had nothing to do with the underlying technology of steam, and the builders knew it. Engineers for the Lima Works and one of its associated companies worked hard on a potentially major improvement: poppet valves. This technology,

brought from Europe in the 20s and later re-engineered for the more severe operating conditions typical on North American railroads, promised a radical cut in fuel consumption. Instead of the older-style piston valves which regulated the flow of steam in and out of a locomotive's cylinders, poppet valves timed the steam flow much more precisely and solved a variety of problems that had always limited steam efficiency. Fuel savings of 15 to 25 percent were promised, with an associated boost in power, especially at higher speeds. The Pennsylvania Railroad sponsored a few installations of the new valves on older locomotives just before and during the war, found them more-or-less successful, and then ordered them installed on a whole new class of 6000-horsepower passenger locomotives for postwar production: the new T1, sheathed in a sensational casing styled by Raymond Loewy. The T1, looking like a horizontal spaceship and capable of speeds over 120mph, threw the gauntlet down before the diesel.

The steam manufacturers had other tech-

Left: *Richard Dilworth and Donald Gordon (right) played key roles in forcing through the diesel revolution. Dilworth was GM's Chief locomotive designer; Gordon presided over CN's dieselization program in Canada.*

Belpaire' design, to improve furnace efficiency and combustion capacity. New boiler drafting and heat recovery systems were in the wings. Welded construction promised to lower both first-cost and maintenance. Engineers designed multiple-cylinder drive systems, and experimented with turbines to eliminate the cylinders altogether. Improved steels and casting methods, improved lubrication systems, light-weight driving wheels, and other advances all added up to a 'high-tech' steam locomotive, cheaper to operate and maintain than its century-long line of predecessors. A modern steamer was, indeed, a *tour de force* of the technology of its era. 'Come what may,' boasted one steam manufacturer in an advertisement in several magazines, 'steam designs are ready to meet every demand of our railroads . . . Steam [will be] the dominating power for railroad transportation for a long, long time to come.'

nological improvements up their sleeves. Roller bearings on all axles and on side rods had proved themselves to be a major improvement in the 30s. Though costly to install, roller bearings cut axle and rod maintenance by two-thirds and virtually eliminated lubrication failures on axles. Engineers researched new boiler configurations, such as Lima's 'double-

Builders and operators of steam locomotives also recognized that maintenance and servicing facilities — the infrastructure of steam — had

Bottom: *Mighty as the power of the steam AC-11 may have been when built in the 40s, the locomotive was obsolescent when photographed here in Los Angeles' Taylor Yard in 1949.*

to be redesigned and upgraded if steam power was to compete economically. Locomotive manufacturers by themselves could do little to effect change in the operating maintenance arena. A railroad led the effort: the Norfolk & Western, a line connecting the port of Norfolk with the central Appalachian coal fields and the Ohio River valley. In the heavy flow of coal and

DIESELIZATION

The last commercially-built steam locomotives for North America left the Lima and the Baldwin plants in 1949. Norfolk & Western Railway built its own steamers for a few more years. But that was the last gasp: during World War II, many railroads had ordered new steam locomotives only because new diesels were not available, and with the end of war in 1945, diesel orders soared.

The cast 'builder's plate' at the lower left tells a mixed tale. Late to take the diesel

revolution seriously, both Baldwin and Lima fielded inferior postwar diesel designs compared to General Motors. In vain hope, Baldwin in 1950 merged with Lima (which had earlier joined with diesel-engine maker Hamilton) to create BLH. By 1956, BLH had built its last locomotive.

There was room in the market, however, for other firms. One was Fairbanks-Morse, which introduced a line of innovative opposed-piston diesel locomotives that sold well for a time.

The only former steam builder to make it

successfully into the diesel era was Alco. General Electric was a neighbor of Alco in Schenectady, New York, and GE made the electrical gear for Alco locomotives. But GE broke off with Alco in 1952. Thus hampered, Alco sales gradually diminished, and the last Alco diesel was built in 1969.

General Motors stole the show, by virtue of generally superior designs with lower maintenance costs than rival diesels. Image-building advertising helped, too: in the 1938 calendar, note the woman checking her makeup.

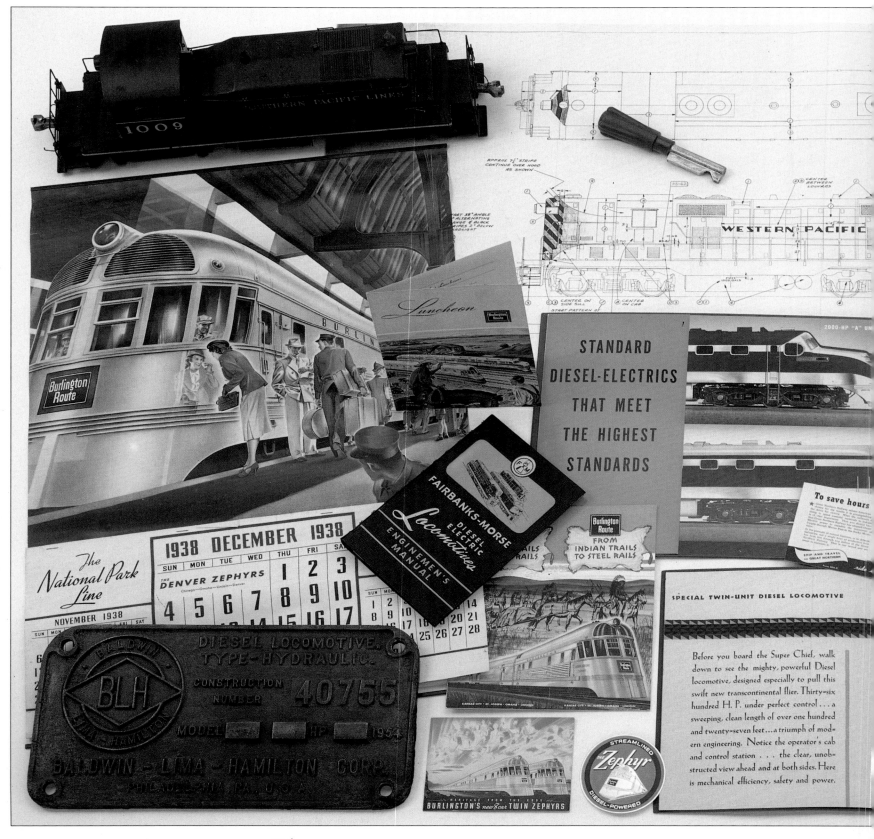

1 1938-9 CB&Q calendar showing a *Denver Zephyr*.
2 Model of SP diesel switcher No. 1009.
3 EMD diesel styling and painting blueprint, 1952.
4 Diesel reverser handle.
5 CB&Q menu cover, 1946.
6 EMD builder's plate, 1953.
7 Models of EMD FA and FB locomotives.
8 Toy train, UP *M-10005*.
9 EMD print of Texas-Mexican Railway locomotive No. 800.
10 1937 UP beverage menu.
11 Inside pages of *M-10000* promotional brochure,

1933.
12 Brochure for the *City of San Francisco*, 1951.
13 Baggage sticker.
14, 15 China cup, saucer, sugar bowl with UP 'Winged streamliner' pattern.
16 Cover, Alco/General Electric brochure for diesel-electrics.
17 Cover, brochure for *Olympian Hiawathas*, 1947.
18 *California Zephyr* brochure, 1949.
19 Fairbanks-Morse *Machinist's Handbook*,

1955.
20 *Super Chief* promotional brochure, late 1930s.
21 GN World War II blotter.
22 Inside panel of Alco/GE brochure (see 16).
23, 24 Brochure for *Silver Streak Zephyr*, 1945; with baggage sticker.
25 Brochure for *Twin Zephyrs*, 1937.
26 Fairbanks-Morse *Enginemen's Manual*, 1957.
27 Baldwin-Lima-Hamilton builder's plate.
28, 29 Covers, UP *M-10000* brochures. 1933, 1934.

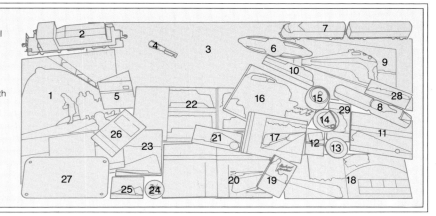

commerce on the N&W, daily operations required many locomotives to be 'turned' — inspected, fires cleaned, fueled, lubricated, given minor repairs, and redispatched — at Shaffers Crossing terminal in Roanoke, Virginia. At this key location, N&W designed and built 'lubritoriums' and modern 'flow-through' servicing bays unlike anything railroads had ever seen. Instead of taking a half-day or more to turn a locomotive, N&W could do it in about an hour. And N&W added a couple of steps. At every turning, workers flushed the locomotive's boiler completely in a few minutes with clean hot water, and other workers applied pressure lubrication throughout the chassis and running gear. The new servicing philosophy, in turn, let N&W staff engineers redesign locomotive lubrication systems. The more-effective lubrication and frequent boiler flushing, together with reduced labor in the flow-through bays, permitted N&W to boost steam locomotive reliability while cutting per-mile repair costs in half compared to some other big roads.

The postwar 'war' between diesel and steam promised to be a donnybrook. The battle was not fought, however, *mano a mano*, machine against machine: rather, a host of subtle factors were to be decisive, and railroaders only vaguely appreciated the significance of most of those factors. The result would transform an industry beyond the imagining of most of the participants.

Above: *The PRR T1 incorporated several innovations — poppet valves promised to give higher speeds with lower fuel costs — but actual tractive pull was poor.*

Below: *Alexander Leydenfrost's* Power, *painted for the PRR's 1945 calendar, featured a prototype T1. Despite this gesture of belief, the last T1 was delivered from Altoona in 1946.*

The insurgent in this war was General Motors, in a classic case of an outsider forcing change. Uninhibited by traditional concerns affecting the railroad-company/locomotive-supplier relationship, GM refused to play by most of the rules. A significant departure was in design collaboration. When the Baltimore & Ohio Railroad, which wanted to help develop a diesel locomotive, offered to underwrite GM's expenses for testing on its lines, GM locomotive designer Richard Dilworth refused. Why, asked the B&O? Replied Dilworth, 'So you fellows won't tell us how to build it.'

Railroad company motive-power engineers had always been intimately involved in the design of their purchased locomotives, working closely with a manufacturer's design staff. Railroad officers rightly insisted on customized steam locomotives suited specifically to the unique topographical and operational circumstances of their railroad. Different prevailing situations of grade, speed, and train size required entirely different steam designs. Given the batch-style production methods used by steam builders — production runs usually amounted to only ten to 50 engines at a time — purchase price per engine was not much reduced by the size of the order, and the railroad received engines best tailored to its specific needs. Real standardization was not an overriding priority. For GM, on the other hand, thoroughgoing standardization had always been a fundamental

part of its engineering and production philosophy. Standardization in high-volume production meant more efficient production methods, lower materials costs, far lower production costs, and the lowest possible prices to customers. Based on its experience with diesel locomotives before the war, GM's renamed Electro-Motive Division (EMD) saw no good reason for collaboration on custom designs; the inherent operational flexibility of its electric transmission meant that a general-purpose diesel locomotive could successfully handle a much wider variety of train sizes, grades, and speeds than could any steam locomotive. The need for custom design did not apply.

In one celebrated incident in the late 30s, a railroad interested in new passenger diesels kept insisting on changes to the GM design. Finally, in exasperation, EMD's Hal Hamilton made an offer. 'We'll build you a locomotive. You tell us what color you want it painted and we'll be responsible for everything else. We'll send you the locomotive without charge, with one of our men in it to supervise . . . You run the locomotive for six months. At the end of that time, you send us either the locomotive or the money.' Six months later, the railroad paid up

Below: *In 1945, two years after this photograph of the N&W's innovative Shaffers Crossing servicing facility was made, a record 141 locomotives were dispatched in one day.*

— and also ordered five more engines.[1]

So GM stuck to its guns, and design chief Dilworth ruled: no departure from massproduced, strictly standardized locomotives. The only real options would be lower gearing for freight service, and higher gearing with trucks (bogies) of longer wheelbase — the longer wheelbase giving better stability at high speed — for passenger service. But with its savvy marketing sense, GM offered to paint their customers' new diesels in stylish, colorcoordinated schemes unique to each railroad. The idea caught on quickly, and EMD established a styling studio.

GM's customer relations did not end there. Electro-Motive set up a network of parts-andservice depots across the country, and trained a corps of field staff to deliver new locomotives, to help establish training programs for its customers' crews and mechanics, and to act as technical consultants and trouble-shooters. No steam builder had ever done such a thing; it was a need that railroads, so long wedded to steam, had never had before. EMD's managers knew, however, that their success depended heavily on railroads adapting to the new locomotives with a minimum of teething trouble.

GM also helped cash-strapped railroads in the critical arena of financing. In response to the issue of higher purchase price compared to steam, GM pointed out that its standardized diesels were far more acceptable as security to

lending banks. In the past, railroads had usually financed purchases of steam locomotives from revenues or from bank lines of credit secured by assets of the company. The steam locomotive builders were indifferent to the financing arrangements. The diesel introduced a new wrinkle. Since the mass-produced diesel models were standard and actually interchangeable from one railroad to another, the locomotives themselves could be readily accepted as security for their own financing. Rarely used for steam locomotive purchases, such arrangements became common for diesels, and a railroad in bankruptcy or in weak financial condition could acquire a fleet of new locomotives this way.

These standardized locomotives ushered in change in many dimensions. The changes can be grouped into two basic categories: operations, and maintenance and repair. In both categories, diesel and steam differed fundamentally.

Railroad operations demand adaptability from a railroad's locomotive fleet. Passenger trains run on fixed schedules; fast freight trains, too, may run to schedule. Many freights, however, run as 'extras,' slotted by dispatchers into the complex flow of other trains. Traffic on a line does not come at a steady rate and is not entirely predictable: there is wide variation in seasonal, weekly, and daily traffic movement.

Topography is another crucial variable affecting operations. Truly flat sections of track are rare. Most track runs up and down hill, even in gentle terrain, with grades varying in severity. Often a relatively steep section will impose on an otherwise flat profile. Mountain districts place special demands, the most serious of which is not so much ascending the grade — which is tough enough — but descending grades safely. Trains coming down long grades must stay in full control, within the limitations of locomotive and car braking systems. Locomotives out on the line must alter their power output frequently — from maximum power, to partial, to idle with braking, to maximum again, in a continuously changing response to load and grade — all to keep the train steady at the posted speed (which may vary from signal to signal), with heavy tonnage in tow (which may vary from day to day), over track with many changes in curve and profile. All these variables require highly skilled locomotive crews. Behind the scenes, these variables require dispatchers and locomotive fleet managers to cooperate closely, often hour by hour, on the careful matching of trains to the capabilities of locomotives actually available for each day's duty.

In the era right after World War II, operations reflected some fundamental characteristics of the steam locomotive, characteristics which had been an inherent part of railroading for over 100 years. First, there was a basic mechanical limitation: a steamer's cylinders, drive rods, and driving wheels are permanently fixed in size and mechanical relationship. The locomotive is, in effect, locked in one 'gear,' with the cycles of the pistons fixed to the rpm of the wheels. This is not as limiting as it sounds, because along with the throttle, the locomotive engineer (or driver) varied the 'cutoff,' which altered the timing as well as the quantity of steam flowing to the cylinders. In skilled hands, the power output of a steam locomotive could be managed very effectively and smoothly at any speed, from starting up to the maximum speed limit.

A RIDE ON THE FAST MAIL

Just before Christmas, 1955, David Plowden — now one of America's foremost railroad photographers — was working for the Great Northern Railway in Willmar, MN. Assigned to the Divisional Office as 'Assistant to the Trainmaster,' David usually worked the night shift. This shift, however, was to be like no other — for he was to catch a ride on one of the last steam-hauled fast mail trains to run on the GN. In an abridged extract from his *A Time of Trains,* David describes the events of a momentous night.

The engineer that night was a man named Brown. He went to work at once settling himself in for the run, ignoring [me] completely. The window on his side had been frozen shut by hundreds of miles of blowing snow. He found a 'fusee' and lit it to melt the ice so that it could be opened. When it came unstuck he kept slamming it back and forth angrily, swearing and spitting tobacco juice, complaining perhaps because he wished this were a diesel tonight. Brown was a passenger man used to the comforts of a diesel's cab.

The signal for the brake test came and suddenly the cab was filled with the deafening sound of the air being drawn off the brake line. Brown turned and thrust his head out of the window and looked back along the train to watch for the signal to release the air. It came almost immediately and once again the hiss of escaping air filled the cab as Brown released the brakes. Then he turned to the task at hand. Almost instinctively he leaned forward and his right hand reached for the power reverse lever and pushed it all the way down into the corner.

A moment later Brown's left hand reached out for the throttle. He pulled it back gently a notch or two and the 2505 [a 4-8-2 type] took a tremendous breath and started to move. I don't remember exactly how many cars we had, perhaps 14 or 15. It was a heavy train though and the engine struggled mightily to get us underway. Brown kept her steady, knowing how much steam to use and never once let the drivers slip. I put my head out of the window and looked up at the towering column of steam and smoke disappearing into the blackness above the engine. The thundering cadence grew louder, drowning out all else, as Brown coaxed the 2505 onward. I felt goose pimples rising on the back of my neck. I looked down from the window and by the light of the street lamps saw the driving rods moving up and down and back and forth, making the drivers roll. Faster and faster now with each revolution as Brown and the 2505 took Second Number Twenty-Eight out of town. As I listened the sound of the exhaust assumed a greater sense of urgency as the speed began to increase. This was the *Fast Mail* after all, 'the fastest long-distance train in the world.' We were hours late, and as they had with the 'silk expresses,' the Great Northern had given us the railroad. There was nothing in our way and Brown knew it.

Once the initial task of getting underway had been accomplished Brown settled back a little in his seat. But his left hand was still on the throttle. He kept pulling it back further and further until I thought he was going to pull it right through the roof of the cab. In spite of the cold he had left his window wide open enough to hear the exhaust, to listen to the sound of the engine. As I watched him I realized that, like most of the other old-timers, Brown never paid the slightest attention to the gauges.

As I watched, the needle reached 80, then a little later 85. The next time I looked over it was at nearly 90. As we approached the outskirts of Litchfield about 25 miles east of Willmar, it had reached 92, and there it stood, hovering on one side or the other of 90 miles an hour — a mile in 40 seconds — 20 miles an hour more than the 2505 was designed to run. I knew that speedometers on steam

Above left and below: *A Canadian Pacific engineer oils his locomotive at the Glen engine terminal, Montreal (above left), while another CP locomotive takes coal at Brownville Junction, Maine (below).*

locomotives were notoriously inaccurate, in fact many had none at all, so we might have been only doing 85, but from the way the engine felt, we could have as easily been doing a hundred. Whatever the actual speed, from the way it felt inside the cab it might as well have been 'warp speed.' The old engine was shaking so much that I had to hold onto the window sill to keep from falling off the seat box. The noise was incredible. The roar of the fire, which was now white hot, the cacophony of clanging and crashing of metal, was deafening. The sense of being propelled forward was so exhilarating that it felt as if we were no longer connected to earth. I kept looking at the speedometer and at Brown beyond . . . Neither moved.

Howling through Litchfield now at 92 miles an hour, the whistle shrieking, the roar of the exhaust [was] absolutely deafening as the town closed in around us and the sounds of the engine reverberated back and forth between the buildings.

In spite of the cold I leaned out of the window as far as I dared to be closer to it all; to feel the wind in my face, to see the headlight piercing the night ahead and the crossing gates coming down on the empty streets, to see the rolling drivers, the rods racing in a blur, and was completely swept along with the engine.

The way Brown was 'scorching the ballast' tonight I felt we might leave the rails at any moment. We roared down the Great Northern's mainline like the proverbial 'bat out of hell,' it certainly seemed as if the old 2505 was going faster than the speed of light. The irony was that we were already so late that the few minutes we might gain wouldn't matter one way or the other. But Brown had a tradition to uphold.

As we streaked onward I wondered if the 2505 was capable of sustaining such speed? Would it still hold together?

After all, it was 32 years old . . . Then there were those 55 and 60 mile an hour curves I knew were coming soon. Would Brown slow down in time? I looked at him again. He seemed as reassuringly dispassionate as ever. If those disquieting thoughts had crossed his mind they were obviously of little concern to him. He was sitting there implacably, stretching the 2505 to the limits, making it reach to even greater heights . . .

And then suddenly without warning it was there in the eastern sky. Almost imperceptible at first, but gaining force, light began to come and with it the terrible realization that the run was nearly over. I turned quickly away and looked in the other direction, but when I turned back it was unmistakably morning . . . with the dawn came the suburbs awakening, people filling the streets, going to work, starting their routine. But this was our dawn, not theirs. We'd earned it. We'd been up all night, racing against the clock, with the Christmas mail.

Then, as if awakened from a dream, we were surrounded by the city; threading our way through Minneapolis and into the cavernous trainshed. We were there a long time as mountains of mail were unloaded, but my mind and body had not yet adjusted to the fact that we were standing still. I was still somewhere out there on the prairie before dawn, not in this alien place. Had we raced all night to catch up with time, our time again?

[After unloading the mail at Minneapolis, 2505 hauls the train onto St. Paul.] . . . Directly across the platform from where we came to a stop was a pair of diesels which had just arrived on the *Northwestern Limited* from Chicago. The engineer was already down on the platform talking to the conductor. No sooner had we come to a halt than Brown suddenly sprang to life. He uncoiled himself from the crouched position he had been sitting in most of the night — he was a tall man, I realized then — and without a word to me or the fireman he climbed down out of the cab . . . He rushed over to the engineer of the Chicago train and, grabbing him by the straps of his overalls, he exclaimed pointing to the 2505, 'Look what I brought into St. Paul this morning!'

By then I had come down from the engine myself. Brown wheeled around and threw his arm around my shoulder and said, 'Boy, can that old girl run. Boy, did we get her worked up tonight. My God, what a run we had, eh? God, what a run!'

Taciturn old Brown. Every time I saw him after that, his eyes would light up and he'd say, 'Boy, do you remember that run we made? Remember that night? Boy, could she run! Will you ever forget it?'

Note

This is a heavily abridged extract from David Plowden's introduction to his book *A Time of Trains* (New York, Norton. 1987), pp. 18-24.

But the rub lay in the power available at different speeds. The fixed geometry of any steamer's drive meant that maximum power and efficiency occurred within a very narrow band of rpm or speed. Although a thoroughly accepted characteristic, this narrow power/speed band severely limited the flexibility of assigning locomotives to trains. The maximum raw pull of a steamer (tractive effort, or torque to the wheels) occurred at starting and decreased as speed rose; therefore the heaviest trains on the steepest grades ran at slow speed. Maximum horsepower and efficiency, on the other hand, occurred only at a defined rpm. Freight locomotives therefore had smaller-diameter driving wheels, with maximum power usually peaking at around 25 to 40mph. Passenger engines had larger driving wheels, for maximum power at 45 to 65mph, but with very poor low-speed performance. At speeds slower or faster than its peak-power zone, a steamer was terribly inefficient, wasting fuel out of all proportion to the tonnage being pulled. Depending on terrain and other factors, steam locomotive designers specified driving-wheel sizes in a wide variety of arrangements, resulting in a welter of custom locomotive designs on any one railroad. The welter of designs was inherent. Variety in the size, power, and speed capabilities of a railroad's steam locomotives was a precondition to the adaptability and economic flexibility of the locomotive fleet as a whole.

The new diesels rewrote the honored, ancient rules. The diesel locomotive's electric transmission, with a control feature known as 'transition,' provided high torque and high horsepower over a wide range of speeds. A diesel can run efficiently at speeds both faster *and* slower than a steamer. Like the steamer, the diesel locomotive also puts its maximum available pull to the rail at starting and slow speed, but the diesel's horsepower and efficiency hit maximum quickly — at around eight to ten mph — and stay high as speed increases. Horsepower does not begin to fall off until 40 to 60mph, depending on axle gearing. The kicker is this: when a locomotive — any locomotive — operates at peak horsepower, its economic and operating productivity for its owner is also at its peak. To a railroad manager, the diesel is the dream locomotive: one that maximizes productivity regardless of speed.

As the GM engineers knew full well, this characteristic meant an end to variety in locomotive design. A single locomotive type could handle effectively nearly any combination of trailing tonnage and terrain. Surprisingly perhaps, designers at other locomotive manufacturers seeking to compete with GM did not understand the implications. Baldwin of Philadelphia, for example, had been the world's largest locomotive builder, making steam engines for railroads all over the globe. Baldwin's engineers began designing diesels in the mid-1920s. But Baldwin squandered precious resources in catering to the old railroad habit of wanting custom locomotive designs. Nearly as much engineering and design time, for instance, went in the 1940s to a Pennsylvania Railroad order for a few special high-horsepower diesels as went for a more universal type for quantity production. Neither Baldwin nor the Lima Locomotive Works managed to escape this trap. Of the three major steam builders, only Alco

understood and survived to become an effective diesel competitor to GM. To make matters worse for the traditional locomotive companies, other manufacturers experienced with industrial diesel engines entered the locomotive market for the first time. One was Fairbanks-Morse, which fielded a line of standardized diesel locomotives for both freight and passenger duty.

The implications of the universal locomotive type went a vital step further. As GM's No. 103 had shown, diesel locomotives could be designed in 'units,' each individual chassis self-contained with a complete engine/transmission/driving-wheel package. Each fully standardized locomotive unit could be built to a convenient size. The No. 103 had four such units, each of 1350-hp for a total of 5400-hp, all answering to a set of controls in a cab at either end. For a short time — a very short time — GM engineers did not appreciate what they had done, billing the 103 as 'a 5400-hp locomotive' that was arranged in four units for flexibility around curves and for convenience in maintenance. Each of the

Below: *Great Northern Railway Extra No. 3387, eastbound near Willmar, MN, in February, 1956. The GN was an early user of GM FTs, and phased out steam quickly in the mid-50s.*

two pairs of 1350-hp units was connected with drawbars, not couplers. Forget the drawbars. If four locomotive units could be put together under a single set of controls, so could three or six — or any number that was required for the train to be pulled. All that was needed to put together a locomotive of almost any horsepower quickly were couplers and plug-in electrical cables. Thus was born the modular locomotive, certainly one of the most important innovations in railroading.

Better to appreciate this aspect of diesel flexibility with multiple units, consider that the largest modern steam locomotive had, at most, eight driving axles. In practical terms, each driving axle on a big steamer or an early road-diesel could generate reliably about the same low-speed pull (about 7½ tons of tractive pull for each axle). The steamer's pull was limited by uneven torque; the diesel's pull was limited by the amount of current that could be sustained in each axle-mounted electric motor. So only two standard diesel units, of four axles each, could generate the pull of the very largest steamer at slow speed. Put four diesel units together — such as GM No. 103 — and you have the low-speed pull of two of the largest steamers built. Six diesel units would equal three of the

biggest steamers, and so forth. And all with one locomotive crew — engineer and fireman — instead of two or three such crews. The comparison is actually more complex; compared to diesels, steamers have greater horsepower per driving axle at high speed, and early diesels often burned up traction motors at slow speed with too much current. Therefore at least three (and usually four) diesel units were needed to

Above: *A Maryland & Pennsylvania ('Ma & Pa') Railroad freight, Baltimore County, 1952. It did not take long for such lines to shrink in the face of competition from trucks.*

Below: *Southern Railway trains at Atlanta's Terminal station in the mid-40s: the all-Pullman* Crescent *(right) is hauled by a new E6, while train No. 40 (left) is steam-hauled.*

replace the very largest steamers, and steamers could compete more competitively on flat topograhy or with high-speed passenger trains. But the bread-and-butter of railroading was then, and remains today, heavy freight. Steam locomotives with eight driving axles were relatively rare; most freight steamers had only four or five driving axles, not eight. Therefore, four diesel freight units with one locomotive crew could replace not just two freight steamers, but often three or four — and three or four locomotive crews. With diesels, furthermore, freight trains could actually run slower when long, steep grades required, at top efficiency, making the best use of a diesel's higher power at slow speeds. The use of 'helper' locomotives — extra engines and crews assigned to help push trains over steeper grades — could be eliminated in all but a very few locations.

Power for pulling, however, was just half of the operations equation. Safe speed control descending long grades had always been a major limitation on the size of trains that could be dispatched in mountain territory. Air brake systems on locomotives and cars were capable and highly sophisticated, having been developed over more than half a century. Nevertheless, they still had two fundamental limitations: the need for considerable skill on the part of the locomotive engineer in managing a train's air brakes on a long descent, and the unavoidable frictional heating of brake shoes and car wheels. The heat and wear of friction was the most serious problem, requiring high replacement rates of wheels and brake shoes.

Diesels came with a valuable device: the 'dynamic brake.' On descending grades, the locomotive engineer engaged a switch, and a

simple set of relays functionally changed the electric traction motor on each driving axle into an electric generator. The high turning resistance of these temporary 'generators' slowed the locomotive and poured out electrical current, which dissipated as heat in grids in the locomotive's roof. This was not a new device; straight electric locomotives often used a similar system, with the current from dynamic braking going back into the overhead wire. But such braking had never been available on non-electrified railroads before. Dynamic braking greatly changed mountain railroading. Since dynamic brakes applied only to the locomotive units, air brakes throughout the train — cars and locomotives — were still indispensable. But with dynamic braking, train speed in descent could be much better controlled, and wheel and brake shoe wear greatly reduced.

Dispatchers quickly perceived the advantages of modular locomotives having frictionless braking plus high horsepower in a wide range of speeds: the combination of these operating features, rather than any single one, was revolutionary. All the old bugbears affecting operations — topography and varying traffic — still applied. Yet now, from a common fleet of standard locomotive units, all the trains on the railroad could be handled.

Above: *Two contrasts in manpower usage. Compare the number of people it takes to service this locomotive in 1944 — and the heavy-gauge machinery and monolithic* infrastructure *(such as the coaling tower) required in the yard — with the lean team fueling this GM diesel at the B&Os Riverside Yards in November, 1953 (below).*

Freight trains in any territory could also be much longer: in both mountainous and flat terrain, any required amount of locomotive horsepower could be assigned to a single crew. And in mountain districts, dynamic brakes permitted longer trains safely to descend long grades, as well as to climb them. Longer trains in turn meant fewer trains. That eased dispatching, and having fewer trains compounded the crew savings brought by the modular diesels; even fewer crews could now handle the traffic. The labor implications were slower to dawn on railroad managers, since diesel-hauled trains were rare at first. But crews began to realize the threat, and knew the threat would increase as more diesels were purchased.

In the meantime, crews out on the road actually enjoyed the clean, new diesels. Many locomotive enginemen had loved the steam era, but many more appreciated the improved working conditions of diesel cabs. Engineer Bill Williams of the Kansas City Southern described his mixed emotions about diesels:

> At first I hated them. But once I got on them, I had to admit, they was easier and cleaner to run. I didn't get that old kick out of them that I got out of those old steam engines. In my heart, I'd rather have a steam engine any day. I wanted to stick my head out of the cab and watch those big drivers roll. My first trip in a diesel, I wouldn't have gotten it, but the other man had to lay off. The other fella was all worked up. He asked me, 'How do you like my engine, how do you like my engine?' I told him 'I don't like diesels. If I wanted to run a streetcar, I'd go down and see old man Jacobs at the Shreveport City Transit.'[2]

As for maintenance and repair in the shops, diesels required new approaches there as well. The new machines required new skills, and just like the engine crews, many shopmen felt mixed emotions about the changes.

The steam locomotive had developed from an industrial era of inch-thick plate steel rolled and bull-riveted together, of huge forgings beaten into shape by colossal steam hammers, of one-piece steel castings 70ft long, of huge

Above left: Between the two locomotives (left: a GM unit; right: an Alco diesel) a mechanic checks the locomotive roster posted on a crew shack at the B&O's Riverside Yards in 1953.

Above right: A Rutland Railroad train crew wash up in the engine room after a five-hour, 120 mile run. Their train was discontinued soon after the photograph was made in 1949.

lathes and machine tools. High precision was needed in limited doses — in axle bearings, rod bearings, valves, and cylinders for example — but even there, precisely machined fits wore away quickly and the locomotive was designed to accommodate the imprecision and to operate tolerably until the next cycle of major repair. Interchangeability of parts on steamers was very limited, even on common locomotive classes, and always required a great amount of individual fitting-up by skilled mechanics. The diesel, on the other hand, came from a different industrial era: the era of machine design for internal combustion, where high precision characterizes nearly every working part, where close tolerances must be maintained for the life of the engine, and where genuine interchangeability of identical parts is the rule.

A diesel locomotive is designed as an array of standard components arranged on a standard chassis. Big components such as diesel prime-movers, electric generators, and traction motors can be directly removed and replaced, with the removed components sent to separate shops for heavy repair; likewise smaller components like blowers, pumps, and controls are readily replaceable with a minimum of down time. A steam locomotive, on the other hand, was designed as a complex structural unity: a steamer's frame and boiler were more-or-less permanently bolted together and shared in carrying the locomotive's weight and working stresses; boiler and frame were not separated except for complete boiler replacement, which was rare. To machine its cylinders or to repair a firebox, for example, the entire locomotive had to be handled as a whole. There was no component modularity; even light repairs to auxiliary components required custom fitting of piping

for steam, water, air, and also lubrication.

The difference between the two technologies, diesel and steam, was no more starkly apparent than in the shops. The great variety of sizes and types of steam locomotives, coupled with the high labor intensity required for every repair, prevented significant routinization or production-style repair procedures. The diesel, with its common, interchangeable, standardized parts, lent itself to enormous improvement in shop efficiency. There was, truly, no way the two technologies could coexist in the same shop building, for either light or heavy repair.

And no matter how well designed the steam repair shop, the availability and utilization statistics for diesel locomotives, compared to steam, told the tale: the average diesel unit was available for duty a far higher percentage of the time — up to 92 percent — and could actually be in use pulling trains more hours every day. Fewer locomotives could do more work, with labor hours drastically cut, simply because maintenance was so much easier.

Thus operations on the road and maintenance in the shops were radically affected, and in ways with serious implications for railroad labor. At the heavy repair centers, new shop buildings rose specifically to handle diesels. Men skilled in internal-combustion engines and in electrical equipment hired on. Younger workers took eagerly to the new skills. For supervisors and old steam hands, retraining was wrenching. As Union Pacific master mechanic Frank Acord (later chief of UP motive power) put it, 'I felt like I was a steam-engine expert. I knew my business, but I get up one morning and . . . I have to learn from scratch.' Acord's friend Charlie Spicka, a shop superintendent, saw his first diesels and declared, 'You're not bringing those streetcars in my shop.' Said Acord of his friend, 'It was like they shot him.'[3]

Older steam mechanics still assumed their skills would be needed for years to come; in the worst case, workers hoped, it would take several decades for diesels entirely to replace steam. After all, there were almost 40,000 steam locomotives to replace in the United States alone. For a while, even some railroad managers felt that the two technologies, diesel and steam, might

Pennsylvania Railroad Class GG-1
electric locomotive, built 1934-1943.

coexist for some time to come. But it was not to be. Railroad finance officers ran the numbers: the expense of maintaining two parallel sets of shop facilities and shop staff for the two types of motive power could not long continue. One set of facilities would have to go.

Meanwhile, crewmen who ran the locomotives saw not only their numbers but their working traditions coming under threat. Engineers and firemen were a close-knit fraternity that had developed over the course of more than 100 years. Firemen not only stoked the coal, they were acolytes in a system that promised them eventual promotion as engineers. Engineers, in turn, served at the top of this supporting social hierarchy. Diesels threatened not only job skills — there was no coal to stoke — but this powerful tradition, too.

The Brotherhood of Locomotive Firemen and Enginemen acted early. In 1937, the union had demanded that firemen continue to be assigned to diesels. The UP and the Burlington, which were then running two of the early diesel streamliners, reluctantly agreed. Managers saw merit in the argument that two sets of eyes should be assigned to the cab of a fast-moving passenger train, and besides, only a few trains were involved. There was no thought in 1937 that diesels would ever fully replace steam on passenger trains, let alone be used commonly on freight trains.

Ten years later, the acrimony over the question of whether firemen were needed on diesels was in full cry. During the war, the unions had argued that a second fireman, and even a second engineer, should be assigned to every set of multiple locomotive units assigned to a train. A board established by the President rejected those ideas. But by 1947, the firemen were on

Left: *A B&O 'Mikado' heads a mixed freight off the old main line westward at the classic Point of Rocks junction station (built 1871-75). Track at right goes east to Washington, DC.*

Electro-Motive F3 diesel-electric locomotive,
in two 'units', built 1946-1949.

Union Pacific 'Big Boy,' heaviest steamer
ever built, 1941-44.

strike for the survival of their profession, and engineers supported them. More strikes followed and it was not until 1963, and a Supreme Court ruling, that railroad managements won the ability to eliminate firemen gradually from some trains.

Despite these ongoing labor disputes, the modular locomotive affected locomotive crew jobs across the board. The diesel's various operating characteristics began to cut deeply into locomotive crew rosters. Even with firemen assigned, railroads could save millions of dollars in employment costs. An example is the Western Maryland Railway, which in steam days often had to assign from four to six big steam locomotives to each coal train wrestled over the spine of the Allegheny Mountains. One set of diesel units, with one engineer and one fireman assigned, could handle the same train, or an even larger one. Two crewmen could do the work of eight to 12, even without confronting the fireman issue.

Railroad operating and maintenance officers discovered that a much smaller stable of diesel locomotives could replace a given steam fleet. Financial officers pointed out that borrowing money to add diesels as fast as possible made good sense; actual operating savings would more than offset the debt. Change came like a whirlwind.

Railroad orders for new steam locomotives evaporated. Alco built its last steamer in 1948, the great Baldwin plant built its last one for a US road in 1949, and Lima turned out the last commercially-built US steamer, a 2-8-4, in 1949. Thousands of skilled workers at these plants lost careers. By 1956, many railroads made their last runs with steam, and by 1958, only a handful of steamers were left. The Norfolk & Western held out alone with steam for a few more years, but to little avail. Soon that railroad, too, threw in the towel. Locomotives only a few years old — in other circumstances having decades of

Above: *A UP 'Big Boy' stands alongside a yellow-painted UP gas turbine at Cheyenne, Wyoming, in October, 1958. The last of the 25 famous 'Big Boys' ran in the fall of 1959.*

service remaining — joined ranks of more elderly engines in long, dead lines, awaiting scrap. By 1960, some 27,000 diesel units had entirely replaced those 40,000 steam locomotives in the United States. The major Canadian lines operated their last steamers in 1962.

The steam maintenance facilities disappeared quickly. Water tanks and coaling towers came down; diesels did not have to stop every 50 miles for water or 100 miles for fuel. A new network of compact diesel servicing terminals arose, much more spread out geographically, to fit diesel needs. The steam backshops converted to diesel repair shops, or shut down entirely.

Communities large and small were affected. From Hornell and Binghamton, New York, to Los Angeles; from Cheyenne and Green River, Wyoming, to Baltimore; from Livingston and Havre, Montana, to St. Louis; from Roanoke, Virginia to Fort Worth; from Sedalia, Missouri to Seattle; from Bangor, Maine to Miami; from Pine Bluff, Arkansas to Denver; from Spencer, North Carolina to Chicago — and from Vancouver to Montreal, Winnipeg to Toronto, and Calgary to Quebec — the geographic extent of the changes was unlike anything in American or Canadian industrial history. In several thousand communities across the continent, the steam shops, fueling stations, and servicing depots gradually came down. Thousands of lives changed forever.

It was a time of pain for many. Sons could no longer follow fathers into well-loved trades; fathers saw their trades disappear as sophis-

American Locomotive Co. PA-1
diesel-electric 'A' unit, built 1946-1949.

ticated skills, acquired over lifetimes, became worthless. From 1,400,000 people in 1946, just after the war, employment on major US lines fell to 700,000 in 1962 — a draconian cut of one-half in just 16 short years. Families moved on. Communities adjusted.

An example is Altoona, a city of medium size in central Pennsylvania. Altoona owed its existence and reason for being to the Pennsylvania Railroad. When the railroad was first surveyed in the late 1840s, planners saw that the foot of the Allegheny Mountains would make a good place for major locomotive and car shops, and so Altoona was born. As the PRR grew, eventually connecting New York and Philadelphia with Chicago, the shops at Altoona grew as well. Eventually 16,000 people worked for the railroad at Altoona's vast complex, and their families built a lively, cultivated city.

In the 30s and 40s, the PRR accounted for ten percent of American railroading. 'Do not think of the Pennsylvania Railroad as a business,' said *Fortune* magazine. 'Think of it as a nation.' The heart of this nation was not its managerial and financial center in Philadelphia, nor its huge and celebrated Penn Station covering a square block in New York City, but its human center in Altoona, where seven out of every 100 of the railroad's workers labored — and where the PRR underwrote sports teams, bands, an accom-

plished orchestra, the library, and a major hospital. Here the self-sufficient PRR designed, tested, and manufactured its own locomotives over the years. At Altoona, the PRR staffed the most extensive research-and-development department of any railroad in the world. The number of engineers, chemists, and physicists the PRR employed rivaled any of the world leaders in industrial research, such as Bell Laboratories, General Electric, or Westinghouse. The shops in Altoona turned out steam locomotives in numbers greater at times than the commercial builders: over 400 of one model, over 500 of another, and nearly 7000 in all.

The diesel locomotive upset all of this. In 15 short years — 1955 to 1970 — Altoona's social and economic fabric had to be reconstructed, as the railroad shops and related departments shrank. Rail employment at Altoona dropped by over three-quarters. In 1968, the PRR itself ended its history in the city, as the company merged with its former arch-rival, the New York Central, to become Penn Central. It took time for the wounds to heal, but Altoona prospered again, its economy moving to a more diversified

Below: *The observation car of the restyled* Hiawatha *at Milwaukee in 1948. Sleek new trains such as this were at the forefront of the railroads' postwar battle to recapture customers.*

base. 'When the Pennsylvania gave up on steam, something in this town died, too,' said one long-time Altoona resident. 'It's a great little city, but it took ages for us to recover.'[4]

Railroads in the United States and Canada adapted to the diesel, reluctantly or otherwise. And they pursued other promising cost-cutting strategies. Between 1950 and 1965, more Centralized Traffic Control (CTC) centers allowed railroads to increase dispatching and operating efficiencies. Larger freight cars, such as Southern Railway's 'Big John' covered-hopper design, cut empty weight in proportion to load. Yards, too, were improved and streamlined.

And another important innovation quietly took hold: widespread use of roller bearings on freight car axles. Introduced in the late 20s, roller bearings were expensive, sometimes doubling the cost of a freight car. Not until the 50s did their use take off, necessitated by the longer trains of the diesel era. 'Hot boxes' were the issue — the all-too-frequent overheating of car axles, due to lubrication failure. Ordinary axle bearings had to be serviced manually, and there were inevitable oversights. Hot boxes delayed trains and sometimes caused derailments when overheated axles failed. Roller bearings virtually eliminated hot boxes and needed little servicing. Just as with diesels, the higher purchase cost of roller bearings was more than offset by big

CLEANING UP

On one of his first postings as a towerman on the New York Central in the 50s, Barry Garland made a mistake that could have cost him his career:

George [Birnbacher, the Chief Signalman] knew I was familiar with SK tower and sent me there one day without posting to cover the second trick. I was confident I could handle it.

There was a lot of traffic in those days with the Putnam Division on one side of the tower and the Hudson Division, or main line, on the other. The four track main splits apart at SK tower, and a passenger car washing facility called the wash rack ran down the middle between the mains. After the famous flyers arrive in Grand Central, they are dragged backwards out to the wash rack by venerable 'S' motors (some in service since 1907 were still running), and then to Mott Haven yard for interior cleaning. The wash trains were interspersed with the main line trains heading west. M0 tower (Mott Haven yard) would ring me up on the speaker phone and let me know the order; train number so-and-so, followed by a wash, followed by train number so-and-so, etc.

I set the signals, lined the switches and sat back to read a copy of *Argosy* magazine that I found in the desk. The sound of a slowly approaching 'R' motor filled the tower (it was summer, and the windows were open). I looked out the window. 'Uh-oh, that's an 'R' motor, not an 'S.' Did he say followed by . . .? Oops!' Moving majestically through the switches, off the main and onto the wash rack was one of the Central's finest crack passenger trains — the *Commodore Vanderbilt* — about to get washed, with all the passengers and crew on board peering out the windows and, I was sure, up at me. I'm certain the conductor was looking at me. He was shaking his fist at me from the vestibule as he slammed the dutch door closed to keep from getting wet.

The wash rack came to life. As water and soap lathered the train, brushes whirled and scrubbed the sides of the cars. More water rinsed off the soap. Was my railroad career going down the drain as well? The train moved slowly — ever so slowly — almost in slow motion. It seemed it was the longest train in the world. Would it never end?

I could see the surprised but pleased faces of the passengers. At least *someone* thought it was fun; certainly not George Birnbacher, when I was called on the carpet the following day!

Note

This is an abridged extract from a piece written by Barry Garland for *Western Railroader* magazine, a publication of the Pacific Coast Chapter of the Railway & Locomotive Historical Society. Barry now works at the California State Railroad Museum, Sacramento, CA.

Above: *The 4-unit diesel loco of the eastbound* Super Chief *passes the full-length dome car of the westbound* Chief. *The dome car was popular, and the service prospered, briefly.*

Below: *The 'Aerotrain,' GM's little experimental train, which consciously borrowed from contemporary automobile style, was tried out by a number of railroads in the 50s.*

operating savings. The new bearings permitted even larger freight cars and safe operation of ever-longer trains.

Passenger trains were not forgotten. It is a myth that railroads did not try to recapture the elusive rail passenger. Fabulous new streamliners rolled out after the war. The *Twentieth Century Limited* and the *Broadway Limited*, the *Rocky Mountain Rocket* and the *Empire Builder*, the *Canadian* and the *Continental*, the *Hiawatha* and the *Daylight*, the *City of San Francisco* and the *Chief*, the *Sunset Limited* and the *Silver Meteor*, the *Crescent* and the *Orange Blossom Special* — all these trains and more rolled out in new, diesel editions. These were full-sized, commodious trains, not compact affairs like the early diesel trains *Pioneer Zephyr* and *M-10000*. The best of the new, postwar trains used

RAILROAD FAIRS

Beginning in the second half of the nineteenth century, the world went on a binge of grand fairs and expositions, beginning with London's Great Exhibition of 1851. These celebrations became sources of national pride, as well as showcases for the latest in technology. As one of the great industrial phenomena of the age, the railroad assumed a prominent role in such events. Railroads held center stage, for example, at the 1893 World's Columbian Exposition in Chicago and at the St Louis World's Fair of 1904. Railroads held fairs of their own, too. In 1927, the Baltimore & Ohio Railroad celebrated its Centennial with the 'Fair of the Iron Horse,' staged near Baltimore. The public loved it and, thus inspired, railroads mounted exhibits at the 'Century of Progress' fair of 1933, and at the New York World's Fair of 1939-40. The latter featured 'Railroads on Parade,' a musical pageant with locomotives passing in review. In 1948-9, right after the end of World War II, American railroads staged the Chicago Railroad Fair, which rivaled the 1927 and 1939-40 events in the number of locomotives and rail equipment involved. After 1949, railroad economic fortunes worsened dramatically, and there were no more industry fairs. With the ascendency of the diesel on the big roads, however, the steam locomotive became of nostalgic interest, and various private groups and museums operated steamers as part of public events. In 1991, the California State Railroad Museum staged the largest railroad fair since 1949 — Railfair '91 — with emphasis on railroading's future as well as its past.

1 Posters for the New York World's Fairs of 1939 (left) and 1940 (right).
2 The 'Smallest Train in the World' was operated by the UP at the Trans-Mississippi and International Exposition, Omaha, 1898.
3-5 Brochures published by different railroads advertising various fairs.
6 'Fair of the Iron Horse' calendar, 1927.
7, 8 UP and GN brochures for fairs in 1909 and 1933.
9 New York World's Fair poster, 1939.

10 Exhibitor's Pass for the Eastern [Railroad] Presidents' Conference, New York World's Fair, 1939.
11 Souvenir brochure, Pullman Exhibit, New York Wor.d's Fair, 1939.
12 Official guidebook to the 'Wheels-a-Rolling' pageant, Chicago, 1948.
13 Artist's rendition of the 'O'-gauge layout at the New York World's Fair, 1939.
14 Map of the Chicago Railroad Fair, 1948.
15 Brochure promoting

AT&SF model railroad display at Golden Gate International Exposition, 1940.
16 Commemorative photographs, Chicago Railroad Fair, 1949.
17 Membership card to the 'Chessie Club,' Chicago Railroad Fair, 1949.
18 GM booklet: 'The Train of Tomorrow,' 1948.
19-25 Commemorative programs and souvenirs from railroad fairs held in Vancouver and Sacramento in the last 25 years.

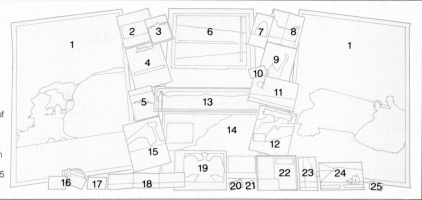

coaches, diners, and sleepers designed by the Budd Co. These cars were built entirely of stainless steel, a major innovation in durability for passenger car construction. The unpainted, fluted exteriors of these beautiful cars gleamed in the sun and created a completely new architecture for rail travel.

Two trains in particular epitomized the attempt to recapture the long-distance traveler: the *Super Chief* and the *California Zephyr*. Santa Fe's *Super Chief* ran between Chicago and Los Angeles, beginning operations before the war. Its splashy look of polished stainless steel and scarlet-nosed diesels painted in 'warbonnet' motif became a Southwestern icon. The train quickly picked up the nickname, 'Train of the Stars,' with its frequent patronage by Hollywood's elite. The *California Zephyr* initiated service in 1949 between Chicago and San Francisco (actually, Oakland) as a cooperative venture of the Burlington, the Denver & Rio Grande, and the Western Pacific railroads.

The *Super Chief* was the posh, upscale train, with fine dining and the celebrated 'Turquoise Lounge.' The *California Zephyr*, on the other hand, aimed at the vacationer, and was launched at a time when rail passengers were disappearing in droves. The creative planners who conceived the new *Zephyr*, however, realized that some attention-grabbers were in order. First was a fare structure better suited to family travelers on more modest budgets. Then came the innovation which became the virtual trademark of the *Zephyr*: the 'Vistadome' car. The *California Zephyr* was not the first train with a dome car, and other trains in the US and Canada quickly introduced dome cars of their own after the *Zephyr*'s initial success. For lesser trains, however, a dome car was an add-on. For the *Zephyr* — which traversed probably the most scenic route in North America, through the sheer-sloped Rocky Mountain canyons west of Denver and the Feather River Canyon of the Sierras — the Vistadome was the main event.

And not just one such car. The regular complement was five of these splendid sight-seeing conveyances, and sometimes up to seven. With these bright bubble-tops in tow, the *California Zephyr* was the 'Silver Lady.' She passed 'Through the Rockies, not around them,' as her official slogan said.

Above: *The domeliner* City of Los Angeles, *the Union Pacific's premier train connecting Chicago and Los Angeles (and operated by the UP and C&NW) pauses at East Los Angeles.*

Below: *SP train No. 99, the* Coast Daylight, *changes crews at San Luis Obispo, CA, in 1953. In the distance, a 2-10-2 helper engine returns from assisting a freight train earlier.*

Above: *Two 1968 studies of the* California Zephyr: *eastbound No. 18 on the D&RGW at Soldier Summit, and (below) westbound train No. 17 passes through Niles Canyon.*

Above: *Engineer Gordon Addis running one of the last* California Zephyr *trains from Oroville, CA, to Oakland in March, 1970. Later Addis took the next-to-last* Zephyr *over the route.*

For a brief time, both the *Super Chief* and the *California Zephyr* brought a renewed interest in train travel. A few other 'name' trains, such as New York Central's ever-famous *Twentieth Century Limited*, prospered briefly, too. But economic success was elusive. By 1960, every train in North America was struggling under a crushing burden of high labor costs and evaporating patronage. Some commentators babbled on that railroads 'were not doing enough' to recapture the passenger trade. A look at the record is sobering, though. Railroads did try, and very hard.

In 1962, freight ton-miles on railroads skidded to their lowest level since the Great Depression; passenger-miles kept plummeting until the creation of Amtrak in 1971. In 1963, a long-term recovery began in freight. Only with the economies brought by the new diesel fleet would railroads have been positioned to survive a reordered transportation market. Of all the economies that diesels brought in their wake, fuel-cost savings were only a small fraction of the whole story. Thirty years later, in 1993, railroads would be prospering, carrying all-time record levels of freight — over a trillion ton-miles a year. The 1945-1960 period set the stage.

Those 15 years marked the end of the Railroad Age. The vast business enterprise of railroading had been the connection between every other business in the land. More than that, railroads had been the social enterprise that physically connected every other human enterprise on the continent. Trains were the way you came and went, no matter where or why, and the way you sent and received all your goods. Trains employed you, or your family, or your friends. Trains were basic. Somewhere between 1945 and 1960, that all changed. Memories remained for many railroaders, but other railroaders did not look back. They pushed ahead into a new era, reshaping their enterprise for a new time.

Jervis Langdon, former president of the Baltimore & Ohio and an architect of the new railroad era, summed up the situation perfectly:

> We had to realize that the diesel was a lifesaver. If we had to compete against the trucks with steam engines, I doubt if the economics would have permitted a competitive operation. But there were many in management who were very reluctant to get rid of the steam engines . . . The hard facts of business can be tough when you're dealing with emotions.
>
> As a kid, I lived in the country up on a hill overlooking Elmira, New York. Down below were the old Delaware, Lackawanna & Western Railroad and the Erie Railroad. I remember I'd wake up in the night and hear those steam-engine whistles coming down the valley. I still hear them in my dreams.[5]

Notes

[1]F.M. Reck, *On Time* (La Grange, Illinois: Electro-Motive Div., 1948), p. 126.

[2]S. Leuthner, *The Railroaders* (New York: Random House, 1983), p.5.

[3]M. Klein, in *American Heritage Invention and Technology,* (New York: Forbes, Inc., Winter 1991), p.20.

[4]Fred E. Long interview by W.L.W., May 20, 1987.

[5]S. Leuthner, *The Railroaders,* p.129.

TOWARD A NEW ERA

THE 1960s AND 1970s WERE decades of turmoil for railroads. Long-distance trucks took more freight away from railroads, and passenger trains slid into a limbo of badly maintained cars, deteriorating stations, and unkept schedules. Shoddy track maintenance became endemic, especially in the eastern and midwestern United States. Conditions became so bad by the early 70s that many people wondered if railroads might soon disappear from the North American scene altogether, passing into oblivion.

The US Interstate Highway System, begun in the late 1950s, grew rapidly in the next two decades. As the mileage of these four-lane concrete ribbons increased every year — funded in large part by gasoline taxes from ordinary motorists — truckers found a bonanza. The new highways meant bigger trucks operating over longer distances, with reduced costs and more convenient schedules for shippers. Truck and trailer manufacturers couldn't turn out new '18-wheelers' fast enough, and truck fleets expanded rapidly. The result was that both the American landscape and the freight transportation business were transformed.

Railroads in both Canada and the US were caught in a terrible squeeze: as freight revenues fell and passenger revenues virtually disappeared, operating costs remained high. Archaic work rules, the result of labor agreements going back half a century, stymied railroad managers in seeking to cut employment costs. For example, a full day's pay for a train crew on the road was based on 100 miles, the average length of a railroad division. Thus a passenger train crew could collect a full day's pay in two or three hours, and a freight crew in little more, depending on how long it took to cover the 100 miles. A train traveling 500 miles needed to change crews five times. And each crew, by union agreement throughout the country and by law in some states, amounted to at least five people — conductor, two brakemen (on a freight train) or trainmen (on a passenger train), engineer, and fireman. This was true no matter the size of the train or the switching (or lack of it) to be done enroute. To some newspaper

editorial writers, this was 'featherbedding' — jobs guaranteed by labor-management contract, but which did not involve any substantial work being done.

Rail union spokesmen bristled in anger at such allegations. Every railroad work rule had been won in blood, union people observed; the 100-mile day had long been part of railroading traditions, and stemmed from an era of work days of 16 hours or more. Union members also recalled that their forebears had had to fight — and strike — just to secure that limit on duty hours, with eight hours' rest between callups. Even in the 1960s, most actual crew days were in excess of eight hours, unions argued, despite the supposed 100-mile day. When a long freight train had a lot of switching to do, picking up cars along the way or setting them out, or when an emergency occurred such as a hotbox or a broken coupler (which happened all too frequently), five crewmen had their hands full.

The most intense squabble was over the fireman, whose job had become obsolete with

Three GE 'Dash 8' diesel units, totaling 12,000 hp, roll a 'double-stack' train of intermodal containers across the Nevada desert (main picture), while (inset) Amtrak's California Zephyr *heads over the Sierras, soon to leave Interstate 80 behind, in November, 1984.*

the onset of the diesel erea (see Chapter 8). The first big railroad to tackle the issue head-on was the Canadian Pacific, which won a Royal Commission ruling that permitted the gradual dropping of the fireman's job on freight trains. Roads in the US began a campaign targeted not only at the fireman, but at crew size across the board. Nearly any train could be handled by four people, managers proposed, and often by just two, depending on the actual demands of a train's particular schedule. Railroads sought such flexibility in crew assignments. Unions fought back, saying that safety would be jeopardized, and that the theories of management did not fit reality on the job. .

The cost squeeze facing railroads included two other major items: in relation to the declining traffic, there were far too many miles of track and too many redundant facilities (shops, terminals, and yards). Corporate mergers seemed the answer. Trackage and facilities could both be substantially reduced if railroad companies consolidated.

In 1968, the Pennsylvania Railroad and the New York Central merged, after years of planning and approvals by the Interstate Commerce Commission. The two old arch-rivals became the Penn Central. Later, four railroads — the Great Northern; the Northern Pacific; the Chicago, Burlington & Quincy; and the Spokane, Portland & Seattle — merged to form the Burlington Northern.

The BN prospered, to become the strongest railroad in the American northwest and upper midwest. The Penn Central merger ended in debacle. In 1970, just over two years after its creation, Penn Central declared bankruptcy in the largest corporate collapse of its kind up to that time. The reasons were legion. Gross financial mismanagement was alleged. More importantly, perhaps, the old competitive animosities dividing the PRR and the NYC had remained, codified in an organizational structure that was divided into a 'Red Team' (mostly former PRR people) and a 'Green Team' (former NYC people). Corporate infighting reigned, service to shippers deteriorated, the regional economy continued its shift away from heavy industry, and rail traffic dropped.

Below: *The Lehigh Valley Railroad station at Wilkes-Barre, PA, in 1964: not a passenger in sight. Passenger operations ceased not long after the photograph was made.*

With the fall of Penn Central, and the consequent drying-up of financing for northeastern railroads generally, other lines fell like dominoes. The Lehigh Valley, the Central Railroad of New Jersey, the Reading, and others — all fabled companies — joined the PC in bankruptcy.

The merger movement went on, undeterred. From the late 1960s and into the 70s, another series of consolidations began in the east and south. The Baltimore & Ohio Railroad — the United States' first chartered line — negotiated merger arrangements with the Chesapeake & Ohio, while the Seaboard and the Atlantic Coast Line joined together to become the Seaboard Coast Line. A bit later, the old Louisville & Nashville, and some smaller lines, joined SCL to create a firm officially dubbed the 'Family Lines.' In the 1980s, the Family Lines and the B&O/C&O came together as CSX Corporation. The Norfolk & Western Railway and the Southern Railway, healthy companies to begin with, joined forces to become the potent Norfolk Southern.

The Penn Central collapse of 1970, however, prompted a frenzy of governmental talk about 'saving the railroads.' With nearly every railroad in the northeast in bankruptcy — later to be

Right: *The Milwaukee Road (along with the Rock Island) followed many of the northeastern railroads into bankruptcy in the 70s. This 1966 photo indicates that not all was well.*

Right, center: *A line of CB&Q 2-10-4s await the torch at the scrapyard in Sterling, IL, in 1962. Most major railroads had ceased steam operations altogether by the late 50s.*

Right, bottom: *CB&Q engines go under the torch, 1962. However sad this sight, it was only the end of 'steam age' working practices that enabled railroads to recover economically.*

followed by two major Midwestern lines, the Rock Island and the Milwaukee Road — debate in Congress reached fever pitch. At one point, almost 25 percent of US rail mileage was in the hands of federal bankruptcy courts. For the industry as a whole, disaster was on the doorstep. Nationalization — a federal takeover of the failing lines — was seriously under consideration by both academic analysts and congressional subcommittees.

Congress first acted to relieve railroads of passenger business nationwide. At last persuaded that passenger losses were unavoidably sapping the financial viability of railroads, Congress created the National Railroad Passenger Corporation — Amtrak — in 1971 to run all intercity trains in the US. At first it was a real struggle for Amtrak. It inherited 1275 passenger cars and 326 locomotives, all decrepit, but no track: the 200 daily trains on the vastly pruned nationwide rail passenger network were to travel on track owned by the freight railroads. Unreliable schedules and frequent breakdowns made rail travel a real adventure. Amtrak became something of a national joke. But the 'host' railroads, paid a trackage-rights fee by Amtrak to cover their costs in handling its trains, were finally relieved of an inherent loss-maker. Some years later, Canada adopted a similar scheme: Via Rail took over passenger train service on both the government-run Canadian National and the private-sector Canadian Pacific in 1977-78.

Back in the US Congress, a number of bills to resurrect the northeastern lines were heading through various committees in 1972 and 1973. An intriguing structure was suggested by Union Pacific Railroad vice president William McDonald: create a new railroad corporation to take over the assets of the bankrupt northeastern lines, but charter that corporation not as a nationalized firm but as a private-sector business in all respects, except that the federal government would own a majority of the stock, based on the government's new investment. McDonald then suggested that, before launching the new corporation, Congress create a new, independent planning agency to assess which trackage should be conveyed to the new firm and which trackage should be sold or abandoned. In that way, stressed McDonald, the new railroad would not be saddled with the same money-hemorrhaging, underused trackage that had helped sink the predecessor companies.

McDonald's ideas found quick favor among key politicians involved in transportation legislation, most notably Rep. Brock Adams of Washington State. Nationalization proposals were not going anywhere, due to conservative opposition, and every other formula being considered contained one feature or another to which some senators or representatives objected. Adams and others added a few wrinkles to McDonald's proposal — giving roles in the planning phase to other turf-conscious transportation agencies like the Interstate Commerce Commission (ICC) and the US Department of Transportation. Interestingly, only one northeastern congressman — that is, living in the affected region — took an active role as an early co-sponsor before the final consensus was struck: Rep. James Hastings of New York (for whom the author worked during that tumultuous time). Other northeastern politicians kept their distance through late 1973, no doubt in case the Adams plan failed.

Signed into law in January, 1974, the new act created a new railroad, the Consolidated Rail Corporation — Conrail. And as important, the act created a new entity, the United States Railway Association, to do the planning. Over the next two years, helped by additional legislation and skillfully led by director James Hagen, the new USRA designed the most complex American corporate reorganization in history.

Conrail began operations in April, 1976, on a streamlined system of track. A competitive company, the Delaware & Hudson, was granted special trackage rights on Conrail lines. Many miles of line owned by the former bankrupt companies were sold, or reserved for sale, for operation under state authority by new 'shortline' railroads.

Conrail's success was far from assured. Some analysts felt that Conrail's early leadership was not focused, and for several years the new railroad lost a lot of money. Across the country other railroads, too, continued in trouble. The Rock Island eventually liquidated, and the Milwaukee Road abandoned its line to Seattle. When he became President of the Association of American Railroads (AAR) in the late 1970s, William Dempsey was worried. 'I thought the industry was headed for nationalization,' he frankly admits. Dempsey became a respected witness before congressional committees, effectively representing railroads' interests in legislative and regulatory issues.

Capable management for Conrail came in the person of L. Stanley Crane, just retired from the presidency of the Southern Railway. Crane realized that a new agreement with labor was essential to survival. The fireman issue had finally been settled nationally a few years before, and further progress had been made in labor-management negotiations to permit four-person crews — and sometimes three-person crews — on some trains on some railroads.

Crane wanted more. He wanted a transition to new work rules in the shops and terminals as well as in the engine cabs. Rather than a confrontation, however, he sought a partnership between employees and management. Through adroit bargaining in many private sessions with union representatives, a new Conrail labor structure was worked out. Labor leaders praised Crane's approach.

Crane also stressed creative marketing. Running trains on time was only part of the equation. Under Crane, Conrail set up marketing groups focusing on the important commodities hauled — grain, coal, automobiles, and manufactured goods in intermodal containers, among

others. Helped by a recovering regional economy, Conrail people turned their fortunes around. Costs dropped and revenues rose. To the great surprise of many observers, Conrail began returning profits, and Crane persuaded Congress to authorize the public sale of its stock. Conrail became a successful company.

Legislatively, one of the most important events for American railroads since World War II was deregulation. In the late 1970s, under President Carter, both trucks and airlines were partially deregulated. Deregulation of trucking put additional competitive pressure on freight railroads, so they demanded equal treatment.

Passed in 1980, a bill that became known as the 'Staggers Act' (formally named for then-chairman of the House Commerce Committee, Rep. Harley Staggers of West Virginia) significantly altered the terms under which railroads and shippers could set freight charges. Simply put, if a shipper and a railroad could openly agree on terms, the two parties could set a contract rate for shipments that could be

Below: A Louisville & Nashville freight crew-change in 1963. By the 90s, L&N was part of CSX, the caboose and 'rear-end' crew were gone, and the boxcars were containers.

substantially lower than the old 'common carrier' tariffs. In a phrase, railroads could now offer volume discounts, which formerly had been prohibited. As before, the ICC still oversaw the process, but the ability of railroads and big shippers to negotiate their own contracts was entirely new.

In the new atmosphere, US railroads began to regain their financial footing. Throughout the 60s and 70s, freight market share had continued to slide: from 44 percent of all intercity freight ton-miles in 1960, to just over 37 percent by 1980. In 1963, total freight ton-miles by rail had begun slowly to increase each year instead of fall, but these increases were overwhelmed by the greater tonnage gains posted by trucks, river tow-boats, and pipelines. In the 1980s, with deregulation, railroads expanded their carriage of coal and grain, accelerated their growth in the shipment of automobiles, and moved an increasing number of intermodal containers. Freight market-share, however, held steady at about 37 percent through the 1980s.

Mergers continued. In the west, the Union Pacific expanded, acquiring the Missouri Pacific and Western Pacific; Burlington Northern brought the St. Louis-San Francisco (the Frisco) into its fold; and in self defense, the Santa Fe and

the Southern Pacific sought to merge. Unexpectedly, the proposed Santa Fe-Southern Pacific union failed to receive ICC approval — industry observers cited failure to address ICC concerns fully, including poor anticipation of anti-merger sentiments by big agricultural firms in California, among other factors. It was a major setback for both companies. Santa Fe, back on its own, and with an innovative marketing effort, recovered. Meanwhile, entrepreneur and oil man Philip Anschutz, who had earlier bought the Denver & Rio Grande Western, bought the SP. It was perhaps a case of Jonah swallowing the whale: Anschutz later decided to operate the combined railroads as the Southern Pacific, and the Rio Grande name, so long a part of railroading in the American West, disappeared.

Railroad deregulation led to the strengthening of major carriers and the creation of a whole new class of railroads: regional and shortline railroads which took on existing routes that major railroads sought to abandon or sell. These new companies could take lines with low traffic flows and operate them profitably because, in most cases, old, high-cost work rules no longer held. Stemming from US legislation in the 1970s encouraging formation of new shortlines, together with a generally supportive approach

Above: *Altoona (PA) Yards, after the start-up of Conrail in 1976. Some cars still bear Pennsy 'keystone', Penn Central, and New York Central logos, others the new Conrail stamp.*

Below: *The Penn Central yards at South Chicago, IL. The track is in deplorable condition. The Penn Central filed for bankruptcy in 1970.*

'THE GOLD COAST'

The private railroad car has always been a status symbol for aristocracy and the extravagantly wealthy. A veritable land yacht on wheels, a private railroad car afforded its owners the luxury of traversing the country within the comfort of elegantly appointed living, dining and sleeping accommodations, attended by a private chef and car steward. Early in 1948, railroad aficionados Lucius Beebe and Charles Clegg purchased their first private car, *The Gold Coast,* from the Georgia Northern Railway at Moultrie, Georgia, when it was GN No. 100.

Lucius Morris Beebe (1902-1966) was born in Wakefield, Massachusetts to an established New England family. A well-known columnist and society writer for the *New York Herald Tribune* and later the *San Francisco Chronicle*, Beebe authored dozens of pictorial railroad history books. With photographer and collaborator Charles Myron Clegg, (1916-1979), the pair realized the dream of many railroad enthusiasts. In March 1948 they purchased a private car in which to make their home in the Carson City, Nevada yards of the Virginia & Truckee Railway.

The Gold Coast was built, or possibly rebuilt, in 1905 in the Savannah, Georgia car shops of the Central of Georgia Railway as CofG officers' car No. 97. Remnants of earlier appointments and discontinued sill and plate truss rods suggest that the Pullman-green car may well have been rebuilt from an older car. The wood car was paneled inside in inlaid mahogany and featured leaded mirrors and colored glass clerestory and transom windows. Some of the linens still on board

the car bear the unique CofG No. 97 monogram.

Early in 1948, Hollywood interior decorator Robert T. Hanley outfitted the car to its present posh appearance. Beebe and Clegg liked to refer to the interior of their car as reminiscent of Leland Stanford's (1824-1893) private car. A linen closet, six built-in seats, two overhead berths and a water closet were removed to create an unusually long observation lounge replete with simulated green marble fireplace. Redecorated rooms included a master

stateroom with shower, a guest room, formal dining room with built-in china cabinet (main picture), kitchen (bottom right), wine and cold storage, and crew quarters. Beebe and Clegg christened the car *The Gold Coast* and wrote three books while living aboard it during the summers of 1948-1950 in the V&T's Carson City yards (below right). They also made occasional excursions with the car to the Bay Area and back. Aboard their private 'mansion on rails,' Beebe and Clegg wined and dined royalty and literary figures.

When the 80-year old Virginia & Truckee

ceased operations in May 1950, *The Gold Coast* moved onto Southern Pacific tracks at Sparks, Nevada. After briefly owning two further private cars, Beebe and Clegg presented *The Gold Coast* to the Railway & Locomotive Historical Society in November 1954. In turn, the car was presented by the Pacific Coast Chapter of the R&LHS to the State of California. After periods in storage and on display, the car was fully restored to its 1948-50 appearance as occupied by Beebe and Clegg. The car can now be seen in the California State Railroad Museum, Sacramento.

from larger connecting railroads, shortlines proliferated. By 1990, there were over 350 shortline firms in the US, with more in Canada. Canadian policy recently has been mixed; Nova Scotia, for example, has reduced regulatory burdens for shortlines, while other provinces have done the reverse.

Some of the new shortlines — most from five to 100 miles long — made it on their own, and some became part of larger companies. One of the most successful of the latter has been RailTex Inc., a Texas-based company with (as of 1993) 21 shortline railroads in the US and in Ontario, Canada. Bruce Flohr is the founder of RailTex, and he and a small staff in San Antonio direct the overall business, while a local general manager at each of the separate lines runs on-site operations.

The largest of the new regional carriers is Wisconsin Central. When the Soo Line (a long-established midwestern carrier) acquired the failing Milwaukee Road in the early 1980s, Wisconsin Central was formed to take over lines the Soo wanted to shed from its newly merged system. WC took over 2000 miles of track, and later purchased more. By building up new rail freight business along these routes, Wisconsin Central is prospering.

Elsewhere in the midwest, various medium-size companies such as the Illinois Central, the Kansas City Southern, and the Chicago & North Western — all with illustrious histories dating from the nineteenth century — have undergone decline and, with draconian pruning of money-losing lines, resuscitation.

By 1981 and its tenth birthday, Amtrak was doing even better than its planners had hoped. New rail cars were supplanting the worst of the older ones, many of the older cars were being extensively rebuilt at Amtrak's facility in Beech Grove, near Indianapolis, and most Amtrak locomotives were new. Schedule-keeping had vastly improved, and more people were riding its trains. Amtrak had also been given some track of its own: in the wake of the Penn Central collapse, Congress authorized transfer of the former Pennsylvania Railroad electrified

Right: *CN freights in Fraser Canyon. By concentrating on cargoes in bulk, from autos to chemicals, railroads posted economic gains in the late 80s and early 90s.*

Below: *SP engineer Susan Bowlus watches from the cab at Sparks, NV. Another aspect of the recent railroad renaissance is that women are now found in every railroad occupation.*

trackage between Washington and New York, together with the main line from Philadelphia to Harrisburg, to Amtrak ownership. Additionally, a multi-year 'Northeast Corridor Improvement Project' was funded to rebuild the deteriorated line extensively, and Amtrak received money to buy a new fleet of electric locomotives. Soon thereafter, however, the new administration of President Reagan began a concerted effort to kill Amtrak's funding.

Congress had originally mandated that Amtrak reach a goal of covering at least 50 percent of its total operating expenses from fares. Amtrak edged closer to that goal, and then exceeded it. Still, the Reagan administration pointed at Amtrak as a highly-visible example of 'government waste.' Amtrak president W. Graham Claytor — former Southern Railway president and Secretary of the Navy under Carter — articulately defended federal investment in the passenger rail system before Congress. At the same time, Claytor overhauled Amtrak's management, improving services and accelerating the improvement in the revenue/cost ratio. A big boost to Amtrak income came from new contracts to haul US mail, predominantly in the northeast corridor, and then on other heavily used routes.

By 1992, Amtrak reached an annual revenue of $1.3 billion, which covered 79 percent of operating expenses. Such a ratio of revenue-to-cost was as good or better than any other rail

passenger system anywhere in the world. In 1992, Amtrak carried almost 42 million riders, 21 million on the national Amtrak system and the rest in contract commuter operations.

Congress still has to fund capital improvements for Amtrak. New cars and locomotives have been vital: double-decked 'Superliner' sleeping cars, coaches, and dining cars now equip all long-distance trains in the midwest and far west, and soon will equip some eastern trains. A new generation of 'Viewliner' sleepers and diners, of conventional height to fit the more limited clearances of the east, have begun to enter service. New diesel locomotives have also been ordered.

Along with the severe restructuring of railroads across the continent, another quiet revolution has taken place. Women are now found in every railroad occupation, from locomotive engineer to dispatcher, from mechanic to executive. After initially resisting, rail unions today — such as the United Transportation Union, the Brotherhood of Locomotive Engineers, and the Transportation Communications Union — are now encouraging this change. Railroad women also have their own organizations, some formed when women took railroad jobs during World War II. In truth, of course, women have been part of the railroad story from its beginning.

Above: *The 125mph* Metroliner *service on the northeast corridor run between New York City and Washington, DC is just one element in the increasingly successful Amtrak story.*

Below: *Electro-Motive Division SD70 model freight locomotive, introduced in 1992. Each unit has 4000hp, a 'wide cab' seating up to four, and microprocessor-based controls.*

For most US freight railroads, the financial successes achieved in the early 1990s represent something of a renaissance. Between 1990 and 1992, stock prices doubled for several major carriers. The excruciatingly low rates of return on investment of the 1930s through the mid-1980s were replaced by more-than-respectable profit margins. In 1992, for example, the Norfolk Southern system posted a profit of over $550 million.

How did this happen? Deregulation has both lowered average rates to shippers in real dollars, and allowed railroads to concentrate on high-volume, 'wholesale' movements. Where once railroads hauled nearly every kind of freight that moved, and distributed it to the loading docks of shippers large and small, railroads have largely abandoned the 'retail' freight business to trucks.

Another indicator is productivity. In 1988, American railroads carried more goods more miles than ever before in their history: over one trillion ton-miles. Over one trillion ton-miles were carried again in 1990. By comparison, the goods carried by rail in 1929 — during a good year in the heyday of railroads, and just before the Great Depression — amounted to less than 50 percent of the current ton-mileage. In the meantime, a great deal of track has been eliminated; in 1990, US railroads used only about half as many miles of mainline track as in 1929. Railroad employment has also dropped sharply: in 1929 over 1.6 million people were needed to run the major railroads in the US; in 1990 only about 230,000 were required. The result is that seven times fewer people, on half the track, are producing twice the work. That is a dramatic productivity increase.

Most of that productivity gain has been made since 1960. In a vastly reordered freight market, railroads have settled into a niche where they carry something over one-third of all US intercity freight ton-miles. Surprisingly perhaps, that is more than trucks, which carry about one-

Below: *CSX car inspector affixes an End-of-Train Device (ETD) to the rear of a freight train ready to leave Louisville, KY. The ETD has replaced the caboose on most freights.*

As long as mainline steam-power was continually replaced by larger, more powerful and impressive steam locomotives, there was little incentive or rationale to preserve the older examples, and their historical importance was long ignored.

It was only following World War II, when the introduction of diesel-electric power meant that steamers were disappearing from entire divisions, that belated and usually feeble attempts were made to preserve the historical legacy of the machine that had changed the face of America. Up until the early 1950s, only the Baltimore & Ohio had preserved an extensive number of locomotives (including a few later replicas) covering the full period of its history. After losing several important

examples, the Pennsylvania Railroad accelerated a preservation program (which included freight and passenger cars, as well as locomotives), but no other railroads embarked on an attempt at genuine preservation of representative types.

A number of companies, most notably the Santa Fe, Union Pacific, Frisco, Southern Pacific and the Soo Line, donated generous numbers of engines to municipalities, museums and historical societies. As the engines were usually displayed out-of-doors, however, they often deteriorated due to vandalism and weather. Railroads had no planned program — or money — to ensure that a good representation of each major locomotive type and era would be saved. The result was typified by the Chesapeake & Ohio,

Above: *BC Rail's ex-CP 'Royal Hudson' class 4-6-4 No. 2860, built in Montreal in 1940, now works regular tourist trains such as this on the line between Vancouver and Squamish.*

Above: *Renovation work underway on one of several steam locomotives preserved for operation at the Steamtown National Historic Site in Scranton, PA.*

which preserved 22 locomotives; however, 12 of these were identical 2-8-4s, and they failed to save a single 4-6-2, 2-8-2, 0-8-0 or 2-10-4. Other lines saved one, two, or a dozen specimens, again often withholding identical machines while junking everything else. American railroad historians can only look with envy at the museums in those countries which have nationalized railways — Great Britain, Germany, Poland, and Japan, for example — where the aim has always been to carefully preserve at least one example of

Left: *The spirit of steam: an evening shot of Union Pacific's 4-8-4 No. 844, as it completes an excursion run. UP maintains two big steamers as emblems of its storied past.*

every major class. The lack of any similar direction or funding were the primary reasons for the haphazard and spotty preservation record of the US from the 100-year-long era of steam.

Locomotive and rolling stock preservation falls into two main categories: static display and operational. The former ranges from forgotten hulks, rusting in city parks, to magnificent restorations maintained under protective covering. The latter come in many varieties, including the Norfolk Southern and

Below: *Norfolk and Western No. 611, one of the most powerful passenger steam engines ever, and built at the N&W home-shops in Roanoke, VA, still hauls excursions.*

Union Pacific, which have re-built their own locomotives, after recalling them from museums or other owners to whom they had sold the engines decades ago. Santa Fe and SP (including its subsidiary, Cotton Belt), have seen groups outside the company restore large, mainline locomotives, then have taken the projects under their wings to run on their own tracks. Burlington Northern, Conrail and C&O have occasionally decided that since a responsible outside organization has restored an indigenous locomotive, they will allow it to run on its former home rails. Because of escalating insurance rates and an increasing shortage of suitable passenger cars, some magnificent and costly ($500,000 is not an uncommon sum to spend restoring a large high-speed passenger locomotive) restored engines have wound up in the melancholy role of a jilted girl on prom night: all dressed up with no place to go.

The quality of operational preserved lines also varies greatly, from historical recreations correct down to the last detail to rather less accurate renditions of how things used to be done. Tourist lines are often very short (1-5 miles), but even they can offer a fine period ride, depending on the motivation and the dedication of the management. Some tourist roads, such as Pennsylvania's Strasburg Rail Road or the Colorado narrow-gauge lines, have become the centerpieces of the local and regional economies, and the revenues earned enable them to invest heavily to ensure the continued quality, and authenticity, of their operations.

While the shorter tourist runs cater mainly to families on vacation with short attention spans (the ride usually takes less then one hour), mainline runs can last from a few hours (a 50-mile romp down the line and back), to week-long extravaganzas in Pullman cars, during which hundreds of route-miles are traversed. Private-car owners, whose rosters include coaches, sleeping cars, lounges, dining cars and both open-platform and streamlined observation cars, often assemble from six- to 10-car trains of their own and then lease the motive power and track from the railroad they have to travel over. The high operating and insurance costs are defrayed (in part, at least) by selling tickets to an eager public.

There seems to be no let-up in the fascination that people feel for the nostalgia of train travel, especially behind steam, although vintage diesels are popular too. Therein lies the deep-rooted national mystique for the once-omnipotent railway. There are few groups who restore vintage DC6 or Stratocruiser airliners, or Greyhound or Trailways busses with the goal of operating them to haul the general public as in the old days, but the phenomenon of restoring steam locomotives and their trains has endured, once again illustrating the hold that the steam locomotive still has on the imagination of the American public.

Contributed by Ron Ziel.

RAILROADS IN POPULAR CULTURE

No other transportation industry has had the deep and lasting romantic appeal of the railroad, and this has seeped into literally every aspect of American popular culture. From that most American popular art form, the movies (after all, the first feature film with a plot was Edison's 1903 *The Great Train Robbery*), to music, books, popular magazines, toys, and the hobby of scale model railroading, images and symbols of the railroad surround us.

Although it has been two full generations since the steam locomotive passed from the daily scene, we continue to immerse our children in representations of railroading. One of the first books we give children to read — or read to them — is almost invariably *The Little Engine That Could*. While there is no organized scheme to promote the railroad, thousands of books and toys inculcate in children a lasting appreciation for the subject.

The consequence of this is to perpetuate in people an almost intuitive appreciation of trains — a national ability to be moved by the sound of the 'mournful whistle in the night,' even though few listeners actually remember the era of the steam locomotive. America is no longer the great railroad society that depended in every degree on the visible comings and goings of trains. Thus for many, the toy train around the Christmas tree or a trip to their local tourist railroad is as close to the railroad as they get. But these same people recognize the sights and sounds of the industry: they have been surrounded by them since early childhood.

1 'Honeymoon Express' toy. Early 1940s.

2, 3 Shaving mug with picture of caboose; razor with handle showing locomotive.

4 Railroad highball glass with swizzle stick.

5 'Instant railroad' capsules. Contemporary.

6, 7 'Snoopy' engine, 1958, and whistle, 1960s.

8 Lionel advert. 1940s.

9 Promotional card for a movie shot on the California Zephyr. Late 1950s.

10 Avon after shave lotion

marketed in 1976.

11 'Night Train Express' fine pear wine.

12 Cigars, from 1930s.

13 Commemorative plate. 1930s.

14 Brochure for movie Rock Island Trail, 1941.

15, 16 Ads for NBC's 'Railroad Hour', late 1930s.

17 Locomotive clock, 1920s.

18 Box of dominoes, 1910s.

19, 20, 21 Sheet music and records with railroad themes.

22 Poster for 1941 movie The Broadway Limited.

23 Locomotive picture

puzzle, copyright 1887.

24, 25 Railroad Stories magazine, April 1933 and October 1936 issues.

26 The Little Engine That Could. 1954.

27 Wrapping paper with locomotive motifs, 1970s.

28 Lionel AT&SF Super Chief, 1950s.

29 California State Railroad Museum patches, 1992.

30 Boxes for 'Railroad Cookies,' 1970s.

31 Glass candy container. 1920s.

32 Cast figure of a railroad conductor.

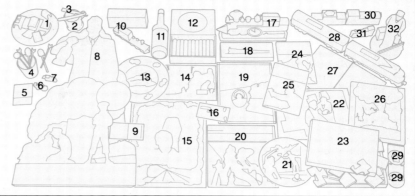

Southern Pacific, which built the first double-stack container cars, in cooperation with ACF Industries (the former American Car & Foundry). Then came American President Lines, which invested heavily in double-stack cars built by Thrall Car to carry containers between east and west coast. Every major US and Canadian railroad soon was handling a burgeoning growth in container trains.

New labor agreements in the 1980s resulted in the final demise of a North American icon: the railroad caboose. Through-freights now run with two- or three-person crews, and these people sit up front in the locomotive, which often has a 'wide body' cab design with comfortable accommodation. At the back of the train is an End-of-Train Device (an ETD), about the size of a breadbox. Hung on the last car's rear coupler, the ETD incorporates a flashing red strobe light and a motion detector, and it is hooked into the train brake air line. The ETD radios air brake pressure and motion information from the rear end to a receiving unit in the locomotive cab. With these readouts, engineers find they can handle mile-long trains more smoothly and safely, with less slack action.

The next major change in overland freight

fourth of intercity freight ton-miles. Waterways and pipelines divide up the rest between them.

Bulk commodities such as coal and grain, usually carried in dedicated 'unit trains,' are the backbone of rail income. Railroads derive 25 percent of their total freight revenue just from coal movement. Other important commodities are bulk chemicals, sheet steel, new autos and light trucks, auto parts, ore, lumber, corn sweetener, and fresh fruits and vegetables.

At the same time, railroads have benefited from the most significant worldwide change to occur in freight carriage in the past 50 years: containerization. The movement of 'piggyback' trailers on rail flat cars was the beginning. But that technology evolved. Standard cargo boxes

— called containers and each about the size of a truck trailer without the wheels — were developed in the 1960s for shipping by sea. In the last two decades, such containers have become the standard method of shipping manufactured goods long distances; they are carried equally well on sea, highway, and rail. Hence the containers are 'intermodal,' that is, entirely interchangeable among the three modes of surface transport.

Both 'trailers on flatcars' (TOFC) and containers began to constitute a growing market for railroads during the 1960s. The innovation of the 1980s that has allowed greater numbers of containers to move more cheaply by rail is called 'double-stacking.' The pioneer was

RAILROADING'S MUSICAL LEGACY

Above: *Bruce (Utah) Phillips, the 'Golden Voice of the Great Southwest'.*

In a controversial essay in 1947, noted folk music collectors John and Alan Lomax wrote that 'It is in the texture of our popular music . . . that the railroads have left their deepest impression . . . listen to the blues, [hot jazz, and other popular music], and you'll hear all the . . . syncopated rhythms and counter-rhythms of trains of every size and speed . . . What you hear back of the notes is the drive and thrust and moan of a locomotive.' The train is found not only in folk songs and Bluegrass, say the Lomaxes, but in 'the distinctive feeling of American hot music.'[1]

To modern musicologists — especially to ones with no experience of pre-1950 railroading — this seems overstated. But consider how ever-present the rhythmic beat of the railroad once was in the aural landscape of daily life. The rhythmic chug of locomotives was everywhere. Then consider the powerful symbolism of trains: trains that took you away and, maybe, brought you back. Or trains that called you out of your despair: 'Hey, come hitch a ride with me,' the whistle said, 'you can escape.' The creative and sensitive people among us were bound to be affected.

In today's railroading, the steam whistle has changed to an air horn, welded ribbon rail has removed the clickety-clack, and the far tracks are not so lonesome in suburbanized America. Nonetheless there are musicians today who are still moved by the call of the railroad. 'Utah' Phillips is one — boomer, tall-tale teller, poet, song writer, agitator — who weaves the train into his haunting songs. He can show you how to imitate on your guitar the echo of a far-off diesel horn or the rumble of a mile-long freight.

Note

[1]*Folk Song: U.S.A.,* (New York: Duell, Sloan and Pearce, 1947), p.245. Copyright John and Alan Lomax.

Above: *A Conrail 'double stack' container train crosses Bear Mountain Bridge, NY, in 1991. Starting operations in 1976, Conrail lost money at first, then became profitable.*

transportation is already underway. It is an invisible change, however — except to rail-roaders and shippers. Trucking companies specializing in truckload lots and railroads are entering into long-term cooperative agreements. The result is, for the shipper, a 'modal blind' arrangement: the shipper need not worry about the mode. Trucking company and railroad work in unison to pick up and deliver the cargo on an arranged schedule. Long advocated in theory, the practical realization of this idea depends on computers and information networks to provide efficient coordination.

Key innovators this time were the Santa Fe, and its then-president Michael Haverty, and J.B. Hunt, a growing long-haul trucking company based in Arkansas. More than a simple piggy-backing arrangement, Hunt's trailers travel by flatcar under a contract that gives both trucker and railroad a stake in timely pick up, transfer between road and rail, reduced damage to lading enroute, and timely delivery. This kind of partnership is spreading rapidly to other motor carriers and railroads. Rail intermodal volume set a new record high in 1992 for the eleventh year in a row.

Another variant on the truck-rail theme is the

dual-mode 'RoadRailer,' a highway truck-trailer specially adapted to travel by rail without a flatcar. First conceived many years ago, Road-Railer has had a long and painful engineering development. Norfolk Southern carried the idea to fruition with its 'Triple Crown' service. Road-Railers travel as conventional trailers over the highway on standard rubber tires. At rail terminals, the RoadRailers are assembled as self-contained trains, carried by railwheels mounted to each trailer's chassis. One type of RoadRailer mounts onto separate rail bogies at the terminal; another type carries its railwheels as a permanent part of the trailer.

Research and development by railroads has picked up in the 1980s and 90s. The Transportation Test Center — a sprawling railway research facility near Pueblo, Colorado, operated by the AAR under contract to the US Department of Transportation — has conducted a great variety of tests on its loops of track, ranging from causes of abrasion on wood crossties, to proof testing of concrete-tie designs, to the behavior of cars under differing dynamic conditions, to the performance of systems to detect overheated wheel bearings, to the effects on track of heavier freight cars, to the safest and most efficient procedures for handling hazardous cargoes.

Burlington Northern is experimenting with an Advanced Train Control System (ATCS), using

Above: *Via Rail's LRC train was equipped with an active tilting system. The LRC cars are still in use, but the tilting system proved unreliable and has been deactivated.*

Below: *Amtrak train No. 11, complete with 'Superliner' coaches, on Cuesta Grade in 1991. Amtrak entered the 90s with new routes, new locomotives, and new rolling stock.*

global positioning satellites to keep track of trains to within 50ft, to monitor locomotive performance enroute, and to give instructions to engineers. BN is also experimenting with locomotives fueled by natural gas.

Track maintenance is another area in which fundamental change has occurred in recent decades. Highly automated equipment for rail welding, rail profile grinding, ballast cleaning, tie replacement, and track alignment now permits small, highly skilled track maintenance teams to do the work once performed by huge track gangs. Lately, pre-stressed concrete ties are being installed on heavily used routes. Construction of entirely new rail lines has been rare in North America for a long time, but two projects stand out. In the 1970s, BN built a heavy-duty line into the Powder River Basin coal fields of Wyoming. This line was later extended, with participation by Chicago & North Western. In the 1980s, Canadian Pacific constructed a second main line through Rogers Pass in the Selkirk Mountains of western Canada, boring two new tunnels, including one 8.7 miles long.

What does the future hold? Much discussion has been devoted to 'High Speed Rail' (HSR) projects for passengers. Studies have been completed or are underway in at least 17 states that look at the future use of high-speed rail trains using French, German, Japanese, or Swedish technology. The administration of President Clinton has encouraged planning for HSR, provided the states also commit funds.

The Texas High Speed Rail Corporation was granted a franchise by that state in 1992 to plan and build the so-called 'Texas Triangle Project,' to link Dallas-Fort Worth, Houston, San Antonio, and Austin with HSR trains using the well-proven, 186mph technology of the French Train à Grande Vitesse (TGV). Initially estimated at $5.7 billion, the difficulty in 1993 has been to secure the rights-of-way and the (non-governmental) financing that is required.

Magnetic levitation (Maglev) is another high-speed passenger technology. Maglev does not use a railway, but a guideway; maglev trains promise a frictionless surface-transport mode for speeds up to 300mph. A German consortium has been perfecting this technology for over ten years, and operates two full-size maglev trains regularly on a large test track in Emsland, north of Bremen. Japan has also invested huge research funding in a different form of maglev. In the late 1980s, a bi-state governmental commission established by California and Nevada looked into the possibility of a maglev line between Los Angeles and Las Vegas.

Amtrak, meanwhile, tried out a version of HSR in the Washington-New York-Boston corridor. In 1993, Amtrak borrowed an X2000 tilt-train from the Swedish State Railways for several months of demonstration runs. X2000 trainsets have operated for several years with great success between Gothenburg and Stockholm. Radial steering axles permit greatly increased speeds in curves on standard track, while a microprocessor-controlled, hydraulically activated carbody tilting system allows passengers to experience a gentle ride despite the curve speeds. The builder, ABB Traction, had solved the technical problems that befell earlier tilt-train designs such as the British APT and the Canadian LRC.

The past may be prologue. The train has sometimes seemed to be a relic of the past. Yet perhaps railroads in North America have turned an historic corner. Inherently conserving of energy and fuel compared to other modes of transport, and able to provide high traffic densities using far less land, trains are becoming responsive to modern needs. It is a new era.

Below right: An artist's impression of the Texas TGV Corporation's train for the proposed high-speed 'Texas Triangle' line between Dallas-Fort Worth, Houston, San Antonio and Austin.

Below left and bottom: The cab of the X2000 (below left), and the X2000 at Lancaster, PA, during the Amtrak test runs in March, 1993 (bottom). Radial axles permit greater speed on the curves of conventional track, cutting schedule-times significantly.

INDEX

APPENDIX

Steam locomotive types are designated by both names and a numerical system. For example, a 'Pacific'-type locomotive is also a '4-6-2', with four guiding wheels in front of the driving wheels, six driving wheels, and two carrying wheels behind the drivers. (Europeans number the axles instead, so there a 'Pacific' is termed a '2-3-1'. In the US and Canada, wheels are counted.) In similar fashion, a 'Consolidation'-type is a 2-8-0: it has two guiding wheels in front, eight drivers, and no carrying wheels behind the drivers. Names have idiosyncratic histories; often the first railroad to acquire a then-new type had the privilege of setting the type's name. Generally, locomotives with four guiding wheels in front are passenger engines; locomotives with two guiding wheels are freight engines, and locomotives with no guiding wheels are switchers for duty in rail yards; but there are exceptions to this rule. Big 'articulated' engines for freight duty, with two groups of drivers, often had four guiding wheels, such as the 4-8-8-4 'Big Boy' or 4-6-6-4 'Challenger'.

PICTURE CREDITS AND ACKNOWLEDGMENTS

The publisher wishes to thank the following organizations and individuals who have supplied photographs, credited here by page number and position. For reasons of space, some references are abbreviated as follows: **AAR**: Association of American Railroads; **B&O**: Baltimore & Ohio Railroad Museum; **CSRM**: California State Railroad Museum; **CN**: Canadian National; **CP**: Canadian Pacific Corporate Archives; **R&LHS**: Railway & Locomotive Historical Society; **UP**: Union Pacific Railroad Museum.

Positions of photographs are indicated as follows: Top: (T); Bottom (B); Center (C); Top right: (TR); Top left (TL); Bottom left: (BL); Bottom right: (BR); etc.

The editor offers additional thanks to the following: W. Graham Claytor, President of Amtrak, and R. Clifford Black IV, Amtrak Director of Public Affairs; Paulette Manos of the Martin P. Catherwood Library, Cornell University; Dorrance Publishing of Pittsburgh and Elizabeth Wilde for permission to quote from *Hobo Over the Hump: Riding the Canadian Railroads in the 30s*; Random House Publishers, New York City, for permission to quote from Stuart Leuthner's *The Railroaders*; St Martin's Press, New York City, for permission to quote from James D. Porterfield's *Dining by Rail: The History and the Recipes of America's Golden Age of Railroad Cuisine*; The University of Illinois Press for permission to quote from Jack Santino's *Miles of Smiles, Years of Struggle: Stories of Black Pullman Porters*.

Endpapers and artifact spreads: Don Eiler; **1**: Wilton S. Tifft; **2-3**: David Plowden; **4-5**: David Plowden; **6-7**: David Plowden; **8-9**: B&O (B); **9**: B&O (TR, CR); **10**: (from top) AAR; B&O; Peter Newark's American Pictures; AAR; **11**: National Railway Museum, York, England; **14**: CN (T); B&O (B); **15**: Peter Newark's American Pictures (T); B&O (B); **16**: B&O (T, B); **17**: Peter Newark's American Pictures; **18**: B&O (T, B); **19**: CN; **22**: Salamander Books (TL); Peter Newark's American Pictures (B); **23**: Maryland Historical Society, Baltimore (T); B&O (B); **26**: (from top): Salamander Books; National Archives; Salamander Books; **27**: Salamander Books (T); Peter Newark's American Pictures (B); **28-29**: UP; **29**: CSRM (T); **30**: Peter Newark's American Pictures (T); CSRM (B); **31**: CSRM (L, R); **34**: UP (T, B); **35**: CSRM; **36**: CSRM; **37**: Salamander Books/CSRM (TR); Denver Public Library (B); **38**: CSRM (T); UP (B); **39**: UP; **40**: Salamander Books/CSRM (L); CSRM (TR); **41**: CSRM (T); UP (B); **42**: B&O (T); Salamander Books (B); **43**: Don Hofsommer (TL); CSRM (TR); **46**: Peter Newark's American Pictures (T); Salamander Books (B); **47**: Special Collections Division, University of Washington Libraries (B); CSRM (TR); **48**: Peter Newark's American Pictures (T); R&LHS (B); **49**: CN; **50-51**: Minnesota Historical Society (B); **51**: Ron Ziel (R); **53**: Salamander Books/Railroad Museum of Pennsylvania (T); CSRM (B); **54**: Norfolk Southern; **56**: Peter Newark's American Pictures; **57**: Peter Newark's American Pictures (TL); CP (TR); CSRM (B); **58**: CSRM (T); Ron Ziel (B); **59**: Kansas State Historical Society (B); **60**: Southern Railway: Southern Railway Historical Association Collection; **62**: Peter Newark's American Pictures; **63**: Salamander Books/CSRM (T); CSRM (B); **64**: B&O; **65**: Minnesota Historical Society (TL); CSRM (TR); Ron Ziel (B); **68**: Minnesota Historical Society; **69**: Salamander Books/CSRM (TL); CSRM (TR); Peter Newark's American Pictures (B); **70**: B&O (T, BL, BR); **71** Minnesota Historical Society; **72-73**: Ron Ziel; **74**: CSRM (C); **75**: Louisville & Nashville Collection/University of Louisville Archives (C); **76**: B&O (BL); **78**: UP; **79**: Peter Newark's American Pictures (TL); B&O (TR); Don Hofsommer (B); **80**: Peter Newark's American Pictures; **81**: Southern Pacific Company (T); CSRM (B); CSRM (TR); **84**: DeGoyler Library, Southern Methodist University, Dallas (T); Minnesota Historical Society (B); **85**: Smithsonian Institution, Anacostia Museum (T); Peter Newark's American Pictures (B); **86**: Peter Newark's American Pictures; **88**: CSRM (T); CP Corporate Archives (B); **89**: Minnesota Historical Society; **90-91**: Don Hofsommer (T); Minnesota Historical Society (B); **93**: USX Corporation (T); Minnesota Historical Society (B); **96**: UP; **97**: Sears Roebuck (TL); Peter Newark's American Pictures (TR); Don Hofsommer

(B); **98**: CN (BL); Don Hofsommer/Salamander Books (TR); **99**: Minnesota Historical Society (TL); Don Hofsommer (TR); Special Collections Division, University of Washington Libraries (B); **102**: Martin P. Catherwood Library, Cornell University (T); Smithsonian Institution/Salamander Books (B); **103**: National Archives/Food & Drug Administration; **106**: Peter Newark's American Pictures (T); Smithsonian Institution (B); **107**: Don Hofsommer (T, B); **108**: Peter Newark's American Pictures (L); CN (T); **109**: Norfolk Southern (T, B); **110-111**: Seth Bramson; **112**: Ted Rose (C); **113**: Collection of Ken Murry (C); **114**: UP (T); Ron Ziel (B); **115**: Burlington Northern Railroad; **118**: UP (T); The Newberry Library, Chicago (B); **119**: Courtesy of NAACP Public Relations (TL); Smithsonian Institution/Division of Transportation (TC, TR, BR); CSRM (BL); **120**: Peter Newark's American Pictures (T, C); CSRM (B); **121**: Peter Newark's American Pictures (TL); Smithsonian Institution (B); **124**: Peter Newark's American Pictures (TL, CR); Salamander Books (TR); B&O (BR); Library of Congress (BL); **125**: R&LHS; **126**: CSRM/Salamander Books; **128**: Allen County Historical Society (T); Smithsonian Institution/Division of Transportation (B); **129**: Smithsonian Institution, Anacostia Museum (TL); UP (TR, C); Don Hofsommer (BR); **130-131**: Ron Ziel; **131**: H. Roger Grant Collection (TR); CN (B); **132**: Ron Ziel; **133**: Minnesota Historical Society (TR); **134**: Don Hofsommer (T); Railroader's Memorial Museum, Altoona (B); **135**: Ron Ziel (TL); Special Collections Division, University of Washington Libraries (TR); **136**: Peter Newark's American Pictures (T); Ted Rose (B); **137**: H. Roger Grant Collection (TL); Peter Newark's American Pictures (TR); **140**: H. Roger Grant Collection (T); Salamander Books (B); **141**: R&LHS (T); UP (B); **142**: CSRM; **143**: H. Roger Grant Collection/Salamander Books (TL); CN (TR); Collection of Ken Murry (B); **145**: Ron Ziel: Frank Quinn photograph (BR); **146**: UP (T, B); **147**: B&O (T); Peter Newark's American Pictures (B); **148-149**: Ron Ziel (B); GM Electro Motive Division (TR); **150**: Boston & Maine Railroad (T): Ted Rose (B); **151**: James Gallagher; **152**: Collection of William L. Withuhn; **153**: GM Electro Motive Division (TL); CN (TR); Richard Steinheimer (B); **156**: Salamander Books (T); Collection of Ken Murry (B); **157**: Kenneth L. Miller Collection; **158**: David Plowden; **159**: David Plowden; **160**: David Plowden; **161**: James Gallagher (T); Norfolk Southern (B); **162**: Ransom-Wallis Collection, National Railway Museum (T); James Gallagher (B); **163**: James Gallagher (TL); Philip R. Hastings/Mark Smith (TR); **164**: James Gallagher (C); **165**: UP (C); **166**: Minnesota Historical Society; **167** Santa Fe (TL); CSRM (B); **170**: CSRM (T); Richard Steinheimer (B); **171**: Ted Benson (TL, TR, B); **172-173**: Richard Steinheimer (B); **173**: Shirley Burman (TR); **174**: David Plowden; **175**: John Gruber (T); Ron Ziel (C, B); **176**: Louisville & Nashville Collection/University of Louisville Archives; **177**: Anna Leopold/Railroaders' Memorial Museum, Altoona (T); David Plowden (B); **179**: CSRM (TR); **180**: CN (T); Shirley Burman (BL); **181**: Amtrak (T); GM Electro Motive Division (B); **182**: CSX Transportation (BL); Joel Jensen (TR); **183**: BC Rail (TL); Wilton S.Tifft (TR); Harold Edmondson (B); **186**: CN (T); CSX Transportation (B); **187**: Richard Steinheimer (L); **188**: Via Rail (T); Richard Steinheimer (B); **189**: GEC-Alsthom (TL, TR); Karl Zimmermann (B).